CONFESSIONS OF A SKINNY-MARINK

When I was twelve years old my brother was already eighteen and was a student at NYU, though he still was living at home. My mother had a weekly mah jongg game in those days, every Wednesday, the game rotating from one home field to the next. One fateful Wednesday, as the mah jongg tiles clackety-clacked, one of the women asked me what I wanted to be when I grew up. "A baseball player," I said. It was my standard response; I had said it a hundred times before. But for some reason my brother chose this night to get annoyed. When I went to my room he followed me in. "Why do you keep saying that?" he asked. "You know you'll never be good enough to be a ballplayer." Then he left the room, leaving behind this shocking reality, this previously unspoken truth.

Deep in my gut I knew he was right. Quietly I began to cry. Picking up my glove and ball, I began to fire the ball into the glove as hard as I could, painfully, again and again and again, while the tears rolled down my cheeks. . . .

BASEBALL
— AND —
MEN'S LIVES

THE TRUE CONFESSIONS OF A SKINNY-MARINK

ROBERT MAYER

Delta
Trade Paperbacks

A Delta Book
Published by
Dell Publishing
a division of
Bantam Doubleday Dell Publishing Group, Inc.
1540 Broadway
New York, New York 10036

Library of Congress Cataloging in Publication Data

Mayer, Robert, 1939–
    Baseball and men's lives : the true confessions of a skinny-marink / Robert Mayer.
        p.   cm.
    ISBN 0-385-30926-0
    1. Baseball—United States—History.   2. Mayer, Robert, 1939–
3. Authors, American—20th century—Biography.   I. Title.
GV867.M39   1994
796.357'0973—dc20   93-26750
                                                                          CIP

Manufactured in the United States of America
Published simultaneously in Canada
March 1994

10 9 8 7 6 5 4 3 2 1
RRH

To La Donna,
who understands

ACKNOWLEDGMENTS

This book would not have been possible without the kindness of my friends Gene Smith, Tony O'Brien, Tom Collins, Jon Richards, Jorge Ramirez, Jaime Dean, and Jerry Ortiz y Pino—and all the others named in the text—who graciously allowed me to usurp a part of their lives.

The genesis of the book I owe to Philip Spitzer, my agent and friend, whose dedication never fails to astonish. Emily Reichert, my editor, responded immediately and was enthusiastic throughout. Craig Schneider copyedited the manuscript with wondrous care.

On the childhood set my brother, Saul, never tired of tossing me grounders into the night; and he lent me his beloved Dodgers. And my parents, long gone, rarely questioned a small boy's curious passion.

Finally, but not least, I am grateful to Pee Wee Reese, whom I have never met: for a child's inspiration, for a grown man's memories.

Because this is in part a book of memory, it is possible that miscues have occurred. I have checked the facts, but if on occasion I've dropped the ball, the errors are mine.

—R.M.

We've been on earth all these years and we still don't know for certain why birds sing.

—Annie Dillard,
Pilgrim at Tinker Creek

Contents

Prologue:
Our National Anthem

The ball is nestled in the pocket of the glove, which is propped on an unpainted wooden shelf above the white filing cabinet near his desk. He takes down the glove, holds the ball in his right hand, curves his fingers around the taut horsehide, feels it press back as if with calm assurance, tight yet gentle, a bit more insistent at the seams. He closes his eyes, loosens his grip, turns the ball lightly in his hand, tightens his palm against it once again, feels the pleasure in his flesh, feels it move up through his palm to the back of his hand, through his wrist, his forearm, to the elbow, all the way to the shoulder: a simple distillation of touch, of tightly wrapped potential. The sensation of well-being is fierce, as always, and not merely remembered—and therefore inexplicable.

In the beginning, he thinks, there is the ball. Not in the cradle, not in the carriage; an infant in a carriage could not grip anything larger than a marble, which might find its way into his mouth. Not then, but in the playpen, perhaps, or on the living room floor, or out on the front lawn. The baby, the small child, clutching some kind of ball in his fragile fingers, feels perhaps this sensuous connection even then: the perfect fit of the ball in the hand. But not all babies. Mostly male babies. Perhaps the difference is genetic, he thinks, carried on the Y chromosome. A worthy subject for scientific scrutiny. You cannot cure a compulsion until you isolate the cause.

He opens his eyes, returns to his surroundings. On the same set of shelves where he keeps the glove and ball is the Muse. It is a sculpted bronze candelabra, burnished brown, from turn-of-the-century

1

Germany. NÜRNBERG, it says on the bottom. Place of judgment. The base of the sculpture is a seated man of the last century, wearing buckled shoes, knee stockings, pants and waistcoat that must have been silk or satin, his hair curled at the sides like a British judge's wig. His elbows are resting on his knees, his chin on his hands. He is thinking—a writer most certainly, in the grip of writer's block—and looks, in fact, constipated. Poised on his back is a lovely naked nymph, long hair flowing down over one breast, flowing further, modestly, between her legs, lips smiling, eyes gazing heavenward in quiet ecstasy. She is grasping a funnellike candle-holder, the point of which is implanted in our hero's head. The drippings of the candle, of his burning thoughts, will enter into his brain the hard way, courtesy of the gentle Muse.

He bought the bronze more than thirty years before, when he first moved out of his father's house. Found it in an antique shop on Hudson Street, prowled the shop for more than an hour, wanting desperately to buy this candelabra, this icon, this Muse, but not comfortable splurging on himself, not for such a luxury. Finally, about to leave the shop, he turned back, sprung for the sixty dollars, took the nymph home with him to his basement apartment. Fingered her hard metal curves, even as he is touching her now, later wrote a poem to her, suggesting the Muse might get better results if she climbed down off his back and into his arms.

He returns the Muse to the shelf. Other trophies are near, in places of honor beside the ball and glove: a horse pulling a cage marked OVERLAND CIRCUS, which he bought in the company of the city girl he married. In the rims of the wheels there is faded evidence that the cage once was painted bright red, a child's toy. But when he bought it for thirty dollars in a shop in Colorado it was already painted black. It stands out starkly against the pure white wall, this empty, horse-drawn cage, reminding him now, as it did then, of Kafka, "A Hunger Artist." Did a beast belong in the cage, or was it a man? And where has he gone, did he truly starve himself to death, and what exactly did he hunger for? Surely it was for more than food.

Nearby are a pair of acrobatic bronze clowns: one lying on his back, his feet raised high in the air; the second clown balancing with both his hands on the first clown's upraised foot; the lower clown grinning behind his false clown mask; the upper clown maskless beneath a pointy hat. This he found at a flea market in Manhattan and took home to the country girl, a *girl whom he also married. The clowns are less archetypal than the Muse, less mysterious than the empty black cage, but in their state of suspended balance they have their own depths not yet plumbed. Something it is these clowns represent—but what?*

He slips his left hand into the Rawlings glove, the webbing much wider than in the vanished glove of his youth; he places the ball in the pocket. The glove feels stiff to the touch. It has been many months, more than a year, perhaps, since he has oiled it. He goes to the kitchen, finds in a cabinet under the sink the small tin of machine oil he bought some time ago for just this purpose. He squeezes a few drops of oil into the pocket. With the fingers of his right hand he spreads the oil into the glove, watching the autumn-orange color of the too-crisp leather deepen to a comfortable brown, feeling the leather soften as he works, works his fingers, works the oil deeper into the pocket, his right hand coated, glistening, the smell of the oil, of the leather, taking him back. He works the oil into the glove until only a dark dampness remains. He places the ball in the sheen, in the pocket of the glove. He presses the fat thumb and fifth finger of the glove together, pressing the ball deeper still. He returns glove and ball to the shelf, pressed into a corner, careful to preserve the shape.

In another room a woman waits; her name is La Donna. In yet another room, a female child; her name is Amara.

He is fifty-three years old. Going on thirty-eight. And I am seven, or nine, or eleven. And he is I and I am he, simultaneous, interchangeable, permanent pilgrims in this mythic green field, voyagers in a parallel reality, nameless starlight in a comet with an ever-lengthening glow: to which we have given the simple name "baseball."

The men in white (the Mudville nine?) are about to take the field, are trotting out, gloves in hand, in slow motion, glowing bright as vapor lights against the brilliant grass. He moves in his cleats to the bat rack, selects a stick, slim, light. He is not a power hitter, he is a leadoff man.

Batting first, he will hear in a moment, in the roar of the crowd, in the jangle of his brain, in the stark reverberation of the years, playing shortstop, number one . . .

But first, ladies and gentlemen, our national anthem.

FIRST

A Puddle of Moral Uncertainty

When I was a kid my mother called me a skinny-marink. I never knew what a marink was, not then, not now, but skinny I certainly was, largely because whenever the Brooklyn Dodgers lost a baseball game I became too upset to eat. And the Dodgers lost a lot. Baseball, by the time I was seven years old, had lodged itself that deeply into my gut. My own national tapeworm. The Dodgers lost just often enough to keep my immigrant parents fearing for my survival. Such mounds of spaghetti and Yankee Doodles they did induce down my gullet I quickly burned off by playing ball from the moment school let out till half an hour past the time you could see the ball in your hand. There was a decided advantage to playing ball after dark; errors could be blamed on God, who'd been dumb enough to invent the useless night.

Strictly speaking, it wasn't baseball that we played. I grew up in The Bronx, in a neighborhood of brick houses and tenements and narrow paved streets lined on both sides with parked cars. We played punchball in a concrete backyard that housed several garages; we played stickball in the street when the steady stream of traffic would allow. But as Humpty Dumpty would surely have instructed Alice, baseball we wanted it to be, and baseball it became, and anyone who says different is a liar. The fact that we used our fists or broomsticks instead of bats, that we hit Spaldeens or worn tennis balls instead of baseballs, never detracted from my

5

certainty that one day I would be playing in the major leagues. I would be the next Pee Wee Reese.

Though we lived a mile from Yankee Stadium, I seem to have emerged from the womb a Dodger fan. This was just as well, because the Yankees in that Joe DiMaggio-followed-by-Mickey Mantle era never seemed to lose; as a Yankee fan I might have become the Goodyear blimp. But rooting for the Yankees would have been like rooting for General Motors. I was congenitally for the underdog, an off-my-trolley Dodger. As was my older brother, for reasons equally obscure.

All my friends on the block were Yankee fans, and my infatuation with the Brooklyn Bums provided all the sweet music of childhood, the endless front-stoop arguments over who was better, Reese or Rizzuto, Mantle or Snider or Mays; all the grand clichés that got us through the wonder years, the true wonder years—the days when girls were that half of the human race who tried to throw a ball with the wrong foot in front. That and nothing more.

My earliest baseball memory is from the summer of '46, late at night, the Dodgers playing a night game with St. Louis, whom they were battling for the pennant that year, my parents and my brother asleep, me in my bed, seven years old, the blanket pulled over my head to hide the light of a flashlight and the sound of a portable radio, listening to the game. It was the top of the ninth, the Dodgers were losing, and a rookie catcher just called up from the minors was sent up to the plate to pinch-hit. It was his first major league at bat. He struck out, and the Dodgers lost. His name was Gil Hodges. You could look it up.

The Dodgers and the Cardinals tied for the pennant that year. They played the first play-off games in baseball history, best two out of three. The Dodgers lost. Born to an ancient tribe of sufferers, I had found my baseball home. The next year the Dodgers, sparked by Jackie Robinson, would win the pennant but lose the World Series to the hated Yankees in the seventh game. "The Bums Is Dead," the *Daily News* would proclaim, while my weight dropped precariously. They would lose the series to the Yankees again in '49. In 1950 they would fail to tie the Phillies for the pennant on the final day, when Richie Ashburn would throw out Cal Abrams at home plate. I was eleven years old then and I still remember the name of the coach who sent Abrams in from third. Milton Stock. Mentioned prominently, I believe, in the *Inferno*. . . .

And then came 1951.

Of 1951 we do not speak. . . .

Through all of this we played our own games, countless boy hours—punchball, stickball, box ball, triangle. Punchball we played in the large backyard behind the houses our families rented. One side of the yard was formed by the windowless rear wall of a warehouse, solid brick. Another side was the solid brick wall of a tenement. Two sides were formed by the backs of brick houses, and these had windows in them. These windows, if left open, often caught our Spaldeens or tennis balls; we would have to beg to get them back; if left closed, when ball met glass—a law of elementary physics—the glass often broke. Mostly this happened to the bedroom window of Mrs. Newman, a frumpy hausfrau who would come waddling down to the backyard in pursuit of us, swinging a broom with which she hoped to box our ears. But there were two sloping cement driveways leading down to the yard, one at either end, and whichever Mrs. Newman chose to block with her huge bulk, we could always scamper up the other. The poor woman never understood Newton's third law of punchball dynamics: that a two-hundred-pound landlady in house slippers will never outrun a fifty-pound skinny-marink. Not ever.

Though I liked to be called Pee Wee, my nickname for one entire year was Slugger. That was because I was the only one on the block who couldn't punch the ball over the fence. But if there was derision in the name it was ill conceived. I had no desire to hit home runs: I was more the hit-and-run type, the slickest fielder in high-tops. Pathologically shy in school, on the ball field I was always the captain, shouting instructions to kids much older than I.

My mother, who did *The New York Times* crossword puzzle every day, was a firm believer in reading, and every two weeks we rode the trolley car together to the Fordham library. And every two weeks, to her chagrin, I came home with an armload of books about baseball. Fiction was dominated by the immortal John R. Tunis; the clackety-clackety-clack of spikes in *The Kid from Tompkinsville* and *World Series* was—since we ourselves played all our games in black high-top sneakers—like music from a foreign land. It was echoed in my childhood only by the clackety-clack of the trolley cars as they switched rails on the way to Fordham Road and the Grand Concourse, the Times Square of The Bronx. In the nonfiction section of the library I read every book available about how to play baseball. I studied as scrupulously as a brash young scientist at work. I knew the game. By the time I was eight years old I knew that on a hit to right field the shortstop had to cover second base, while on a hit to left field he had to go out for the relay. I knew that with a runner stealing and a left-hander at bat he had to cover second. I knew that to sacrifice a runner you squared around and caught the ball on the bat while laying down the bunt. And that bunting for a base hit was another matter entirely; hour after hour in the small front parlor of our apartment, where I slept, I stood with a bat in my hands and practiced dropping the bat on an imaginary ball, laying the ball down the third base line even as I broke toward first. I knew, therefore, nearly everything important about life. The only thing I didn't know was how to stop being afraid of the dark.

When I was six years old my brother took me one Saturday afternoon to see my very first movie, at the old Surrey Theater on Mount Eden Avenue, fourteen cents for kids. The attraction was an animated Walt Disney film called *Make Mine Music*. It featured, as I recall, *The Little Engine That Could*, a bunch of penguins freezing their butts off on ice floes, and assorted other inspirations and amusements. Unbeknownst to me, however, there was also a second feature, which my brother wanted to see. It was *The Phantom of the Opera*, with Lon Chaney. As we watched the film I took particular note of the Phantom's acid-eaten face. I did not venture into a dark movie theater again for two more years. I did not go to bed with the light off in my room for three.

"How can you be a baseball player if you're afraid of the dark?" my frustrated mother asked, trying a bit of psychology.

"What's that got to do with anything?"

"How will you play night games?"

"There's lights."

The trouble was, even if the naked light bulb was burning on the ceiling of your room, when you closed your eyes to go to sleep, darkness inevitably descended. To rid myself of the monsters that immediately filled my brain, I began to chant, that summer of 1947, first summer of my fandom, the same refrain, over and over in my brain: *The Dodgers are gonna win the pennant! The Dodgers are gonna win the pennant! The Dodgers are gonna win the pennant!* Since I had never in my life seen a sheep, counting Jackie Robinsons and Pee Wee Reeses scoring runs was far superior to the traditional escape. The problem was, the Dodgers actually did win the pennant that year, so when October turned to November, and then to winter, the mantra of the Dodgers winning lost some of its soporific effect. Which gave new meaning to the perennial Brooklyn refrain, Wait till next year.

If the Dodgers did win the pennant that year, they maintained their traditional role as heartbreakers by losing the World Series to the hated Yankees. It was during that series that I learned an important lesson, however. While Dodger fans could run like hell, Yankee fans could fly.

It was the fourth game of the series, played at Ebbets Field. The Yankees led, two games to one. Now, in game four, Bill Bevens of the Yankees was still pitching a no-hitter with two out in the ninth inning. To be no-hit in the World Series—that would be too much even for a Dodger fan to bear. I was listening in our two-story house, in our apartment that covered the entire first floor, when two men reached base on walks, and Cookie Lavagetto came up to pinch-hit. The Yankees were ahead, 2–1. Lavagetto swung. The ball sailed deep into right field—all this coming over a yellow plastic radio in the moderately hoarse voice of Red Barber, the voice of the Bums, the original music man of my youth. The ball hit the wall high over the right fielder's head. Two Dodgers raced around the bases and scored. The no-hitter was broken, the Dodgers had won the game and evened the series, all with that one swing, the most dramatic hit in history up to that time, and, for Dodger fans, for all time to come. (We do not mention 1951.)

This little-known substitute player, Cookie Lavagetto, who would never play another season, had found instant immortality—this player who until then might have been to the vast uncaring public, or to my parents, some arcane vegetable, like a zucchini or a squash. *You don't get any dessert till you finish your lavagetto.*

Light-headed with joy, I raced out the door and down the three front steps to rub it in to my neighbor and best friend Jackie Brownstein, who lived two doors away and was two years older and was a Yankee fan, antagonist in all my childhood arguments, William Buckley to my Bill Moyers. To my eternal astonishment Jackie, who lived on the second floor, and thus had to churn his solid body down a whole flight of stairs, Jackie, who should have been brooding in solitude about the sudden turnabout, about the terrible loss, as I would have been doing had our roles been reversed, Jackie was waiting for me in the street before I got there, waiting to chatter excitedly about the unbelievable ending. As if he knew his Yankees would triumph anyway. As they did. As in those days they always did. But how had he gotten into the street so fast? How had he beaten me, for I had raced for the door in a flash? There could be only one explanation. He had leapt without fear from his upstairs parlor window. Yankee fans, it seemed, could fly.

This observation has held up fairly well throughout my life. In the byways of my mind Dodger fans and Giant fans and now Mets fans tend to ride the buses or hitch with their thumbs, hoboes drinking beer at synaptic gaps. While Yankee fans drink Chivas Regal and fly first class, no matter how well, or, in recent years, how badly their team is doing. They need the wider seats for their mental bottoms. They do not suffer, they do not quit eating, when the Bronx Bombers lose. They are not now, nor have they ever been, either skinny or marinks.

A day or two after Lavagetto's Hit came Gionfriddo's Catch. With two men on base and the Dodgers leading 8 to 5, Joe DiMaggio belted a long drive into left-center field. A Dodger scrubbini named Al Gionfriddo, filling in in left field, raced far back to the wall and caught the ball as it passed over the low fence into the left field bullpen. Television had not yet reached Townsend Avenue in 1947, so this, too, I heard on the radio. A picture of the catch appeared in the next day's newspapers, and has been reprinted many times since. It shows Gionfriddo with his arm bent at his waist, over the bullpen fence, the ball in his glove. I studied the picture that day and have studied it many times since and still can't figure out if this was the follow-through of a traditional leaping catch, or if indeed he caught the ball in that curious position. It remains one of the abiding mysteries of life, along with the origin of the universe and how anyone can eat boiled okra.

Despite the immortal heroics of Lavagetto and Gionfriddo, however, the Dodgers lost this Subway Series, this first World Series in which I was an active participant. On the seventh day God rested; He ceased His miracles; He let the Philistines win. When the afternoon of the seventh came I was riding downtown with my parents in the family car, going I know not where. I heard the tragic ending on the car radio. Minutes later we passed through Times Square, which was thick with traffic, with noisy people in the streets, as the electric lights on the Times Tower spelled out the Yankee victory. People were shouting and cheering and throwing confetti, and I, feeling sick to my stomach, could not imagine what it was they were celebrating. Didn't they understand that the Dodgers had lost?

The next day my friend Jackie's father, Harry Brownstein, who was a policeman and a Yankee fan and had heavy jowls, came by our house and handed me a small white card. It was rimmed all around in black. In tiny letters in the center, surrounded by white space, were the words: BROOKLYN DODGERS.

I didn't get the joke. I asked my mother what the card meant. She said it was the kind of card people gave out when someone had died: a black border with the dead person's name in the middle.

I didn't think it was very funny.

I still don't.

He no longer lives in the city that gave him birth, the city that gave him succor, an education, a job. He moved away more than twenty years ago, for good and sufficient reasons. He lives now at the base of a mountain range, where the air is clean and perfumed in spring by the sweet scent of lilacs. But the city is in him still; the most obvious link is through the snakelike black wire that connects his house to a cable TV system, the cable that connects much of America to the televised games of the New York National League baseball team. For thirty years, since the first day of their existence, he has been rooting for the Mets. For the past twenty years he has been doing this across two thousand miles of American countryside.

Today he is apprehensive, and eager. Today he prowls the hours like a tiger in the zoo. It is April 6, 1992. In the world of baseball it is Opening Day. His Mets will be playing the Cardinals in the evening, and the game will be televised.

On this night he will not be dining with his wife, his daughter. On this night, they understand, he will carry his plate, his drink, into his office beside the bedroom, he will eat at his desk, he will watch the baseball game. The ritual, they know, is sacrosanct; they do not mind. They have shows of their own to watch.

His anticipation is a distilling of high hopes. The Mets are going to win the pennant this year. And perhaps the World Series. This is not only his conviction, but the forecast of most experts. To a pitching rotation of Dwight Gooden, David Cone, and Sid Fernandez, they have added the Cy Young winner from Kansas City, Bret Saberhagen. The fifth spot is up for grabs, but this appears, at the season's start, to be the best rotation in baseball.

There are questions, of course. Gooden is coming off of arm surgery. His soundness has yet to be proved. But there are always questions. . . .

In the batting order they have added Bobby Bonilla, the most prized free agent of the off-season. To sign him they offered the salary equivalent of the Empire State Building, but between the foul lines such matters of high finance are irrelevant. With a middle-of-the-lineup punch of Bonilla, Howard Johnson, and Eddie Murray, the Mets should score many runs.

And so, eating and drinking and making believe he is relaxed, he watches tensely the first game of the season. He watches Bobby Bonilla blast his first home run as a Met. The game goes into extra innings. He watches Bonilla hit his second home run as a Met. He watches the Mets win.

A Puddle of Moral Uncertainty

*Reluctantly, but happy, he snaps off the set, returns to human form,
rejoins in another room his wife, his child. His team is undefeated, with
161 games to go. An average of three of these games each week will
travel in electric impulses through the cable that brings the pictures and
the sounds into his home. This multispotted miracle, amid life's inevitable dark corners, holds out the prospect of six months of comfort, of
light.*

Sparks splattered out of the dark ceiling like electric fireflies. I
zoomed in and out of traffic on the oval surface. I was driving a
bumper car, my favorite amusement-park attraction, but I did not
like getting bumped, did not care to slam into others. A hook-
slider, a bailer-outer, in the Coney Island of my youth.

It was the last weekend in June, school had let out the day
before, we were on our traditional family outing to the other end
of the city. To the farthest corner of Brooklyn. We climbed out of
the bumper cars and walked along the boardwalk, saw the dark
Atlantic rolling onto the beach, stopped for hot dogs and french
fries at Nathan's, played miniature golf in the sweet salt air,
passed advertisements and shills for freak shows featuring snake
charmers, sword swallowers, bearded ladies, and assorted other
aberrations that I did not care to see or imagine. Finally my brother
and I and a bunch of the other kids went into a penny arcade.
While the bigger guys played pinball games, I spotted a baseball
card machine.

Some of the boys on the block, David Portman in particular,
would buy pack after pack of bubble gum, throwing away the
brittle gum but keeping the smallish baseball cards. That always
seemed a waste to me. I preferred the postcard-sized cards that
you bought for a penny each out of a machine. The cards were
sepia. They had no information or statistics on the back, but that
didn't matter: I could keep as many statistics as I needed in my
head. It was the pictures that counted (and the facsimile signa-
tures), those large soft images, Carl Furillo finishing his swing, Pee
Wee Reese bending to scoop a grounder, Preacher Roe pitching.
Most of the batters, in fact, were finishing their swings, as I recall,
not captured with the bat out over the plate—probably because

the extended bat would not fit onto the vertical card. This occurs to me only now.

There were card machines in the candy stores near PS 70. Some of the kids bought cowboy cards—Bob Steele, Hopalong Cassidy; some bought movie stars cards—Bette Davis, Barbara Stanwyck. But baseball was my only vice. And now here was a machine at Coney Island, way out in Brooklyn, with all the attendant possibilities of a new selection of cards: fewer doubles, more originals. I took a penny from my pocket and placed it in the coin slot, pushed the silver metal handle all the way in, slowly pulled it out, my heart pounding with excitement at who the player might be. I don't remember, now, who it was. What I remember, what was astounding at that moment, was that two cards came out, instead of one. This had never happened to me before. The cards must have been stuck together, I thought. What luck! I fed another penny into the machine. To my amazement another two cards came out. I tried it again. And again. With five pennies I now held ten penny baseball cards in my hand. The unexpected provender of the Coney gods.

My brother and the others came to see what I was doing. I showed them. Two cards for a penny, every time. My brother pushed me out of the way. He tried a penny of his own. Two cards. He tried another penny. Two cards. All of them crowded around now, excited, yet trying to be quiet, so as not to attract attention, filling their hands with this bargain. I, the youngest and smallest, had been shuffled to the rear, out of the inner circle.

Here I must pause momentarily, for a warning. What follows is not for the squeamish. But I have determined in this baseball memoir to pull no punches. Only the strong need read on.

Wandering through the arcade, aimless, alone, I suddenly found myself face to face with a fat belly, with a dirty apron. The apron had large pockets, which hung heavy with coins. Above it the unshaved face of a large man loomed. I hesitated, then tugged at the fat man's apron.

"What do you want?"

"That machine over there," I said, excited, a cub reporter with a scoop, the cub reporter, perhaps, that I would later become. "It's giving out two baseball cards for a penny, instead of one."

"Is that so?" the fat man said.

He patted my light brown hair with appreciation. He strode toward the machine, pushed through the knot of my slavering friends, pushed my brother away from the machine. He took a penny from one of his heavy pockets, shoved it into the machine, pulled the silver-colored handle. Two baseball cards came out. He tried it a second time, with the same result.

"That's all, beat it," he said to my brother and the others.

"What do you mean, beat it?" my brother asked.

The fat man produced a gray canvas bag. He pulled it over the machine, as if he were blindfolding a prisoner at the gallows, and he tied the bottom of the bag with a cord.

"The machine's broken. No more cards today. Beat it."

His look had turned mean. He was prepared to get physical if the guys didn't move. They seethed out into the bright glare of the boardwalk. The sun shone directly on me, like a spotlight in a police station.

My brother looked at me. "You told him! Why the hell did you tell him?"

"Because the machine was broken."

"Idiot! Stupid schmuck!" And he punched me in the shoulder, hard, with a knuckle protruding, the only time he hit me hard in my life. It hurt like hell.

The others, too, looked at me. Then they turned and walked away, disgusted. I stood alone in a warm puddle of moral uncertainty. All I had done was tell the truth! But in so doing I had become the bearded lady, the two-headed calf, the freak show I dared not witness.

Why I did it I cannot say. Perhaps, by the time I was eight, my parents had already instilled in me some ancient Hebraic notion of absolute rectitude. Or perhaps, as my brother said, I was merely a schmuck.

I still can feel today the touch of the fat man's chubby hand on my hair. As if it was a violation.

15

And that is only half the agony.

I continued to collect the penny baseball cards throughout my youth, paying a full cent for each one ever after, one chiseled round portrait of Lincoln for every Gus Zernial and Phil Cavaretta and Hoot Evers. In those pretelevision days they were the only way to learn what players looked like, especially players from other cities or the other league, whom you never got to see on the field. One year I did make an exception; I started collecting one set of nickel-a-pack bubble-gum cards. I don't recall the brand, but the small, squarish cards were black and white, which I liked, and unlike with most cards the accompanying pink bubble-gum was softer than a manhole cover. It wasn't anywhere near the quality of the Fleer's Double Bubble we sidewalk connoisseurs preferred, but it would do. There were forty-eight baseball cards in this particular set, and within a few months one summer I had acquired forty-seven of them. Only Buddy Kerr was missing. Nickel after nickel went for more cards in search of the Giants' shortstop. Nickel after nickel he remained elusive. I went to a Giant-Dodger game at the Polo Grounds, proved to myself that Buddy Kerr did in fact exist, saw him in the flesh. But I never obtained his card. I never even saw his card. I suspect now, in the well-honed cynicism of my years, that they never printed any—well, perhaps one; that Buddy Kerr was somehow chosen to be the Holy Grail we nickel-dropping urchins would never obtain, the bottomless black hole in our childhood galaxy.

A red rubber band wrapped tightly around the set—I was one card short of a deck, then as now—I placed the forty-seven cards in a cardboard box and went back to collecting the postcard size. Sometimes I would trade cards with my friends, sometimes we would flip cards, sometimes we would toss cards against a wall, closest to the wall wins, sometimes, using a clothespin, we would fasten the cards to the wheels of our bicycles, which made the spinning spokes roar like a motorcycle. But these divergences I would indulge in only with my doubles. My singles I would not gamble with. When I was twelve years old my family moved from our apartment in the West Bronx to a house my parents bought in the Pelham Parkway section. My box of baseball cards—it was a multicolored box that had once held jars of finger paints—I placed on a shelf in my closet as I turned my attention to the homework of junior high school, to my fear of the opposite sex, to the pimple which like some unwelcome guest perpetually revisited the point of my nose, to all the other mysteries of adolescence. The box of cards remained at the top of the closet throughout my high school years, throughout college.

It was around this time in the lives of most men that their treasured baseball cards disappeared, never to be seen again. For some it happened when they were away at college, learning the lingo of their future professions. For others it happened when they were in the service, defending their country's honor, its military-industrial complex, whatever. Not so in my case. In my case the wound was self-inflicted.

I was twenty-two years old. I had just taken my first long-term newspaper job. I had fallen in love for the first time. And I decided it was time to grow up. This meant, in the madness of my ardor, two things. First, it meant letting my hair grow out. Since the age of twelve I had worn my hair in a crew cut, a brush cut. It was world class. My hair was so thick and full that every time I went to my favorite barber on Eastchester Avenue, Rudy would unwrap a newly sharpened pair of scissors. He would use it to trim my crew cut. Then, when he was done, he would toss it into the drawer of scissors that needed to be sharpened again. My hair wasn't merely cute, it was tough. And it was me. It stands up firm and proud in my high-school yearbook picture. It does the same in my college graduation picture. It was a part of my identity. But now I was out in the real world, and in love, and it was time to grow up. I let my crew cut grow out. But that action was fairly painless. It did not seem to complete my rite of passage. It did not assuage the part of my soul that knew I could not remain a little boy. A further task was demanded, something more painful, more drastic. And I knew what it was. One dark night I poked around in the top of the closet of the small room I had long since outgrown. I found the box that had once held finger paints, I wiped off the years of dust, first with my hands and then with a paper towel. I opened the box, and in it, neatly stacked, neatly preserved, were all my hundreds of sepia baseball cards. Pee Wee and Duke, Gil and Jackie, Roy, Preach, all the others. Still in perfect condition. A rubber band marked off a small pack of doubles. Perhaps, I thought, if I just threw *those* away. . . . But a stern inner voice said no. A stern inner voice said it was time to do away with childish things. With a minimum of ceremony I closed the box, carried it down the stairs and out to the street, where our garbage can stood. Like a burial at sea, but without so much as a prayer of farewell, I slid my baseball cards into the trash. Then I turned and walked under the stars back to my house. I had become an adult.

Or so I thought.

The memories those cards would conjure today are priceless. And how much money would the cards be worth? I have no idea. I have never tried to find out. I dare not speculate. Hundreds of dollars, for sure. Thousands, most likely. Tens of thousands is not out of the question, in the strange, burgeoning baseball-card market.

But my cards are gone to limbo, like most men's childhood cards. With this one burning difference: I was cheated of the lifelong pleasure of blaming it on my mother.

And what of the inner child that I was trying to kill off?

It lives inside me still. Crying, *Schmuck!!!!!!!!*

He goes to the door and takes in the mail. Nothing today but two magazines. One is his copy of Modern Maturity, *sent to him unbidden by the American Association of Retired Persons, not because he is retired but because he is over fifty. The other is his copy of the Victoria's Secret catalog, from which he occasionally orders a pretty, lace-trimmed nightgown for his wife, or a flowered print robe for his teenage daughter. These orders are rare, but the enticing catalog keeps coming. He opens this new one, flips through the pages: gorgeous young models in nightshirts, in swimsuits, in body stockings, in see-through underwear. It has become, by far, his favorite magazine.*

He does not open Modern Maturity. *At fifty-three he is not yet prepared to claim such grace.*

* * *

When I was growing up we lived at 1707 Townsend Avenue, in the Grand Concourse section of The Bronx. Four two-family brick houses extended north from Clifford Place. The one in which my family rented the ground-floor apartment was the fourth. The remainder of the block was filled with six-story apartment buildings stretching to 175th Street, where we bought our bread for fourteen cents a loaf and our milk for seventeen cents a quart at Barth's grocery store; where we drank egg creams and bought chocolate-marshmallow twists at Goldstein's candy store; where my mother rented for three cents a day the latest Daphne du Maurier best-seller from the lending library in Harry's candy store; where we got our hair cut at a barber shop whose name I forget; and which we traversed to go to the A & P supermarket under the Jerome Avenue El near 176th Street. Virtually every family on our block was Jewish. Virtually every family on the block north of 175th was Italian. Not a single black family— colored, then—dwelled in the entire neighborhood.

Until I was eight years old there was only one black person in my life. She was a beautiful young woman named Virginia. Every Thursday for half a dozen years she came to our house to do the heavy housework—to wash the floors, to polish the furniture, to vacuum, to clean the windows. My father called her "the *schvartze*," which was commonplace bigoted Yiddish for "the black." Virginia was the object of one of my earliest inner conflicts. I did not like Thursdays because of the disruption her cleaning and moving furniture caused in our stable household; at the same time I was a little bit in love with her.

The second black to enter my life was Jackie Robinson. A standout player with the Montreal Royals, he was given a Dodger contract by Branch Rickey in the spring of '47, the single most important act in all of baseball history. Robinson, with his dark skin and his pigeon toes, quickly became the most exciting player in the game. His dances off the bases at first or third, his mad-dash steals of home, drove opposing pitchers frantic. His brilliant fielding and clutch hitting led the Dodgers to the pennant. If I had chosen the Dodgers as my team out of some unconscious desire to root for the underdog, their claim to moral superiority was now established before all the world.

My father, a gentle Jewish man, a product of his time, also called Robinson "the *schvartze*."

Having emerged from the womb a shortstop, I naturally gravitated to Pee Wee Reese as my idol, my hero, my alter ego. I worshiped him for the smooth way he glided behind second base to cut off base hits up the middle, the speed with which he went into the hole between short and third, planted his feet, and threw out the speediest runner at first, the grace with which he leapt over murderous spikes to complete a double play, the sure way he laid down a bunt, the singles he so often delivered to drive in runs in the clutch. One year my childhood bible, *Sport* magazine, did a feature story on Reese. Under a half-page picture of Pee Wee swinging the bat, the familiar number 1 on his back, the caption said: "He may never hit .300, but it won't be for lack of trying." That same year he hit his career high of .309. Pee Wee knew how to show 'em.

Reese, it would emerge later, was truly among the nobility of his time, something that in my eight-year-old innocence I did not understand then. The admission of Jackie Robinson to major league baseball stirred up the racism that was latent not only throughout the national pastime, and throughout America, but right in the Dodger locker room. My second favorite player was the Dodgers' right fielder, Dixie Walker. When, after the '47 season, the Dodgers traded "The People's Cherce" to Pittsburgh, I was astonished, hurt, by this lack of loyalty by so brave a baseball man as Branch Rickey. Not till many years later did I understand that Dixie Walker, a prisoner of his nickname, had been a bigot who did not want to play on the same team as Robinson. Reese, on the other hand, a former marbles champion from Kentucky, had befriended the black man, had welcomed him to the team, had set an example for the others, had helped Robinson blaze the trail for the hundreds of black players who would follow. My choice of proper heroes apparently was instinctive—though in later years they would have a tendency to attract the bullets of assassins.

Virginia worked for us for several more years, following us

across The Bronx when we moved. Then she became ill and cut back on her hours. One day her husband came around to say she would not be able to work anymore. Though my parents hired other cleaning women, they rarely stayed for long. And none of them were as efficient or as lovely as she. For a few more years we received Christmas cards from her. Then, if memory serves, we heard that Virginia died young.

Thinking back, I would like to remember the time when, while she was polishing the furniture, or while she was eating her bologna sandwich, which she always liked for lunch, I had chatted with her about baseball; about the Dodgers; the time I asked her what she thought about Jackie Robinson. But I can't seem to recall the conversation. Probably it never took place.

Unlike my hero I was never a marbles champ. When we did play marbles it was usually a simple game. We'd cut rectangular holes in a shoe box and try to roll marbles into the holes from a few feet away: one point for getting it into the largest hole, five points for a smaller hole, ten points for the smallest opening. I did all right, but in my low-key marble career there was just one roll that I felt was worthy of the master. I was walking to my grandmother's house one day, four blocks away on Walton Avenue, carrying in my hand a sack of marbles—I never called them immies, like some kids—when I passed a group of punk kids I did not know. They were playing marbles in the street; seeing my bulging bag, they fastened on an easy mark.

"Wanna play?" one of them asked.

I shook my head no.

"Whatsamatter, you chicken?"

They had placed a marble against the curb, and had drawn a line with chalk about ten feet into the street. The object was to roll your marble from behind the line and hit the one at the curb. If you missed, you lost your marble; if you hit it, you won five.

"How many from across the street?" I asked. Not sure why I was asking. Not sure why this bravado.

The three punks looked at one another; no one had ever asked that before.

"From all the way across?"

I nodded. They looked at the far curb. It was thirty feet away at least.

"A hundred marbles," one of them said.

"Okay," I replied. And I walked across the street while they eyed my sack of marbles hungrily.

Near the far curb I pulled a marble from my pouch. I knelt. The target marble across the street was lonely and distant as the only star in a broad night sky. Barely taking aim, I let fly. My marble rolled and jumped and skidded across the street. And flattened out and rolled the last five feet straight and true, smooth as a golf ball on a putting green, and careened with a sharp clack into the target.

I stood and sauntered across the street, feeling a thumping, like the beating of wings, somewhere near my chest. The punk kids looked at me, their jaws slack. I held out my open hands, cupped together. Too stunned to protest or get tough, they counted out a hundred marbles and poured them in.

I think they wanted to dare me to do it again, but were afraid. I walked away, my small sack of marbles now bulging, off toward my grandmother's house, retiring undefeated, wondering how I had done it. Regretting only slightly that, like that tree falling in a forest, my deed had gone unwitnessed by anyone who mattered. But not really caring too much, for I knew what I knew.

Every so often comes a day in your life when an angel sits on your shoulder. That day was one of them.

Batting first, playing shortstop, number one, Bobby Mayer. . . .

This was the poetry, pouring forth from some heavenly public address system, that echoed through the chambers of my youth. Filled with glory, filled with deceit. There was no Bobby Mayer. He did not exist.

My given name was Robert. No middle name. I never missed the absent middle name—we came from a poor family, I used to explain—and *Robert* was just fine for most purposes. But not for playing ball. *Robert* was not a big-league shortstop; *Robert* would look clunky in a box score; *Robert* would stumble awkwardly in an announcer's mouth; *Robert* couldn't sign a baseball card. Only *Bobby* could gracefully don the Dodger blues, the Dodger grays. There should have been no problem, there should have been a natural metamorphosis, Robert into Bobby, graceful as a butterfly. But *Bobby* though I always wanted to be, *Bobby* I never became.

The fault was Bobby Brownstein's.

Jack Brownstein, my Yankee-worshiping friend from two houses down, was two years older than I; his brother, Bobby, was one year older. Because Bobby had been on the block first, and because neither of our mothers saw any point in shouting out the window for "Bobby" and having two of us respond—or neither of us respond—an agreement was reached between them, which set a precedent for life: Bobby was Bobby and I was Robert, and so it would remain.

The arrangement was logical and I never questioned it; my parents, my brother, my cousins and my uncles and my aunts, never called me anything but Robert. In school I was Robert through elementary and junior high. At the Bronx High School of Science, which was in another neighborhood, I graduated into Bob. Short, simple, and not really me. Bob I remained through college and into the real world. While Bobby Mayer, the sure-handed shortstop, fielded endless grounders in the shadows of the night, waiting to be discovered.

The funny thing was that Bobby Brownstein did not like baseball. He did not like any sports. He joined in our ball games when we needed an extra man, but he was awkward in his motions, unlike his brother, unlike me. He would rather put on a puppet show than hit a homer. He didn't need *Bobby* the way I needed it. Whatever his ultimate path in life—I have no idea what it was, but I'm sure it was not in sports—*Robert Brownstein* would have served him just as well; *Bobby* was not a job requirement. But I never asked him to trade and he never offered. I fielded my grounders deep in the hole and waited for someone to come along who would see into my soul and call me *Bobby*.

Each morning he makes a cup of eye-opening cappuccino, fetches the newspaper from where it has been tossed more or less accurately into the driveway, settles into his favorite wing chair, still wearing his blue terry-cloth robe that's faded with age, and turns to the sports pages. He does not find it congenial to converse with wife, child, or beast until he has perused the scores, the standings, the deals, the box scores. Normally this addiction is riveted to the National League; the other league is situated psychologically somewhere to the south-southeast of Uzbekistan. But on this particular morning his eye traverses the globe to the Republic of Kansas City, where everything is up to date, where the barbecue delights even Calvin Trillin, and where the baseball team, he discovers, is dwelling in the cellar, with a record of one win and sixteen losses. This terrible start for the Royal family surprises him. It also dismays him, because three of the Royal regulars are really Mets—Gregg Jefferies, Keith Miller, and Kevin McReynolds, all of whom were traded in the off-season for the strong right arm of Bret Saberhagen. He had been hoping they would tear up the junior circuit; they still have a claim on his loyalty; they are his friends.

Rashly, he makes a vow. Not every day, but at least once a week, he will check on them in their unfamiliar landscape. See how they are doing. Empathize. He owes them that much.

His conscience assuaged, he kisses his wife on the lips, he touches his daughter's cheek. In response to a certain brute insistence at knee level, he tousles the hair of the dog, and starts the day.

That summer of '47, while the Dodgers struggled toward their first pennant in six years, the first pennant of my fandom, my parents decided to go on vacation with Harry and Clara Brownstein; they would drive to Canada, visit the Thousand Islands, see Niagara Falls. To make this possible Jack, Bobby, and I would be sent to camp. We envisioned some exciting Indian refuge—Camp Mohawk, perhaps, or Camp Geronimo, something rich with bows and arrows, with knives and tomahawks. Instead, the place my parents chose was Camp Separation Anxiety.

Okay, not exactly. But close enough. The real name was Camp Away. I was eight years old, short, skinny, had never before been separated from my parents. Camp *Away*. Thanks, guys.

My parents calmed my fears with a single word: *baseball*. There was a real baseball field there, they assured me. Baseball—or softball, but that made no difference—would be played every day. And so, only half kicking, only half screaming, and totally out-voted, I went. Away.

There were nine bunks at Camp Away. The first three were for the senior boys, the middle three for the intermediates, the last three for the junior campers. I was placed in bunk nine. The youngest and therefore the lowest of the low.

The very first day we went swimming. There was a lake at the camp with a raft anchored in it, about fifty yards offshore. Closer in was a rectangle in the shallow water enclosed with wooden sides. This was for the kids who couldn't swim. It was known, derisively, as the crib. Some of the bigger kids plunged into the water, swam in smooth strokes out to the raft, climbed up onto it as it bobbed like a small white oasis on the lake, dove off its edge into the water. Intermediate kids swam and splashed near the shore. We junior kids were ushered into the crib. I watched with jealousy as some of them swam the length of the crib, others swam the width of the crib. I splashed about and made believe. But I didn't know how to swim.

"In two weeks you'll all be swimming," a voice said.

Right. And in three weeks I'll be playing in Ebbets Field.

I flailed my arms and kicked my feet and whipped my head from side to side, straining to keep my jaw above the water.

"Not like that," the voice said. "You have to put your face in the water."

I did not want to put my face in the water. I do not like the water.

I dried off and waited for the baseball game. There was no baseball game. There was lunch, and arts and crafts. Then it was time to swim again. I held on to the edge of the crib, let my body float up. I kicked my feet. I learned to kick my feet very well, holding on.

"Put your face in the water," the voice said.

I did not want to put my face in the water.

The next morning there was still no baseball. Junior kids, it seemed, were considered too young for baseball. Especially the kids in bunk nine.

What!!!!!

"Change into your bathing suits. It's time for swimming."

I hid under my bed.

They found me. They led me down to the lake.

"It's easy," said the voice of someone standing beside me. "Keep your feet on the ground. Just bend over and put your face in the water. You'll see it's not so bad. Like this." And he bent over and put his face in the water and kept it there. I thought he was going to drown standing up.

"Now you," he said when he pulled his dripping face out.

I bent over. I put my face in the water. The water stung my eyes. I closed them. I tried not to breathe through my nose or through my mouth. The water pressed back with the strength of the earth itself. I couldn't not breathe any longer. I breathed. The water swam up my nose like an eel, the water swam into my mouth like a snake. I choked, I coughed, I swallowed water. I raised my head, but I couldn't seem to get my face out of the water. It seemed to take ten minutes to get my face out of the water. . . .

The next day there was still no baseball game. There was swimming. I ran off into the woods, I hid behind a tree. They found me and dragged me down to the lake. Kicking and screaming.

After that I did not hide anymore. I went to the lake like a good little boy. And stepped gingerly into the crib. And held on to the edge and kicked my feet. No more screaming. Just kicking.

I did not put my face in the water.

The counselor had a girlfriend. Her name was Phyllis. She was a counselor at the girls' camp across the way, dark haired, very pretty. He began to bring her to visit us after lights out. One night, in the dark, as I lay in bed, she kissed me on the cheek. She went down the line of bunks and kissed every boy on the cheek. The next night she did it again. The third day someone had an idea. We stuffed clothing under our blankets, in the shape of our bodies. At the place on our pillows where our heads should be, we made fake faces out of dirty underwear. Dirtiest side out. We envisioned Phyllis kissing these stains. . . .

We hid under our bunks. Phyllis arrived as usual. I don't believe she actually kissed the underwear. But she was not amused.

She never came again. I missed her good-night visits.

Day after day the biggest kids played softball. The intermediate kids played softball. Even Bobby Brownstein played softball. And hated it, I'm sure. But for Bunk Nine there was swimming every morning, swimming every afternoon. One after another the kids learned to swim the length of the crib and back; they passed their swim tests, they graduated out into the lake. Soon I was alone in the crib, holding on to the edge, kicking, kicking.

Like the Boston Braves of the era, I prayed a lot for rain.

Great tides of baseball knowledge churned through the depths of my mind. Facts darted to the surface like the minnows in the lake, then swooped out of sight while other facts darted up. The fact that Leo Durocher, the manager of the Dodgers, had been their shortstop before Pee Wee came along in 1940. The fact that Reese and Reiser were the Gold Dust Twins. The fact that Durocher had been suspended by the commissioner for associating with gamblers, and that the Dodgers this year were being managed by Burt Shotton, a gray-haired old man in street clothes, the first manager to wear street clothes since Connie Mack. The fact that Babe Ruth had started out as a pitcher, that Ty Cobb used to slide with his spikes up, that Carl Hubbell struck out five straight batters in the 1934 All-Star Game, that Dizzy Dean hurt his arm because he kept on pitching after he broke his toe. The as-yet unprovable fact that the Dodgers were gonna win the pennant.

The counselors didn't care.

"Put your face in the water," a voice said.

One Sunday in August was visitors' day. Our parents, home from Canada, came to see us. That afternoon the counselors—future politicians, perhaps—trotted us juniors up to the ball field to play a softball game. It was the only day all summer that we had touched a bat, a ball, a glove. It was a farce. Most of the kids stank.

"We had a lovely vacation," my mother said. "Did you have a nice summer?"

I never went to camp again. Not till I was fifteen, not till I was a counselor. Not till I could stand by the side of the pool, and look down unctuously, and smirk, and say: "What are you, afraid? Put your face in the water!"

I could have said it, but I didn't. Let St. Peter note that in his book. I hit them fungoes, I hit them grounders, I called balls and strikes, I kept their batting averages, I taught them to choke up on the bat, I taught them how to slide. I never, ever, made a scared kid put his face in the water. Not once. Some joys, in this brief life, we must forego.

He rubs his forehead, his eyes. He is astonished. He cannot remember with absolute certainty the first major league game he saw. He recalls with clarity assorted other manly firsts. If pressed he could name names, could list approximate dates. But the precise details of that first ball game have vanished.

He comforts himself. Probably he can't remember the details because it was an exhibition game at Yankee Stadium. In the country of baseball few events mean less.

In those days, when the teams arrived in New York from their spring training bases in Florida, the Dodgers and the Yankees would play exhibition games the weekend before the season began, just as the Mets and Yankees do now. My first major league game, I am fairly certain, was an exhibition at the Stadium at the brink of the '47 season. Memorable, one would think, because it was Jackie Robinson's first appearance. Each year after that I would watch the Dodgers play the Yankees in the spring, because that was the closest they ever came, the Stadium only a mile from my house. I would go with my brother, Saul, and later with my cousin David, and sit in the bleachers for fifty cents and look down into the Dodger bullpen. Once I brought my Brownie Hawkeye camera and took pictures of Carl Erskine warming up. Oisk. But the games did not count, so the hits and runs and strikeouts have disappeared, leaving K's in the computer of my brain for memories that signify.

The first genuine, certified, everything-goes-into-the-record-books games I saw were at the Polo Grounds. The Dodgers versus the Giants. This hate-filled rivalry. Maglie. Furillo. But the most memorable moment of all was my first night game. This is true, I have discovered, of every male baseball fan I know.

It was not even the Dodgers. It was the Giants versus the Phillies. For a reason.

Harry Brownstein, the policeman, a traffic cop, was walking a beat near the Polo Grounds one day. He saw a black limousine parked beside a fire hydrant. As he took his summons book from his back pocket and was about to write a ticket, a well-dressed man hurried up and asked the officer what was wrong.

"You're parked by a fire hydrant," the officer said.

"I'm Horace Stoneham," the man said. "I own the Giants."

"If this is your car," the officer said, "it's still parked by a fire hydrant."

"Do you have any kids, any boys?" Stoneham asked.

"Yes, I do," Officer Brownstein said.

"Perhaps they would like to see a ball game," the owner said. "Compliments of the Giants."

"I think they would like that."

"How many boys do you have?"

Mr. Brownstein thought of Jack and Bobby at home. Then he kindly thought of their best friend, little Robert Mayer.

"Three," he said.

Horace Stoneham reached into his pocket and pulled out a wad of tickets and handed the officer four tickets to the Giants-Phillies game the following night. The officer thanked him and put away his summons book.

"Stop by the clubhouse on your way into the game," Stoneham said.

I remember Mr. Brownstein recounting the scene, in more or less those words, when he came home from work that night. Mr. Brownstein asked me if I would like to come to the game. Most assuredly, I would.

It's only the Phillies and the Giants, I thought; *the Dodgers won't be playing. But it's a night game.* I had never been to a night game. *There's lights. . . .*

The next night Mr. Brownstein took us to the game. On the way up to our seats in the grandstand, we stopped outside the clubhouse door. Mr. Brownstein went inside. When he came out he was carrying a large box. He removed the lid from the box. Inside were a dozen baseballs. Twelve. They were not brand new, they were scuffed and worn, more brown, in truth, than white; clearly they were balls that had been used by the Giants in batting practice and then become too worn even for that. But who cared? Official National League baseballs, signed by the president of the league. They had been touched by the flesh of major leaguers.

Mr. Brownstein reached into the box. He handed me a ball. To keep. The Brownsteins would keep the other eleven. Fair enough.

He covered the box; we walked on up the ramps till we emerged at the proper level. And there like a miracle it was, spread far below, major league grass under major league lights, the most luminous green I had ever seen, the dark brown diamond cut into it perfectly, the bases aglow as if with a light of their own, players in bright white scampering through infield practice like toy angels. The image burning, burning, burning itself not into my eyes but into my heart. An exquisite sensual pleasure impossible to have imagined beforehand. The first good kiss.

The game was invented for the day. But the night is its fourth dimension. The night lends a vibrant tension to the abstract poetry.

I relish, now, with cynicism born of the years, that I discovered this wondrous beauty because a businessman gave a doughnut to a cop.

More purposeful than sentimental, I did not put Horace Stoneham's baseball under glass. (It was not, after all, a Dodger ball.) I put it to good use. My brother threw me pop flies with it, in the concrete backyard, deep into the dusk. He threw me grounders with it—high bounders, low ground-hugging scarifying skippers, little dropped bunts that made me charge the plate. All the knowledge of how to field that I had gleaned from the books at the Fordham library I put into practice with that ball, till the stitches wore through and the seams of the ball came apart. Then I took off the horsehide cover and wrapped the ball with black electric tape and rubbed it in some dirt to clear the stickiness, and my brother threw me more pop flies and more hard grounders through my ninth year, and my tenth, and my eleventh. If you wanted to be a major leaguer, you had to work at it.

But mostly there was the punchball, the stickball, the triangle—all the childish games that became in our childish eyes the real thing. I was the best fielder on the block, the fastest runner, and if I knew this was not real hardball, no problem. That would come later. There were no hardball fields in our neighborhood. The Little League had yet to reach The Bronx.

When I was twelve years old my brother was already eighteen and was a student at NYU, though he still was living at home. My mother had a weekly mah jongg game in those days, every Wednesday, the games rotating from one home field to the next. One fateful Wednesday, as the mah jongg tiles clackety-clacked like the spikes in John R. Tunis, one of the women asked me what I wanted to be when I grew up. "A baseball player," I said. It was my standard response, I had said it a hundred times before, and it was God's honest truth. But for some reason my brother chose this night to get annoyed. When I went to my room he followed me in. "Why do you keep saying that?" he asked. "You know you'll never be good enough to be a ballplayer." Then he left the room, leaving behind this shocking reality, this previously unspoken truth.

Deep in my gut I knew he was right. Quietly I began to cry. Picking up my glove and ball, I began to fire the ball into the glove as hard as I could, painfully, again and again and again, while the tears rolled down my cheeks. Hour after hour I did this, long after the mah jongg ladies had left, long after the house was dark, till my hand was as red and as sore as my heart. At last, after many hours, I cried myself to sleep. When I woke up in the morning, I had a realistic new goal: I would be a sportswriter.

A writer I eventually would become, first of sports and then of other heartbreaks. But a little piece of my soul died between second and third that night. And though I never casually pronounced it again, I wanted to be a ballplayer still. I wanted to be a major league shortstop. I *expected* to be a major league shortstop.

Whether or not I was good enough had little to do with it.

The Whales of Summer

Most men go through life with-
out ever seeing their own sperm cells. I saw mine at the embarrassing age of sixteen. So did all my classmates. Half of whom
were girls.

I was a senior at the Bronx High School of Science, taking an
elective course called Advanced Biology. It was known more pop-
ularly as "Blood and Piss," because that was what we studied, in
great detail. One day in the second half of the semester, we were
told to each bring in a sample of our own urine from that morning's accumulation. In the laboratory, after much coaxing from the
teacher, we sucked the liquid into pipettes, placed a drop on a
slide, slipped the slides into our microscopes; we would be performing tests to isolate the various minerals and other elements
present. The teacher moved from student to student, peering into
our scopes, making appropriate comments. When he looked into
mine he became ecstatic; he called the class to attention; there were
wonderful, intact sperm cells visible on the slide, he announced
with obvious pleasure; everyone was to gather around Bob
Mayer's microscope to see.

My nearest neighbors pushed in first. Then from all corners of
the room they came, these senior boys and senior girls, the girls in
their light spring dresses, girls whom I was much too shy to ask on
a date, and they formed a line to view my sperm cells. I could feel
my face grow hotter and hotter; I could feel it glowing red, as red a
hothouse cherry.

In retrospect my embarrassment returns. I imagine these nubile girls nudging one another, giggling, flirting sly glances in my direction. But in fact it was not like that at all. The line was quiet, solemn, like a queue of reverent Catholics waiting to view La Pietà.

If I had to conjure today what they saw in my microscope, it would be a bunch of tiny baseballs. Happy little baseballs, wagging their tails.

The anomaly is that, unlike their studly host, the little buggers could swim.

There is nothing in my ancestry to suggest I would be born with a congenital weakness for the game, that my DNA would register Dodger blue. My maternal grandparents fled Russia ahead of the pogroms, paused in London in 1903 long enough to have their first child, a girl named Anne, who would later become my mother, then made the long ocean voyage to New York. My grandfather, a tall, distinguished-looking man, left Russia with the name Mordecaiwolfe Borevyetski. By the time he was processed out of Ellis Island, a harried immigration clerk, as was the practice at the time, had rechristened him Max Wolff. *(Fleet-footed centerfielder? Good glove, weak bat?)* His brother, Jacob Borevyetski, emerged from a different line of immigrants as Jack Borough. *(A pitcher, definitely. Probably with a knuckleball.)* Max and Mary Wolff became naturalized citizens in time, and the seven children that followed Anne (five of whom lived to adulthood) all were U.S. citizens by birth. But it never occurred to Max and Mary, as they made their new lives here, that little Anne, an infant in their arms when they debarked from the boat, had to be naturalized as well. For the next fifty years my mother assumed she was an American citizen, till the fact that she was not came to the attention of the snuffling minions of so lofty a personage (if that is the proper word, and it isn't) as Senator Joseph McCarthy of Wisconsin. The FBI was ordered to investigate this she-devil in our midst. As they say in Hollywood, complications ensued.

My father's father, Abraham Mayer *(no suitable position; not even in the front office)* was a rabbi in a small town outside Vienna, who emigrated to America in 1905. He came alone, gave Hebrew lessons to the children of other immigrants for nine years, till he had saved up enough money to send for his wife and his two sons, Max and Joseph. They arrived here in 1914, just as the guns of August exploded across Europe.

Anne Wolff graduated from high school, a substantial achievement for immigrants of the day, and went to work as a bookkeeper to help her parents support their large family. Max Mayer, after completing grade school, also went to work, first carrying sample cases for salesmen of men's work clothes, then becoming a salesman himself. In 1927, the year of Lucky Lindy, the year Ruth hit sixty, the year of Murderer's Row, the two young people met while working for the same firm, Anne keeping the books, Max selling clothing wholesale from store to store. Their courtship lasted three years. They were married on June 15, 1930, and set sail on the *Leviathan* for a two-month honeymoon in Europe, even as the Depression was beginning to descend upon the land.

In October of 1932 Anne Mayer gave birth to their first child, Saul, a light-haired, blue-eyed child whose features resembled his mother's. More than six years later their second child arrived, with brown eyes, blond hair that would later turn brown, and features that resembled his dad's. This one they named Robert. My mother informed me later that as a babe in arms I visited the 1939 World's Fair at Flushing Meadows. I have no recollection of that, but it's reasonable to assume that I burped once or twice at the very spot where years later they would build Shea Stadium.

I do remember being taken frequently to the park by my grandpa Max to feed the pigeons. These outings took place when I was very young; Max Wolff died when I was four. The memory of those visits surfaced years later when I was writing a novel called *The Grace of Shortstops*, which was published in 1984, and which, unless I know you by your first name, you did not read. The book was fiction, but certain passages, such as the following, were true.

Probably some of the others did take him to the park after that. If they did, he didn't remember. All the boy would remember afterward was feeding the pigeons with his grandpa Max. And if something else was going on then, unknown to both of them, who is to say? Surely in the spring and summer months, within earshot and eyeshot of the man and the boy, there would have been older boys playing ball after school in the park that surrounded the special bench. The sights, the sounds of baseball, at least in its city-park incarnations, could not have helped but fill the wartime air on every side. And if the boy in his later memories would recall only the struts and coos of the pigeons, only the comfort of the old man's lap and the bristles of his white moustache, who could argue that baseball hadn't invaded his being even then?

Who, indeed?

Abner Doubleday is widely celebrated as the man who did not invent baseball. Despite much diligent research I have been unable to uncover the names of the Zen masters who did not invent punchball, stickball, triangle, stoopball, box baseball, and all the other national or regional pastimes with which I idled away my childhood. But their names are of no consequence, nor were the names of the games we played. Put a ball in my hand and I was transported to Ebbets Field each time on the soft white wings of a dove.

A brief elucidation of those childhood contests is, like the whale descriptions in *Moby Dick*, an informative, if indulgent, diversion. The wildly impatient may skip the next few pages and get on with the plot wherever they can find it.

Punchball, the principal form of life in the 1940s Bronx, we played in the brick-walled backyard, two on a side, a first baseman and a shortstop; three bases, home, first, and third. You tossed a rubber ball in the air (always called a Spaldeen, A. G. Spalding corrupted), smote it with your fist, and ran the bases while the opposing team fielded the ball. The center field wall consisted of garage doors, above which metal runners formed triangles in the manner of basketball hoops. A ball punched through the hoops on the fly was a home run. But a foot above the hoops began a brick wall, in which were set the windows of a telephone answering service. After enough windows had been broken by our Spaldeens, to the extreme but tolerant annoyance of the ladies speaking into their telephone chin-sets like refugees from a Norman Rockwell cover, we declared that anything that hit above the brick line on a fly was an out. This cut down drastically on our home runs, but did serve to reduce the volume of broken glass, so in a modest way we helped hold down the cost of some telephone bills. Balls pulled into the left field window of Mrs. Newman were also outs, but sometimes we could not resist taking aim, in the hope of enlivening a lopsided game with a blood-curdling low-speed chase.

If six kids were available, three on a side, punchball was played in the street in front of our houses, the extra man providing each side with an outfielder.

Stickball, which was not invented by Willie Mays, always was played in the street, three or four on a side, using a Spaldeen or a worn tennis ball. You threw the ball up, hit it with a bat made from an old and weathered broom or mop handle, and ran the bases, playing normal baseball rules. Anything that hit a parked car or landed on the sidewalk on either side of the street was a foul ball. But a hit into the leaves of the trees that overhung the street on the right field side was in play. If Carl Furillo could play the indented wall in Ebbets Field like Casals playing the cello, we became equally adept at catching a ball as it cascaded groundward through the thick green leaves of maple branches. The residents of the block lived in constant fear of being hit by the ball, especially the old people who liked to sit of a spring evening on wooden folding chairs in front of their buildings. I recall no injuries, but there must have been some close calls. Every so often a police car would come cruising up the block, summoned no doubt by the elderly residents. "Cheese it, the cops!" someone would yell, and whoever was holding the mop-handle bat would toss it under a parked car, and the rest of us would stand around innocently, as if discussing the Marshall Plan or some other interesting topic of the day. Sometimes the cops would stop and fish the bat from under the parked car and drive off with it. Other times they wouldn't bother, knowing that as soon as they drove off, someone would go into his house and bring out another. What "Cheese it" meant I did not understand then, and do not understand now. (The older kids said "Chickie, the cops!" This seems to offer little additional enlightenment.)

A more highly evolved form of stickball—the one I much preferred—included the use of a pitcher and a catcher. But the scarcest talent on Townsend Avenue in those days was the boy who could catch a pitched ball, inches behind a swinging broom-stick, without flinching, without closing his eyes. It was a talent that neither I nor anyone else on the block ever really mastered. This led to an average of about one wild pitch or passed ball out of every three pitches thrown, which caused a great deal of time to be spent waiting for the catcher to retrieve the ball from down the street. At the corner of Townsend Avenue and Clifford Place the curb gave way to the grimly smiling mouth of a sewer. At least once a week the ball would dribble down into the sewer before the puffing catcher could reach it. At this point the game would be delayed while the manhole cover atop the sewer was pried up by the older players. A tin can on a long string, always kept in readiness, was lowered the twenty feet or so down into the sludge below. And the ball, floating in dark, gummy gook, would be raised to the surface like water being drawn from a well in the distant villages from whence our parents had come. Sometimes the lowered can bobbed and floated and the ball could not be induced to settle into it. At that point one of the braver souls climbed down the footholes set into the walls of the sewer for the benefit of maintenance men, leaned out precariously over the muck, holding on with one hand, and fished out the ball with his other hand. I was never one of these braver souls. Why we did not merely chalk up such sewerfied balls to the expenses of the game and continue playing with another is a matter for speculation. Perhaps it was economics. More likely it was simply pride.

Sometimes our games were delayed by the vegetable man, who came clumping up the street in a creaky wooden wagon drawn by a swaybacked horse. "Vegetables, get your fruits and vegetables," he would shout in a thick voice, and as he pulled the moping horse to a stop on home plate or second base our mothers would stream from their respective doorways to pick selectively from the open wooden crates that covered the wagon, crates of cherries and peaches and plums (the good stuff), of broccoli and cauliflower (the bad.) Other times our games would be delayed by the knife-sharpener, who would arrive in an equally creaking wagon pulled by an equally decrepit horse, and our mothers would stream from the doorways to get their best knives and pairs of scissors sharpened. Eventually, however, both the vegetable man and the knife man replaced their sorry nags with trucks, which speeded up their traverse time. And not long after that they disappeared altogether, losing out to frozen vegetables and hardware stores, and the streets once more were returned to the stickball players for whom God had intended them.

A two-man form of stickball, which was in some ways my favorite, was also available. This required a walk to the school-yard, where a large rectangular box was painted on the wall of a handball court. In this form, as the pitcher pitched a tennis ball and the batter batted, balls and strikes were determined by whether the pitched ball struck the wall inside the painted rectangle. The drawback to this game was that a pitched ball could be lobbed in so that it crossed the batter's box high over his head and then dropped into the rectangle for a strike. A sharp-breaking curve—which should have been a ball—could also send you bailing out as it headed straight for your head or shoulder, then curved around the plate but into the rectangle for a strike. The advantage of this version, however, was that because only two of you were playing you could easily be entire major league teams. The Dodgers versus the Yankees, if I was facing Jack Brownstein. The Dodgers versus the Cardinals, if I was facing my cousin David and he got to choose the Dodgers first. We would go through the respective lineups, batter after batter—Erskine winds up, delivers, Terry Moore swings—and by being the Cardinals I could practice batting left handed, which I loved to do. Unlike the Bums, for whom only the Duke was a port-sider, the Redbirds featured lefties Stan Musial and Enos Slaughter. And Red Schoendienst switch-hit. Since I shared the common though chickenhearted tendency to bail out on sharp-breaking curves, learning to hit left handed would be increasingly valuable, I figured, when scouts came around to take a look.

When there were not enough men around for stickball—we boys somehow grew into men at playing time—there were other, minor-league diversions. Triangle—called slap ball in some neighborhoods—was played from curb to curb, crosswise. The pitcher lobbed the ball underhand, on a bounce, often digging his finger into the ball as he let it go, which caused it to curve sharply when it bounced. The batter slapped the ball with an open palm, then ran the bases as in baseball—but only first, third, and home, hence the name triangle.

When only two players were available there was box baseball. You faced each other across four concrete squares on the sidewalk. The pitcher bounced the ball into the last square. You slapped it back into the first. If you missed the first box, the batter was out. If you hit the first box, you got a single, double, triple, or home run, depending on how many times the ball bounced before the pitcher grabbed it.

Another two-man ball game was stoop ball. The batter stood on the sidewalk and fired the ball into the slope of three brick steps that fronted each house. The fielder stood in the middle of the street. If the first bounce of the ball was on the pavement, the batter was out. If the fielder caught a ball on the fly, the batter was also out. But if the ball bounced in the street, the traditional baseball rules prevailed: one base for every bounce.

Thousands of childhood hours we invested in every one of these games. The skills they required were no closer to real baseball—to hardball—than was whistling or flying a plane. But if hardball did not exist in the paved streets and concrete yards of the West Bronx, denial was the neurosis of the age. I read my library books, I listened to the Dodgers on the radio. I was well on my way to the major leagues.

In the lives of my parents baseball was a radical new element, introduced by my brother and transformed to a biological need by little me. They accepted it with amazing grace. My father usually did not get home from his route as a salesman until eight o'clock at night, so my mother, my brother, and I would eat supper without him, usually sitting down at the kitchen table about six-thirty. As we ate, we would listen, on the yellow plastic radio that sat on a nearby shelf, to Kenneth Banghart with fifteen minutes of the news, then to Stan Lomax with fifteen minutes of sports. Most ball games were played in the daytime back then, and Lomax would let us know how the Dodgers had fared, a fact upon which hung the delicate matter of how much dinner I actually could consume. At seven o'clock came the treat my brother and I had been waiting for: *Today's Baseball,* with Ward Wilson, Marty Glickman, and Bert Lee, Jr. Those three worthy gentlemen spent every weekday evening recreating in half an hour two ball games played by the New York teams that day—the Yankee game, the Giant game, or the Dodger game, two out of three. They offered a play-by-play of the game, in condensed form, complete with sound effects so artificially real you could almost smell the ballpark hot dogs. *Thwuck* was a solid two base hit; *thwack — roooohr* you knew was a homer. We would listen to these games on the edges of our seats—no matter that Stan Lomax had already told us the final scores. The only thing worse than hearing a Dodger loss was hearing the Yankees and then the Giants, hearing no Dodger game at all. My saintly mother sat there with us, finishing the sandwich she always preferred over the food-group meals she prepared for her kids; drinking her coffee, smoking her Pall Malls, tolerating our intensity till the games were over and she could return to her crossword puzzle or to the latest best-seller—John Hersey's *The Wall* perhaps—that she had rented from Harry's lending library.

My father, a small, balding man, only five feet two, an inch shorter than my mother, with no athletic interests, had muscular arms with which he carried cases of samples of the dungarees, sweatshirts, and athletic socks that he sold to army-and-navy stores and sporting goods stores throughout the city. One day when I was seven or eight he took me with him on his rounds to Brooklyn, deep into the promised land itself, where in one store, amid the pungent smell of leather, he bought me the baseball glove of my choice. In another store, which smelled of wool and flannel, he was to buy me a Dodgers uniform, which I long had coveted. The only Dodger uniform on display had the word DODGERS written across the chest in red block letters. This was wrong, I informed the salesman; Dodger lettering, I told him, was blue, and written in script. When the unamused salesman said such uniforms were not produced for kids, I was deeply distressed at the insensitivy of the world in general and adults in particular. But I soon was convinced by my practical father that a red block Dodgers was surely better than no Dodgers at all. I settled. And I wore the uniform proudly for several years, a red number 1 on the back. My brother took pictures of me in the backyard, in front of a brick wall, in full uniform, peering at an imaginary pitcher, my brown baseball bat held high. That summer, in the mountains, he took more pictures of me in uniform, demonstrating my sliding technique (the base in the foreground of the black-and-white snapshot is a rock) and kneeling on the grass, as if waiting on deck, the bat across my knee. The blend of innocence and determination in my face, shaded by my peaked cap, made the on-deck picture my favorite.

Batting next, the shortstop, number one . . .

Despite their tolerance, however, somewhere along the way my parents succumbed to the subversive notion that there were things in life more important than baseball. To my mother one of them was culture. To my father one of them was God.

One day when I was nine years old my mother decided it was time my brother and I learned to play musical instruments. My brother chose the clarinet, to which my parents quickly agreed. I would have preferred to stick to the sweet heavenly music of bat on ball. *Thwack — roooohr.* When pressed to make another choice I decided to play the drums.

Thought my mother (with this sentiment, if not these words): *Over my dead body.* My parents went downtown without me. They came home with a clarinet for my brother and an accordion for me.

"That's not a drum," I said, observant little brain that I was.

This was in the era known to social historians as the Dick Contino Age. Every Sunday night my own family and millions of other American families listened on the radio to the *Horace Heidts Show.* Dick Contino was a guy from Fresno, California, who played the accordion, and who began to win as best performer on the amateur hour week after week, month after month. Ten weeks, twenty, thirty, forty, fifty. A new world's record. Dick Contino playing "Lady of Spain"; Dick Contino playing "The Flight of the Bumblebee." He became a household word, the greatest American musician since Francis Scott Key. Across America ten million mothers looked at ten million little boys and thought: *If only . . .*

So my parents came home with an accordion.

I picked up two knives from our best set of silverware and began to drum with them on the kitchen table, as I often did. "I want to be a drummer," I said. "Like Gene Krupa."

My mother sat down to offer me a logical explanation. As a child I was never abused mentally or sexually; but I was abused with logical explanations.

"If you play the drums," my mother explained, "you'll have to find three or four other boys before you can play songs. Nobody listens to the drums alone. With an accordion you're a one-man band. You can play at weddings and bar mitzvahs. You'll be able to make money someday, to save up for college."

It was all very logical. Though my heart drummed to a different beat, I began to take accordion lessons.

From the outset I did not like the sound an accordion made; it seemed whiny and ineffectual, unlike the crisp and powerful drum. I did not like the way you played it; pulling and pushing bellows in and out lacked the violent drumbeat outlet that I needed, obedient Jewish boy that I was. But dutifully I sat on a chair in my room, because the accordion was too heavy for me to hold standing up, and I practiced my chords and then my songs while though the windows I could see Jackie Brownstein and David Portman having a catch, waiting for me to join them so some necessary game could begin.

Every Saturday morning I rode the D train to Times Square by myself to take an accordion lesson at the Wurlitzer Company. I resented not only the travel but the prime punchball time being stolen from my life. "Every Good Boy Does Fine," the instructor said, teaching me how to read music. Every Good Boy But Me.

After thirteen weeks of this my parents promoted me from Class C in the music league to Class A. They traded in my leased, fairly small accordion on the $125 purchase of a snazzy new one. One that I would "grow into." Never mind Pee Wee Reese; in my mother's eyes I was the next Dick Contino. The heavy new accordion was undeniably beautiful, but it made my shoulders hurt like hell. I gritted my teeth and learned to play "Home on the Range," while the sounds of baseball filtered in through the window. Maybe, I thought, I would enjoy the accordion more if the songs were not so dumb. So I asked my parents to buy me the sheet music for my favorite pop tune of the moment, "Buttons and Bows." They did not know it was my favorite song because it had been sung in a Bob Hope movie—*The Paleface*, I believe—by Jane Russell, whose luscious figure and raven hair had made her the object of my first true lust. But "Buttons and Bows" was difficult, as was every other tune I attempted—perhaps I should not have played with a baseball glove on either hand—and after two years of this torture my parents finally admitted defeat, stopped the lessons, and put the accordion in a closet.

The coda to this experience was played out a year later, when I was in the sixth grade. A baldheaded music teacher named Mr. Tuttleman called me to his office and said that according to his records I played the accordion, and the school was putting on a musicale in the auditorium in a few weeks, and he wanted me to play a song. I told him his information was not current, that I had quit playing the accordion a year ago.

"Well, practice one song," he said. "Surely you know one song."

I was too awed by authority figures not to obey. I went home and dug out the accordion and began to practice "Home on the Range." Day after day while the other kids were out playing ball in the street I once again was alone in my room, making the buffalo roam.

Finally, the day of the musicale arrived. My father drove me to school with the accordion. Before I knew it I was in the center of the stage of the school auditorium, looking down at hundreds of pupils in their white assembly-day shirts and red assembly-day ties. I began to play "Home on the Range." But in my nervousness I could not find middle C, and what I heard as I played was a series of discordant notes that would have sent both the deer and the antelope fleeing had there been any in earshot of The Bronx. After perhaps twenty seconds of this, bald Mr. Tuttleman walked out onto the stage, put his supercilious arm around my puny shoulders, muttered something about "stage fright," and led me off to the wings, to the scaffold, to the guillotine of pure humiliation.

I learned several important lessons from this forced cacophony. I learned never again to say yes to an authority figure when my heart was screaming no. And I learned never again to set foot on a public stage. To both of these adages I remain faithful still.

I also learned that I had no choice but to live my life, to craft my words, to the drumbeat of some inner poetry: ever distrustful of logical explanations.

The second impediment to my budding baseball career, in addition to the accordion, was Hebrew school. From the time I was seven until I was twelve I had to spend an hour every day after school, Monday through Thursday, and another hour on Sunday morning, turning my back on Reese-to-Robinson-to-Hodges, learning instead about Abraham-to-Isaac-to-Jacob. A good student, I begrudged not so much the learning as the hours I had to spend without a ball or a bat in my hand. Every so often, of a Sunday morning, I would sleep late enough to miss class, so I'd would be ready to hit the concrete playing fields. On those occasions, and only those occasions, my father would whip me with a belt, lashing out at my butt, my thighs, my knees, whatever part of my anatomy he could reach as I twisted in my bed. Despite this a few weeks later I would risk another whipping.

Then one miraculous day—or so it seemed—baseball and Hebrew school came together. The teacher, a shaky, white-haired gentleman named Mr. Strauss, announced that the following week, as a reward for being good students, the class would be taken to a baseball game at the Polo Grounds.

When the big day came we packed sandwiches in paper bags, gathered at the Mount Eden Center, where the Hebrew school was located, and took the subway downtown. We sat in the left field stands and watched the Giants and the Pirates knock the stuffing out of the ball. Doubles, triples, homers, flew in every direction. At the end of six and a half innings the Pirates were leading, 8–6. The Giant fans in the stands stood for the seventh-inning stretch. So did Mr. Strauss.

"All right, boys," he announced. "It's time to go."

"It's only the seventh inning," we protested.

He made a dramatic point of looking at his watch. "It's getting late," he said. "We have to get back."

This was sacrilege. The Giants still had three more times at bat. Anything could happen. What if they tied it up? There might be extra innings. . . . Disconsolate, we walked down the ramps. As we reached street level, too low down to see the field, too late to turn back, we heard a great roar erupt from the crowd. There could be only one explanation. One of the Giants had hit a home run.

In the street Mr. Strauss formed us up into two even rows. As he did, another, greater roar erupted like a volcano, rolled across the sky, soared heavenward.

"Another homer!" I told the kid next to me. "It had to be!"

Mr. Strauss acted as if he hadn't heard; it's possible that at his age he hadn't; it's certain that if he had, he would not have cared. He marched us off toward the entrance to the subway.

Just as I stepped onto the first step, a third great crescendo erupted from the stadium, a roar even louder than the others, and continued on and on till it echoed off the clouds above.

"Jesus!" I said.

Mr. Strauss whirled around, searching out the blasphemer in our midst. No one snitched. We continued down the stairs into the darkness below, feeling cheated, outraged. I did not really care if the Giants won or lost, but to some events you want to be a witness.

At home that night I listened to *Today's Baseball*. I confirmed the truth of it. In the bottom of the seventh, in our shuffling wake, three consecutive Giants—if memory serves, they were Whitey Lockman, Sid Gordon, and Willard Marshall—had hit back-to-back-to-back home runs. The Giants had won the game, 9–8.

"And Sid Gordon is even Jewish!" I muttered (a notion that was probably incorrect).

My attentiveness in Hebrew school plummeted sharply thereafter. I had little faith in any instructor, however exalted, who left a game in the middle of the seventh.

That was more than forty years ago. Now, in my sixth decade, I am more certain than ever that my childhood incredulity was precise. No God is worthy of the name Who does not stay the full nine innings.

He is watching the Mets on television, his drug of choice since 1962. They are running themselves into limbo. Bobby Bonilla, who has a five-year contract for $29 million, races from first to third on a single but is tagged out as he overslides third base. A few innings later Dick Schofield is tagged out as he overslides second base. He thinks: This is the big leagues, fellas.

In the house in which he grew up there was a long hallway extending from the living room past doorways on the left that led to the kitchen, the bathroom, and a storeroom, all the way to his brother's room. Down this linoleum-covered hallway, painted a dark green, he and his cousin David Skolsky would spend hours running at full speed, wearing socks but no shoes, and then sliding into the doorjamb at the end while the other one, glove in hand, applied a tag. That's how you got to Ebbets Field. Practice. Practice. Sometimes the constant sliding raised painful strawberries on his hips or thighs, but it was worth it. Even though you did not slide in punchball or stickball or stoopball, he would have to know how, a singles hitter like him, when he made it to the majors.

Watching the tube, he despairs at what he has seen. Schofield's father, Ducky, was a major leaguer: he must have taught his kid how to slide. And Bonilla! In the apartment where you grew up in The Bronx, Robert Bonilla, surely there must have been a proper hall. . . .

It was my family's practice every summer (except for the soggy hell of Camp Away) to rent a bungalow for July and August at a working-class resort in the Catskill Mountains, about ninety miles north of the city. There the women and children would escape the fetid city air for two months, and the husbands would commute on weekends, arriving in their cars on Friday evening, returning to the city on Sunday evening for another week of working bachelorhood. My parents' place of choice was called Fogel's, a former farm a few miles from a village with the storybook name Mountaindale. There, one day in August of 1945, someone ran out of a bungalow, shrieking with maniacal glee: "The war's over, the war's over, the war's over!" In each of the white-painted bungalows, including our own, radios were quickly switched on to confirm this momentous event. Then the women began streaming out the front doors onto the sunbaked, yellowing lawns, banging with spoons on pots and pans, shouting with genuine joy and relief the same happy refrain. We kids, copycats as ever, ran inside for our own pots and spoons and joined the noisy celebration. The war was over! We had beaten the Japs at last! Uncles and brothers and cousins would be coming home! Before long a spontaneous parade formed, and we dozens of women and kids, with not a man around, began to parade down the two-lane blacktop at the entrance to the place, shouting and singing and scaring every bird in the trees with our clanging pots till we reached the nearest hotel, half a mile away, where another celebration was under way. It was a memorable celebration, an outpouring of homespun patriotism that was as smooth and unquestioned and American as chocolate pudding (which I much preferred to apple pie).

The concept of disloyalty was something I did not encounter till three summers later. It emerged in the context of baseball. The traitor in question was Leo (The Lip) Durocher.

For seven years, from 1939—the year that I was born—to 1946, Durocher had been the manager of the Dodgers. He was also a shortstop, that rare breed of playing manager, until Pee Wee Reese came along in 1940, and Durocher the manager was smart enough to see that the marbles champion from Kentucky was the better shortstop, and therefore benched himself. Durocher was a flamboyant character who loved to argue with umpires—hence his nickname—flamboyant enough that the commissioner of baseball had suspended him for the entire 1947 season for consorting with gamblers, the prime consortee apparently having been actor George Raft. The Dodgers won the pennant without him under the gentle Mr. Shotton in his business suit, but in 1948 Leo the Lip was back at his old post. Until the middle of the summer. Then he quit. Worse yet, he crossed the East River and became the manager of the hated Giants.

In the heat of the summer day when this became known to us in the Catskill Mountains—Fogel's had been sold and renamed Gelfand's—it was almost too much to comprehend. The Dodgers could do all right without Durocher, they had proven that the year before; the notion of his leaving the team was only slightly cataclysmic. But for him to go literally overnight to an opposing team—and not just to any opposing team, but to the Giants!—this was a new order in the world of a nine-year-old. This was deserting to the enemy. This was Benedict Arnold country.

Just a few years later, reading Kenneth Roberts, I would come to understand that history has probably given General Arnold a bad rap; that morality doesn't come in black and white. But that was later. In the summer of '48, having absorbed through Durocher's treachery the concept of disloyalty, I welcomed it into my heart and made it my own.

On a cool evening in August a bunch of the boys and girls were gathering after supper to play hide-and-seek or ringolevio. As I began to sprint out the door into the failing light to join them, my mother told me to put on a sweater.

"I don't need one," I said.

"Put on a sweater," my mother insisted. "I don't want you catching cold."

"None of the other kids are wearing sweaters," I argued.

"I don't care about the other kids," my mother said.

"I won't," I said.

"Then you won't go out at all," my mother said. "Go up to your room."

I had pushed too far, and I had lost. Tearfully I marched up the wooden stairs. I closed my door and sat on the soft mattress of my bed and punched the brown metal frame. From the darkening lawns below I could hear the shouts of the kids, including Elaine somebody, who for a few brief weeks had become my first childhood crush. My face was hot with the unfairness of my fate. I picked up my ball and glove and began to pound the ball into the pocket of my mitt as hard as I could, which was my chief outlet for stress in those days and still serves the purpose (along with some cheap Chablis) today. A bare bulb illuminated my room. I realized I was a visible target for pity from the lawns below. I pulled down the black shades that covered the two windows—one of those seemingly inconsequential actions whose momentousness we cannot predict at the time. But because that darkening evening I was angry at my mother for making me a prisoner, and seeing the expanse of unsullied black window shade in front of me, I picked up a pencil that I usually used to score ball games, and wrote in huge letters on the inside of one of the shades the words FUCK YOU MOM.

I blanched as I pulled back from the window and saw what I had done. The unthinkable outburst had eased some of my anger already, but the words I had written were indelible. The pencil was black lead, the shade was black cloth: I had not exactly announced my sentiments in red paint on the George Washington Bridge; with the shade up, as it would be in the daytime, the obscenity would be invisible; with the light in the room out the obscenity would also be invisible. But with the light on as it was now the glow from the bulb caught enough of the metallic sheen of the writing to make the words stand out plainly.

My feeling of guilt, of betrayal, was overwhelming. As was my fear of being discovered for the rotten kid I truly was. What if my mother came in and saw the words? The punishment that would be mine beggared the mind. I thought of trying to erase the words, but there was no way; that would have torn the shade, and I would certainly have been discovered. The games of tag continued in the darkness outside as I twisted in my self-made hell. Three weeks remained before we would return to the city, three weeks during which, at any time, if she happened by chance to pull down the shade, my mother would be confronted with my shocking treachery.

Eventually I fell asleep. When I awoke in the morning I hoped it had all been a dream, but I turned and looked and the dread words still were there on the window shade. There was nothing to do but raise the shade so that the words wrapped around and around themselves and disappeared; nothing to do but hope they stayed that way.

Anxiety and guilt—the one born of the other—pervaded my skinny-marink body as I dressed that morning and went downstairs. Seated at the kitchen table was a stranger drinking coffee. It was my mother. But it also was not my mother. The mother I had known every day of my life till then was the most beautiful woman in the world. Not even Jane Russell came close. The woman seated in my mother's chair that morning, drinking her coffee, smoking her cigarette, was not ugly, not by any means, but she was—ordinary. She was—okay looking. She was—alas—no different from the mothers of my cousins (who were her sisters), no different from the mothers of my friends.

My mother had been demoted to the minors.

And it was all my fault. It was the fault of the terrible words I had scrawled on the window shade.

I hurried back upstairs, to see if perhaps my mother's transformation had removed the words from the shade; to see if she had lost her looks in order to absorb my sin. But it was not so. When I pulled down the rustling black shade, the words still were there, obscene and indelible.

I rolled up the shade again. I returned downstairs. My mother was as I had left her, her ethereal beauty vanished, a hostage to my dark disloyalty.

I lived in the shadow of that window shade for the remainder of the summer. When we returned to the city I had not been discovered; I never was. But in my own consciousness I had joined Leo Durocher in the Hall of Fame of traitors. There was more cruelty in the world, I was beginning to understand, than a little boy's heart could accept. And, like it or not, I was destined to be a part of it.

He is having lunch at Diego's, a neighborhood Mexican restaurant, with his best friend, Gene Smith, an abstract painter and lifetime second basemen. They did not grow up together but have known each other for twenty years: the Keystone Kids in their fifties. He is wearing a Brooklyn baseball cap, royal blue with a white B on the front. He's had it for years but has just begun to wear it in public. Smith, who grew up a Dodger fan in Bayonne, admires the cap; he hasn't seen it before. Then, while they wait for their enchiladas, Smith rails apoplectic about Tommy Lasorda, about the Dodger game he'd watched on the tube the night before.

"It's the ninth inning," Smith says. "The score is tied. The Cardinals have a runner on second, and Ozzie Smith is coming up. Smith is hitting .222. Lasorda intentionally walks Smith to get to Felix Jose, who's hitting .370. Who's tearing up the league. Jose hits the ball so hard, it knocks Lenny Harris into right field. And the winning scores. I couldn't believe it. How can Lasorda be so dumb? Where was the guy's head?"

Smith has long been convinced he can outmanage Tommy Lasorda. Usually, he does.

The conversation turns to childhood. He tells Smith, amid forkfuls of beans and rice, how back in The Bronx his mother used to call him a skinny-marink.

"Bolink," Smith corrects.

"Bolink?"

"Skinny-bolink. Not skinny-marink."

"Marink. I was a skinny-marink."

"I was a skinny-bolink," Smith says.

"What's a bolink?"

"I don't know. What's a marink?"

He and Smith view baseball identically in every respect but one. In this exception he soon discovers the subtle definitions. A bolink was a kid who, when the Dodgers were dragged by the dastardly O'Malley across the continent to Los Angeles, would continue to root for them. A marink was a kid who wouldn't put up with that shit.

My childhood was a radio marathon of Brooklyn games: listening to Snider and Hodges and Roy Campanella belting Old Goldies and then Post Toasties into the short left field stands or, in Snider's case, into Bedford Avenue, as described in the southern drawl of Red Barber, in the straight-man tones of Connie Desmond, later joined by the eager, insightful eye of Vince Scully. Of all the games I heard on the radio, none, including Lavagetto's hit, is more memorable to me than a humdrum game in the summer of '48, or possibly '49. The Dodgers were playing the Cardinals in

Brooklyn. At the end of seven and a half innings the Bums were losing, 8–0. There in our bungalow at Gelfand's it had been a day of scoreless torture, and by the middle of the eighth inning even God might have been excused if He had turned off the radio and gone outside into His bright summer sunshine to have a catch. But that was something I was never able to do. Though the prospects were bleak as the room in which I sat, I always had to listen until the end.

That memorable day, in the bottom of the eighth, the Bums shook off the collar and began to hit. Single, single, double, double. Maybe a homer or two. I do not recall the exact details, but I do know this: The Dodgers scored four runs in the bottom of the eighth, to cut the Cardinal lead to 8–4. Then, with another clutch rally, they scored five more in the bottom of the ninth, and they won the game, 9–8.

When the game ended, I could scarcely move. I could not walk without stumbling, without enduring patchwork needles of pain. All my limbs were numb, asleep, because for two innings I had not moved a muscle. I had not uncrossed my legs, I had not moved my arms, I had not scratched my head, which was itching something awful in the summer heat. Nothing. Because if I had stirred a single limb the Dodgers would have lost.

This is an aspect of baseball understood only by the staunchest fans: that the outcome of major league games is determined not by the players, not by the managers, but by the most subtle movements of little boys or even grown men miles away from the park.

I am not talking here about promises to God, as in: *Let the Dodgers win and I will go to church every Sunday.* Or: *Let the Dodgers win and I will eat my cauliflower.* Or: *Let the Dodgers win and I will stop playing with myself.* These attempts to bribe the Higher Power are indulged in not only by baseball fans but by football fans, basketball fans, hockey fans, probably even lacrosse fans. (*Let the Lakotas win and I will tend the fire faithfully.*) But they do not work. God is too smart for that. He well knows that if in response to such desperate promises He lets the Dodgers win, or the Jets, or the Knicks, or the Rangers, or even the Lakotas, hardly a week would go by before the unappreciative sinner would once again be sleep-

ing through church or Hebrew school, be stuffing his or her cauliflower deep into the bottom drawer of the bedroom dresser while
Mom is not looking, be onanizing with renewed energy, be posturing for the squaws while the tribal fires flicker and die.

That's not what I mean at all. What I mean is much more
immediate than that. What I mean is that, when your hair falls
over your eye, tickling your forehead, it is fine to brush it back
with your hand when the Dodgers, or the Mets, or whomever
you're rooting for, are making outs. Indeed, it may be essential to
brush your hair back, for the hair falling over your forehead may
be the very thing that is keeping your team from hitting, just as a
horse tied to a post will keep a Navajo baby from being born, and
the horse must be untied before the baby is free to emerge from the
womb. But if your team gets a hit, and you notice your hair
tickling your forehead, you must not touch it. If you leave it be,
Reese will probably follow Gilliam's single with a hit-and-run
single of his own; if you leave it be, Cleon Jones will most assuredly follow Wayne Garrett's walk with a homer. But if at that
moment you interfere with the natural order and brush back your
hair—or uncross your legs, or whatever—then a double play is
sure to follow.

This phenomenon does not exist in any other sport. Cynics will
scoff that it does not exist in baseball either; they will say it is a
trick of the bumbling mind, a wishful desire for godlike omnipo-
tence. But true fans know otherwise. To prove this beyond dispute
I eagerly await the day when the *Elias Baseball Analyst*, or James's
Baseball Abstract, will make available the necessary stats.

In the scorecard of my early years there must be a thousand
fielding plays I still remember. Catches made with my back to
home plate, like Willie Mays off of Vic Wertz—*before* Willie Mays
off of Vic Wertz—just as I slammed into a set of peeling wooden
garage doors in the backyard that was the stadium of my youth, a
stadium without fans, which nonetheless echoed in my childish
head with the clamor of multitudes. Or catches in the street, in
fully extended webbings, microseconds before the straining elbow slammed into the windshield of a parked car, the windshield

winning this encounter, the arm bruised but still proudly clutching the ball in the battered glove. Amid all such remembered brilliance—which still exists in some beautiful timescape parallel to adulthood—I shall recount two terrible moments: because they occurred in that critical nexus where baseball and life intersect, with consequences. As they often do.

The first moment took place around the corner from our Townsend Avenue house, on Clifford Place, a wider yet less trafficked street where the older kids of the neighborhood often played stickball. These kids were sixteen or seventeen—my brother, Saul, was one of them—and on this particular day, when I was only ten, they asked me, for the very first time, to join their game, because they were short a man. I was grateful for the honor, determined to prove myself worthy. They placed me at first base, where I could certainly catch the ball, and early in the game a fellow on the other team hit a high bounder in my direction. If I waited for the ball to come to me he would beat it out for a hit. Instead I charged the ball, grabbed it, and with one broad swipe of my right hand as he ran by I ticked the back of his jacket with the ball.

Or did I?

"Out!" I shouted instinctively.

"He missed me, he missed me," the batter insisted loudly.

"I got him, he's out," I said, my face growing red with excitement.

Both teams joined the argument. Finally my brother trotted in from his outfield position and quieted both sides. "Did you touch him?" he asked me, before this gathered jury of my more-than-peers.

"I nicked his jacket," I said.

At which point Saul solemnly informed the others: "If he says he got him, he got him. My brother doesn't lie."

That put an end to it, and we proceeded with the otherwise unmemorable game. But I have never forgotten that warm spring day in 1949, because the truth was that I had missed the dashing runner, missed his blurry back by no more than an eighth of an inch, but missed him nonetheless. In the excitement of wanting so badly to tag him I had shouted "Out," and having shouted that, I could not back down. The moment troubled me on the couch of a psychologist more than a decade later; it troubles me still. I am hardly a saint; in the years since then I have told my share of necessary lies to bosses and to women and to myself. But on that distant day the lesson I learned was that some things in life are sacred, and baseball is one of them. I haven't lied about it since.

The second fielding play I will relate touched yet a deeper, darker place. It occurred a year later, when I was eleven, at Gelfand's in the Catskills. Our summers spent there were the glory days of my youth, perhaps of my life. There was a day camp for us boys all week long, and every morning at nine-thirty, before going swimming, we played a softball game, the same two teams battling each other all summer. There was no greater heaven on earth, it seemed to me, than to play a real, ten-on-a-side softball game every day. I was the captain and shortstop of one team. The only better player, a fellow named Paul Pfeffer, who was a year older than I, was the captain and the pitcher for the other team. My brother was the counselor, and he kept records of the two teams all summer long: batting averages, runs batted in, everything. I batted .431, as I recall. Paul Pfeffer batted .512.

One Sunday, when all the parents were present, standing or sitting in lawn chairs along the foul lines, our two teams combined forces to represent the bungalow colony against a team from the hotel down the road. It was the Dodgers vs. the Yankees in miniature. Pfeffer, who actually came from Brooklyn, was on the mound. I was ensconced at short. At a critical moment in the game, with us good guys clinging to a one-run lead, our opponents had a man on first with one out. At that moment a vision formed in my eleven-year-old mind, a vision of what I wanted to happen next, of what I *knew* was going to happen next. The batter was going to hit a grounder back through the box. Breaking quickly to my left, I would snare the grounder in my glove just as I crossed second base. Then I would fire to first, where my cousin David, an apprentice Gil Hodges, had a sure pair of hands. I warned myself that this vision could not come true, because any bounder up the middle would be snared by the agile Pfeffer on the mound. Then he pitched, then the batter swung, then the ball was scooting up the middle, under Pfeffer's glove. The ball snuggled into my Pee Wee Reese model mitt at the exact instant that I dragged my foot across second base—just as it had in my hopeful premonition. I fired to first to complete the double play, my cousin David caught the ball routinely, and I trotted off the field as happy as I ever get. I found the spot on the sidelines where my mother was standing, watching. I dropped my glove beside her. I waited just a moment for the compliment I was due.

"Wasn't that a wonderful catch David made?" my mother said.

This mother that I loved above all other humans on earth. *Wasn't that a wonderful catch David made?* Nothing else. No mention of my incredible reflexes, my brilliant stop, my smooth glide across the bag, my steamy and accurate throw. Nothing.

I hated my mother then. This was far deeper than the momentary anger caused by having to wear a sweater; this was a wound that touched the core of my being, a wound that would endure. I should have forgiven her—what did she know of baseball?—but I resented her with the heat of the tears that stung my eyes as I found a bat and took my turn at the plate. I don't remember if I got a hit, or what the final score was, though I believe we won a thriller, 2 to 1. But I never forgot this profound new knowledge: learning you could hate the ones you love.

Ten years later there was an echo of that moment of which I am not proud.

On my last day at the Columbia Graduate School of Journalism I received a fellowship, which was awarded only to the top three students in the school. It was the fulfillment of a year-long goal. My mother was in Montefiore Hospital at the time, recovering from an operation for cancer, and I telephoned her with the happy news. She asked me to come visit her that evening. I told her I could not, that my friend Vic Ziegel and the girl I was dating were going to a ball game that night—a game at Yankee Stadium—and that I wanted to celebrate with them. But I would come to see her the following afternoon.

I went to the game that night and I was bored; I was always bored watching the mechanical Yankees. On the way home I had a fight with the pretty girl I had dated all that winter—a ridiculous fight she purposely picked, it seemed to me—and we never dated again; a week later she left the city to be a camp counselor for the summer, and when she came back she was engaged. The day after the ball game I went to visit my mother at the hospital. She was well enough to get out of bed and she walked with me to the day room, a large bright room with a television set at one end and a lot of Formica tables and folding chairs. We sat at a table in the middle of the room, but there were not many visitors at that moment and I don't think anyone could hear us as we spoke. My mother told me how disappointed she had been that I had not come the previous day; she had been so excited, so proud of my winning a fellowship, she said, and had wanted to show me off to her fellow patients. Then she told me the news she had been withholding till school ended, so that I would not be troubled, so that I would win my fellowship. She told me the doctors had given her only six months to live.

I was stunned by her revelation. She'd had several cancer operations in the previous few years and none had led to this. I was stunned by my own blindness, by my ignorant selfishness. If she had told me the truth earlier, I would certainly have been at the hospital the day before; I would have postponed my own celebration. But I have wondered since if I would have been there anyway if in the Catskill Mountains ten years earlier she had offered a bit of motherly praise for my wizardry at shortstop. How I had hungered for that. How I still do! Never mind that I could write, Mom. I could goddamn field!

My mother died two months later. That was more than thirty years ago. I haven't been to a Yankee game since.

Bazeball
Been Good to Me

I am sitting in my rocking chair in Santa Fe, New Mexico, where I have lived for more than twenty years, and I am watching the Mets on the tube. This I do on most Tuesdays, Fridays, and Sundays, courtesy of our local cable company and WWOR-TV. It's a quiet evening in June, the Mets are stalled at the .500 mark, 28 and 28, three games behind the Pirates, and they are playing a not particularly significant game at Montreal. Doc Gooden is on the mound, breezing with a 5–1 lead. With runners on first and second in the middle of the game, he induces a sharp ground ball to the right side. Willie Randolph scoots to his right, shoots—not flips—the ball toward second with a broken-wristed backhand motion. Dick Schofield coming across the bag from short takes the throw and, leaping toward the outfield side to avoid incoming spikes, fires on to first, where the fleet Delino DeShields is out by several steps. It is not a spectacular double play but it is far above routine, and something in my chest reacts, quivers with exquisite pleasure, as at the plucking of some archetypal chord.

My mind unbidden closes the cliché gap—leaping shortstop equals ballet dancer—and I remember a night years ago when my friend Marilyn Berger got us tickets to the Bolshoi Ballet at the Metropolitan Opera House in New York, the last attraction there before the city fathers would tear the old building down. The Bolshoi was doing *Don Quixote,* and for two acts we sat enthralled as the dancers in their brightly colored peasant costumes leapt and spun across the stage while the story played itself out. It was not the traditional image of ballet until the curtain rose for the last act, and the lights came up on a line of ballerinas strung across the stage in gleaming white tutus. I turned to Marilyn and said, perhaps slightly above a whisper: "I thought it would *never* start!" Marilyn giggled, and so did the couple behind us, who overheard. One of them leaned over and repeated my remark to his neighbor, who also laughed, and passed it along to the person beside him. As the first strains of the music came up and the ballerinas began to dance, this small eruption of laughter gradually moved in little explosive pops counterclockwise around the horseshoe-shaped balcony of the Met.

There are only two joys as succinctly wondrous as sitting beside an appreciative young lady and upstaging, for an instant, the infinite grace of Maya Plisetskaya. One is watching the turning of an exquisite double play. The other, longer lasting, is turning one yourself.

Sitting in my rocking chair, I recall what Doc Gooden said when, after his first few seasons, opposing batters began laying off his high fastball, and reduced him from a brilliant pitcher to a routinely good one. "I miss being great," Gooden said.

I visualize my good glove at ages nine through eleven. I, too, miss being great.

Unfortunately, as is my lifetime compulsion, I watch this game till the end. Gooden relinquishes most of his lead in the bottom of the eighth, and when John Franco is brought in to relieve, he blows a save for the first time this season. At the end of eight the score is tied, 5–5. My cheerful evening has slipped, with the suddenness of a spring shower, into a vague uneasiness.

In the top of the ninth Howard Johnson inspires hope with a one-out double. Eddie Murray follows with a long blast to right. Expo right fielder Larry Walker races back, then stops and turns as if he will catch the ball. Johnson, leading off second, races back to the bag to tag up. But Walker is only faking; the ball hits the wall far behind him. As it bounces quickly back toward his glove, Johnson, taken in by the act, can only advance to third on Murray's double. My vague depression sharpens knifelike into futile exasperation.

The Expos walk Bobby Bonilla to fill the bases. After a pitching change Chico Walker is sent up by manager Jeff Torborg to pinch-hit. The count goes to 2 and 0. Way to go, Chico. A walk will force in the lead run. I wince as Walker, who is no Stan Musial, swings at the 2–0 pitch. But he lines a sharp single to right, Johnson, his sin absolved by the hit, trots home, and the Mets take a 6–5 lead into the bottom of the ninth. Exasperation tilts its face toward a watchful wariness.

Bottom of the ninth. With one out Bonilla in right breaks in for a line drive. Then he slams on the brakes and watches the ball sail over his head for a double that should have been caught. The ghost of Metsies past watches and grins. Can't anybody here play this game? Franco uncharacteristically walks the next batter on four pitches. The tying and winning runs are on base. Wariness slumps, sunken chested, into resignation.

Earlier in the game I had eaten dinner in front of the set: roast skinless chicken breast, roasted potatoes, carrots, onions. Tasty and heart-wise. The empty plate has long since been removed to the kitchen sink, but a napkin and a toothpick are on the small table in front of me. I move the napkin, the toothpick, from the table to the desk beside me.

With the Mets about to blow another, John Franco stretches, pitches. The batter slams a sharp grounder up the middle. Franco spears it on one hop. He turns and fires toward second. The throw is high and to the right, is headed toward right-center, but Schofield (again!) leaps high, somehow manages to flag the ball while still keeping his foot on the base, evades another set of incoming spikes, and completes the double play. The game is over. The Mets, undeserving, have staggered to a victory.

I slump in my chair. The dinner is churning in my stomach. The Mets are now 29 and 28. Would it really have mattered, in the universal scheme of things, if they had ended this night at 28 and 29? What's Torborg to me, or me to Torborg, that I should churn for him?

Idly, I glance toward my telephone. He won't even call, I'm sure of it. He won't even call to thank me for moving the napkin, the toothpick.

* * *

There were days in my youth when the Dodgers did not play. Off days. Rainy days. There was also, out of obscure meteorological necessity, winter. In that chilly, sometimes snow-laden time, when the sky was still dark when you awoke to go to school, and was already dark again when you came home from Hebrew school and practiced the accordion, on those days, in other words, in which God had missed the point altogether, my parallel reality was a board game called All-Star Baseball. It was a board game, however, only in the literal sense. More precisely, it was reality cubed, because in this game real ballplayers played games, on the floor of my room, that they never really played—but games that assumed an interest, if not quite the eat-or-perish importance, equal to games played at Ebbets Field.

The primary accoutrements of this game were a simple metal spinner, and dozens of round cardboard cards with a cutout portion in the center that fit over the spinner. Each card bore the name of a major league player—an All-Star. The circumferences of the cards were divided into fourteen numbered spaces. Number 1, if the spinner landed on it, was a home run. Number 2 was a double play. Three was an error, 5 a triple, 7 a short single that advanced the runners one base, 11 a double, 13 a long single that advanced the runners two bases. The other numbers were assorted ground-outs, fly balls, strikeouts, and walks. The genius of the game was that the cards of the players were based on actual major league statistics; they accurately represented the prowess of each player in each department; so that Joe DiMaggio and Ted Williams had number 1's—home-run boxes—more than half an inch wide, while Marty Marion's was the merest sliver; and so forth. The cards were so accurate that they became in my mind not mere cards but the players themselves. As the players batted you moved pegs around a diamond that was also provided, and kept the score up to date on an outfield scoreboard.

The game was meant to be played with the National League battling the American League. But since my cousin David and I were both National Leaguers, we mixed all the cards together and chose our own teams. Whoever got to make the first selection—

the usual first choice was Williams or Stan Musial—the other person chose the next two. After that we alternated until all the players were chosen. These teams remained intact for the entire season. To make things more interesting I kept player and team records in a lined composition book, an entire page for each player. In this record book I kept track of at bats, hits, runs batted in, singles, doubles, triples, home runs, and walks, as well as the won-lost records of the pitchers. One year the manufacturer—I believe it was Parker Bros.—came out with a set of Old-Timer cards you could purchase, with spinner-cards for Ruth, Gehrig, Cobb, and all the other greats. For many months I resisted, a nine-year-old purist. Then, for the sake of variety, I gave in and bought those cards as well. We chose new teams that mixed the former greats with the current players, and established a new record book for the new era. Sometimes I played with David or my brother managing one team and me the other; sometimes I played alone, managing both teams, always scrupulously unbiased in my choice of pinch hitters and other substitutions. The integrity of the game demanded this, no matter which team my heart was rooting for.

All this was long before J. Henry Waugh was a gleam in Robert Coover's eye—though Coover in his own childhood must certainly have done the same. (And probably also wished they'd call him Bobby.)

My All-Star game and my record books did not get thrown into the trash with the same willful self-destruction as my baseball cards, but they vanished nonetheless, at some unknown time, to that mysterious Valhalla where most childhood loves repair to die.

One day many years later, during a period of necessary loneliness that followed my divorce, I prowled the local toy stores in search of the latest version of All-Star Baseball, wishing perhaps to revive my well-spent youth. None of the clerks had ever heard of it. I left each store with an increasing sense of loss, not so much for myself as for all the generations of the young who would never know the pleasure of this game. It was one more casualty, I suppose, of television. And yet . . . what of rainy days? And what of winter? They still do not televise baseball games in winter.

* * *

My friend Hope Aldrich, who is the same age as I am, told me a few days ago that when she was little her father and her brother used to argue about baseball every morning at the breakfast table. I find this of interest because Hope's given name was Hope Aldrich Rockefeller. Her father was John D. Rockefeller III; her brother Jay is a senator from West Virginia. Her father, a devoted philanthropist, was a fierce Dodger fan, Hope recalls, especially after they signed Jackie Robinson; her brother, now a leading spokesman for the rights of the poor, was an ardent Giant fan; the two never ceased to battle about the merits of their teams.

This echo of Townsend Avenue on Beekman Place is oddly comforting, in a democratic way. I cannot explain why. Certainly an interest in baseball bestows neither humanity nor grace. It is well known, for instance, that George Bush, our erstwhile president, played first base for Yale. With no knowledge whatever, I would lay five to one that he was a Yankee fan.

My favorite remark about Mr. Bush—I don't know who said it first—is that he was born on third base and thinks he hit a triple.

1951.

I suppose I cannot postpone it any longer. We must dispose of it as quickly as possible—whistle past the graveyard, as it were—and move on.

But first a necessary word about the media.

In addition to our getting news and sports reports from the radio, my father bought *The New York Times* every morning. And the Bronx edition of the *New York Post* was delivered to our door each afternoon. I devoured the sports pages of both. My favorite sportswriter in those early days was Arthur Daley, the sports columnist of the *Times;* I loved the anecdotes he spun about the ballplayers of old. Sports sections in those days were still the toy departments of newspapers, as someone once said, and browsing in Arthur Daley was like a visit to F.A.O. Schwarz. Red Smith was doing much the same at the *Herald Tribune*, but we never got the *Trib*. By the time I entered college I would understand the superficiality of this warm and cozy approach. A new cynicism and caustic humor would be

63

brought to the sports pages by Dick Young of the *Daily News* and by Leonard Shecter, Leonard Koppett, and later my buddy Vic Ziegel at the *Post*. Out on Long Island a more probing kind of sportswriting would be developed by Jack Mann, Stan Isaacs, George Vecsey, and Steve Jacobsen of *Newsday*, who would set a new standard for the coverage of ballplayers as complex human souls. But that was later. For sharp-edged insight in those early days—a kind of antidote to Daley's soothing milk—I turned to the opinion page of the *Post*, to the columns of Murray Kempton. If Pee Wee Reese was my baseball hero, Kempton, with his incisive language and his biting irony, was the journalistic equivalent, Plisetskaya at the typewriter. His columns inspired the trade I would turn to when my brother's hard-nosed prophecy came true and the majors stood exposed for what they were: an impossible dream.

But I digress. I was about to speak of 1951.

My family did not yet own a television set in 1951.

Television came to The Bronx in 1948. The first time I saw it was one June night when my parents were out and my brother was baby-sitting me. A heavyweight championship fight was being waged that night, one of the first to be carried on television. A radio repair shop on Jerome Avenue had a TV set in the window, which it left on for the entertainment of passersby, a common merchandising ploy at the time. My brother told me to put on my robe and slippers and he led me three blocks through the night, and we stood under the Jerome Avenue El and watched through the window of the repair shop as Joe Louis knocked out Jersey Joe Walcott to retain his heavyweight championship. I never would become a lug-nut boxing buff, but from that day forth, until the demise of Muhammad Ali, I tried not to miss a championship fight. Later that year the Portmans became the first in our circle to buy a television set. On Tuesday evenings we would gather in their living room to watch Milton Berle's *Texaco Star Theater*. I never cared much for Berle's cross-dressing and ridiculous posturing, but I loved the singing signature:

> *We are the men of Texaco,*
> *We work from Maine to Mexico. . . .*

As television proliferated, the Berle show became so popular that the local parent-teacher association, which held its meetings on Tuesday nights, had to switch them to Monday nights in the face of plummeting attendance. Not long after, the meetings would be switched again, when Everyone Loved Lucy on Monday nights.

I would also go to the Portmans to watch an occasional ball game. I remember being there one night when Rex Barney was pitching for the Dodgers. After a few innings the game was delayed by rain. We waited out the delay, play was resumed for a time; then there was another rain delay. I had to return home and go to bed. In the morning I learned that after the second delay the game had been completed, and that Rex Barney, despite a bunch of walks and a bellyache he got from eating a hot dog during one of the delays, had pitched a no-hitter.

Televised baseball notwithstanding, my parents were in no hurry to purchase a TV set. One reason was the high cost. Another was the distraction it would be from our schoolwork. I do not recall lobbying for one either. I was quite content with baseball on the radio; my imagination could supply all the pictures necessary.

In 1950 my cousin David's family bought a set. They lived half way across The Bronx, in the Pelham Parkway section, and every Saturday I would take two buses to their house. David and I would play ball in the morning, then camp in front of the large TV set in the basement playroom to watch the Dodgers. We envied the Little Leaguers who vied for prizes on *Happy Felton's Knothole Gang*, which preceded each home game. Three kids our age, in full uniform, would field grounders and pop flies, and one of them would be chosen as the leading prospect. It was not difficult, with my knowledge of the game, to anticipate each winner. How I envied them! Then came the game itself. Watching the pitcher throw from the top of the screen to the batter at the bottom was a distortion of the baseball aesthetic that was displeasing. But it did not take long to adjust; baseball was baseball, any way you looked at it. Win or lose, we sat before the set to the very end, like primitive moon worshipers, before emerging from the dark basement into the summer sun to resume our own careers.

In the spring of 1951 the house in which we lived was sold. The new owners coveted our apartment, and we were told we would have to move. Instead of renting again, my parents purchased a brick row house in the Pelham Parkway section, only six short blocks from the Skolskys. They got a good, quick deal on the house because the owner was a corrupt policeman who was on the lam in Florida amid a scandal rocking the New York Police Department. We moved at the end of June, and because my mother would spend the summer furnishing our new house, we did not go to the Catskills that year; we would never go again. The daily softball games in which I had so reveled and so excelled were gone forever. I could not know it then, but that cessation ended the purest time of my childhood. Ahead lay the typical turmoil of adolescent angst, in which I fell so far I tried to take up golf.

But that was later. First there was the summer of '51: in which the Dodgers, the beloved boys of summer—Gilliam, Reese, Snider, Robinson, Hodges, Campanella, Furillo, Cox, and the pitchers bold—were streaking to recapture the flag they had lost on the last day of the season the year before; in which the season should have been declared over in the middle of August, when the Brooks were ahead of the second-place Giants by 13½ games; in which my mother had our new living room painted dark green; in which the Giants went on a rampage just as the Bums began to stumble, the Giant comeback so stunning and the Dodger streak so feeble that the Giants caught them, tied them, on the next to last day of the season. No team had ever been so far ahead so late in the season and failed to win the pennant. The Brooks were flirting with total ignominy.

On that last day the Dodgers were playing at Philadelphia. The Giants won their game quickly; the Dodgers now had to win theirs or lose the pennant. I huddled beside the same old yellow plastic radio, now in the kitchen of our new house, along with my brother, my mother, my father. That Sunday evening was the start of Rosh Hashanah, the Jewish New Year. We would be going to temple at sundown, the first Jewish holiday we would observe in a new synagogue, in our new neighborhood, with a round-faced new rabbi named Samuel Weiss. Though my father, for our sake, wanted the Dodgers to win, there would be a six-block walk to the temple, and he wanted the game over quickly so we could get going. But it was not to be. The score was tied into the ninth, the tenth, the eleventh. In the bottom of the twelfth the Phillies threatened. One more base hit and the Bums would be dead. In all my life I never have prayed before the open Aron Kodesh in a temple, before the unrolled sacred Torah, nearly as hard as I did in front of that yellow plastic radio. Certainly it was true that day. I implored God not to let this happen. And God, in the image of Jackie Robinson, listened. The batter laced a line drive toward right-center field. It had base hit, as they say too often, written all over it. The game appeared to be over, the season appeared to be over, the most devastating turnaround in baseball history appeared to be over. Except that it wasn't. Robinson, with the fierce determination that made him great, dove headlong for the ball, his body stretched full length as if in flight, parallel to the ground, and he snared the liner for the out that saved the game.

We all breathed out our relief.

"Okay, let's go to shul," my father said.

Right, Dad.

Neither Saul nor I was in the habit of flat-out disobeying our father. This time our stance was firm as well as righteous. No way.

My father took his siddur, his yarmulke, his talith bag, and set off by himself; we promised we would join him in temple as soon as the game was over.

Another extra inning followed, then another. The tension had strung the season out hours beyond what the schedule-makers had intended. Until, in the top of the fourteenth, Robinson the Hero did it again, swung his quick bat with his ebony hands, belted a home run, to give the Dodgers the lead, to give the Dodgers the game, 9–8, to give the Dodgers a tie for the pennant.

A tie. Like kissing your sister, people have said. A week earlier we would not have settled for this. But from the jaws of defeat the Bums had snatched on this final day at least the aching molar of a tie. Better this than no pain at all. The annual credo of the Dodger fan: I hurt, therefore I am.

A three-game play-off with the Giants would begin the next day, a play-off that would have to be anticlimactic after this incredible final game. Saul and I hurried off to temple, to discuss this turn of events with the other young men; to make believe, in the House of God, that we were praying; maybe even, this time, to say a little prayer for the Brooklyn men.

For the schoolboys of New York the next two days were fortuitous. Because it was Rosh Hashanah, we Jewish kids did not have to go to school. Because the great majority of the city's teachers were Jewish, only token classes would be held for the other kids, a baby-sitting operation that was not taken seriously. Any young ball fan who wanted to could stay home and listen to the games. So it was that we listened at home and compared notes at the temple as the Giants won the first game, 3–1, as the Dodgers came back to take the second, 10–0, behind the shutout pitching of rookie Clem Labine. Now, again, a single game would decide the pennant. And on this frustrating day there would be school.

The year before, I had entered Wade Junior High, in our old neighborhood. I had completed the seventh grade in a Special Progress class, which meant that I would skip directly to the ninth grade. When we moved across The Bronx that summer, I legally should have transferred to the local school. But there was no junior high in the area; I would have had to enter the eighth grade and lose the year I was skipping. Instead, my parents decided I would use as my address, for school purposes, the apartment on Walton Avenue that had been my grandmother's until her death three years before, and in which my aunt Sarah, who had never married, still lived. This meant that, though only twelve, I would travel to school for forty-five minutes on two public buses each morning and travel home forty-five minutes in reverse each afternoon. We all agreed it would be worth it. Aunt Sarah worked downtown as a bookkeeper at the insurance firm of one of my uncles; she was away all day; I was given a key to her apartment in case I wanted to go there for a snack or some other reason after school before my bus ride home. So it was that, on the day after Rosh Hashanah, on the day of the third and final game of the 1951 play-off between the Dodgers and the Giants, I hurried from school the four blocks to my aunt's apartment building, pushed into the cool, dark lobby, unlocked the door to the first-floor apartment that somehow still smelled of boiled cabbage years after my grandmother had died. Until I snapped on the radio there I had no idea of the score; there had been rumors at school that the Bums were winning, but I could not be sure.

As the radio came on, the top of the ninth was ending. The Dodgers were indeed ahead, 4–1. The joy of the New Year was in my heart. But when Alvin Dark singled, and Don Mueller singled, and Whitey Lockman doubled down the left-field line, the score was 4–2, and the tying runs were on.

And there is manager Chuck Dressen walking out to the mound. And there is Brooklyn ace Ralph Branca walking in from the bullpen. . . . And there is Giant batter Bobby (Bobby!) Thomson stepping into the box. . . . And there is his long-armed swing, there is the high line drive soaring toward the short left field stands, there is Leo Durocher, the Giant manager (Durocher!), jumping up and down and pounding Thomson on the back as he rounds third, there are all the Giant players—as I would see in filmed highlight far too many times later—pounding him into submission. What I actually saw, then, at that moment, was the sad, dark apartment of my spinster aunt, me standing beside the radio in the kitchen, then slumping into a chair as Giant announcer Russ Hodges went out of his mind on the air, screaming over and over at the top of his voice: "The Giants win the pennant! The Giants win the pennant! The Giants win the pennant!"

As if anybody cared.

I snapped off the radio, took my schoolbooks, locked the apartment behind me. I walked up the hill to the Grand Concourse and waited for the bus. I was too numb to feel any pain. There was just this crying behind my eyes, this fighting back of tears. When the bus came there were no vacant seats. I held on to a shoulder bar as my body, my mind, in an act of self-preservation, fused its white-hot pain into as close as it could come to art. A poem began to write itself in my mind.

At Fordham Road I had to change for a bus going east. On this one I found a seat, near a window at the rear. I opened one of my notebooks, I took out a pencil, I wrote down the poem that had been forming. Stanza after stanza flowed out of me onto the paper, each one four lines, eight stanzas at least, maybe more. In twenty minutes, to stifle my tears, I wrote the poem, to the meter—as close as I could get it—of "Casey at the Bat." The name of the poem was "Branca on the Mound."

There was no joy in Pelham Parkway as I got off the bus and dragged myself the five blocks home.

My understanding mother commiserated with me on the Dodger loss. I showed her the poem I had written. Always supportive of my writing (if not of my glove!), she thought it was wonderful. She was going to send it somewhere, she said, somewhere where it would get an audience. And she mailed it off to Marty Glickman at *Today's Baseball*.

What she expected I do not know. The season had just ended, the program was going off the air for the year, and they never read poetry anyway. They recreated baseball games. *Thwack — roooohr. . . .*

We never got a response. I think this hurt me then, but what, after all, could Marty Glickman say? There was no comfort he or anyone could offer, short of recreating a Giant ninth in which Thomson, mighty Thomson, would strike out.

In those days there was not a copying machine on every street-corner, a fax in every garage. It's likely my mother mailed off the original of my epic. In any case, no copy of "Branca on the Mound" has survived. This is no great loss to the Library of Congress, or even to Cooperstown.

But the moment survived indelibly in my brain; it helped to create a permanent mind-set. Evidence of this emerged four years later. By then I was a senior at Bronx Science; in addition to "Blood and Piss" I had to choose a second elective from among Advanced Chemistry, Advanced Physics, and Advanced Art. Though I could not draw a straight line, no less a pleasingly crooked one, I enrolled in the latter to avoid the former two. One of the assignments in Advanced Art was to do an oil painting in class, which we worked on for several weeks. The painting that emerged on my vertical canvas was mostly green—a series of tall green lockers in a locker room. All of the lockers were closed except one. A bare lightbulb hung from the ceiling. In front of the open locker, on a plain wooden bench, sat a ballplayer. He was wearing his road uniform—Dodger gray, Dodger blue. He sat slumped with his head in his hands, long after the other players had left. What the painting lacked in technique it perhaps made up for in its feeling of defeat. The name I gave to it was *Losing Pitcher*.

Of all the infinity of subjects possible for my first oil painting, I had chosen Ralph Branca, still beaten after all these years. But it was also, of course, myself, a rendering of a pointless but powerful despair with which in my adolescence I had come to identify. He was me and I was him in this gloomy locker room. In this locker room of . . . life?

The painting received an A from the teacher. I informed my mother that it did not really deserve an A, that everyone in the class had received A's on their oil paintings, because the teacher liked the seriousness with which we had thrown ourselves into the project. This explanation did little to modify my mother's pride. She bought a ready-made wooden frame, inserted the 11″ × 14″ painting into it, and hung it on a corner wall in our living room. There it would remain for the next five years while she battled cancer and lost; there it would remain while my father, a widower with his own fierce and frightened loyalty, lived alone with her memory for twenty years more. Alone in the green living room.

The Mets have just released Rodney Maes. This news, mentioned over the tube at the start of a game, I find startling in its unexpected brutality.

Maes is a young outfielder, slim, black, left-handed, very fast— the kind of player that the Cardinals always remain contenders with but the Mets rarely seem to obtain. He gained widespread notoriety a while back when he ran through a wall during a minor league game while attempting to catch a fly ball. He did not crash into the wall, as Pete Reiser used to do, as Reiser ruined his great career doing; Maes ran right through the wooden wall. I did not see the replays the day it happened, but a fairly dumb program called *Sports Bloopers* comes on Channel 2 every Sunday right after

Siskel & Ebert, and part of the introduction to the program features the tape of Rodney Maes running through the wall. He never takes his eye off the ball. He never looks to see where the wall is. He never slows. He merely at full speed crashes right through the wall, chin first, and disappears from view. In the intro to *Sports Bloopers* they show his disappearing act three times in quick succession. He is running full speed, he goes through the wall. He is running full speed, he goes through the wall. He is running full speed, he goes through the wall. They never show him climbing back sheepishly through the hole he made—if, in fact, that is what he did; it is not even clear if he held on to the ball, which he seems to be catching at the instant he disappears. It is a baseball moment suspended forever in the twilight zone. Each week after *Siskel & Ebert* I watch Rodney Maes run through a wall three times before I click off the set. Watch him disappear through the end of the universe.

Early this season the Mets, lacking speed, brought Maes up, to be used primarily as a pinch runner; to be inserted into the game in a late inning as the tying run on first, or as the winning run, as a man who could steal a base at a crucial moment so they did not have to waste an out with a sacrifice. So they would have an extra chance to score. I loved the image of Maes running through the wall into infinity and I loved the Mets having the luxury of keeping this speedster around; he ran the bases like a Thoroughbred.

Unfortunately, Maes developed an unexpected habit. He began to get picked off first base as often as not. This is not a good practice for any ballplayer. It is especially problematical in a pinch runner.

Several times the Mets sent him down to Tidewater. Each time, as an injury opened up a spot on the roster, they recalled him. He even won a game for them with a crucial, unexpected base hit. But each time his habit of getting picked off asserted itself. And the Mets apparently had no Twelve-Step group for pinch runners.

It would not have surprised me if the Mets had sent him down yet again, for further coaching, further seasoning. This would probably have been unavoidable. But instead they have released him. They have not sent him down to the minors, they have not traded him to a more patient organization. They have released him outright. This is a vindictiveness that, barring serious injury, is almost never shown with a promising young ballplayer.

Unless he can sign with another team on his own, the determined young man who ran through the outfield wall will be gone from baseball. I find this curiously disturbing. There are sudden and unexpected places, it seems to affirm, from whence there is no returning.

In the early spring of 1951, a few months before we moved, a story appeared in the *Post* announcing the formation of the first Little League in the West Bronx. Would-be players were instructed to report to a certain public school on a certain day in the company of a parent or guardian. On the appointed day I was tense with excitement as my mother and I went by bus to the school.

Several long folding tables had been set up in the dim gymnasium of the old school building. Hundreds of boys were lined up at the tables with their parents, obtaining forms, filling out forms. As I think back, the scene brings to mind those old photographs of immigrants lined up at Ellis Island, through which both of my parents had passed, my mother as a babe in arms, my father as a boy of twelve—my very age that spring afternoon. Indeed, I viewed this day as an important passage, my long-awaited entry into another country. I would leave behind the tattered remnants of punchball and stickball in concrete backyards and auto-ridden streets; I would sail into the American dream, real hardball, real bats made in Louisville, real uniforms, smooth green fields with bright white bases, foul lines and batter's boxes, umpires dressed in blue, crowds cheering, bunting and stealing allowed, and all sweet provender. I would find out, once and for all, if I was good enough.

I filled out the form provided—there was a prominent space for Age—my mother signed her permission, we stapled to it the clearance form signed by a physician, which we had been instructed to bring, certifying that I was a healthy, if skinny, kid. Play ball!

As we turned in our forms, we would-be players were told that we would receive further instructions by mail—where to report next, how teams would be chosen, and so forth. I returned home feeling a lot more grown up than when I had left. For the next week, and the weeks after that, I pounded a ball into my well-oiled glove and waited eagerly for word. But no word came. Then there was a follow-up story in the newspaper. Plans had indeed been laid for a Little League in the West Bronx, the story said. But it was too late in the season for games to be played this year. The league would get off to a flying start the following spring.

I could hardly rejoice at this optimistic news. The upper age limit for playing in the Little League was twelve. As I read the story, slumped in my father's easy chair, I felt the crushing burden of my years. By the following spring I would have turned thirteen.

Later on I would become involved in three—count 'em, three— games of pickup hardball in city parks and a high school field. In one I would even come in to pitch when our starting hurler got wild, and I would preserve our victory. But that single application sheet, with a physician's approval attached, marked the beginning and the end of my career in organized ball.

What was it Garrett Morris used to say? *Bazeball been berry berry good to me.* . . .

Television, which finally was installed in our new home in 1952, would change the very essence of baseball as an American experience. The combination of television and baseball would become woven into the fabric of tens of millions of American marriages. The weave would more often be coarse than smooth. All too often, to switch metaphors, it would irritate like a boulder of sand in an otherwise loving eye. The primary reason was that you could listen to a ball game on the radio while you were doing something else. Something useful. Even work. This was a grand tradition. Whereas to watch baseball on television you simply sat, lazy as a frog on a log, and watched.

My friend Jonathan Richards grew up in Woodstock, New York, with his parents and his brother, Tad. Like Saul and me, Jon and Tad both became Brooklyn Dodger fans, for reasons they cannot explain. I cannot prove that the Dodgers of those days attracted more free-floating souls—souls, that is, which did not reside in Flatbush—than did other teams, but I feel certain that is the case. An invisible creative energy emanated from that particular team, a silken web that attracted and held fast. It was as if the other major league teams played Baseball, but the Dodgers played Life.

(This feeling may be mere childish provincialism—*me, me, mine, mine*—but the terrible fates and early deaths that befell so many in that Dodger lineup suggest otherwise.)

Jon and Tad played catch, like most boys, and it was always Furillo or Snider circling under the high fly ball in Woodstock. Using baseball cards they invented their own indoor game. They built a stadium out of their parents' books; they propped up cardboard players at each position. The pitcher rolled a marble from the pitcher's mound; the batter swung a pencil. If the marble hit a player, it was an out, if it went between the players it was a hit. The modern era came to this particular game when they cut a playing card in the shape of a spatula and attached it to the pencil. This introduced fly balls into the game. It was like the coming of Babe Ruth.

This game Jon and Tad played when there was no Dodger game on television. Their family did not own a set, but one man in Woodstock did. He was a deaf-mute—or almost deaf—who lived a mile down the dirt road. Whenever a Dodger game was on, the two boys would walk down the road and knock very loudly on his door. The man would open the door and make a lot of unintelligible noises as he let them in. Then the three of them would sit and watch the Dodger game on a snow-ridden black-and-white set that looked like a washing machine.

Every winter Jon and Tad saved up their money. As soon as the Dodger schedule was announced, they sent away for box seats to one game. And once each summer they were allowed to travel alone, by bus, these ten- and twelve-year-olds, from Woodstock to Manhattan, and then by subway to Ebbets Field. After the game they retraced their subway ride, their walk through Times Square, their long bus ride. Usually it was dark when they got home, the two boys alone, in that innocent and simpler time.

As it is for most real fans, the day was dark or bright depending on if their team had won. Later, when Jon was living in New York, when the Dodgers had left and he was a Mets fan, he would go out and buy a newspaper on days after the Mets had won. But if they had lost, he would not buy a paper. The sports section is what he cared about, and who wanted to read bad news?

Jon does not know why baseball is so important to him. Like most true fans he cannot explain it, any more than a butterfly can explain its wings.

Tad is a more emotional person than Jon. At times he gets very depressed. "You can't kill yourself," Jon has advised him. "You don't know who's going to win tomorrow."

Jon lives far from New York now with his wife and two daughters. He cannot understand how this game that is still so much a part of his life can be ignored by an entire sex. He once asked his wife if she could name the three outfield positions. She replied: "Infield, outfield, center field."

In his house on a hill he watches the Mets on a huge color television screen that overhangs the large living room. But if he is watching a game and he hears footsteps coming—his wife, one of his daughters—he quickly snaps off the set and tosses away the remote. "It's like I'm an addict," he says, "throwing the coke spoon under the bed."

At such times, in some small unconscious part of himself, I would not be surprised if he longs for the days when he and Tad used to watch the Dodgers, free of guilt, on the small, snowy black-and-white set that looked like a washing machine, in the company of the man who could hardly hear and couldn't speak.

I have referred several times to the failure of the Bums to tie for the pennant on the final day of 1950. I have dwelled at length on the trauma of '51. The next baseball images in my mind are from the World Series of 1954: watching the Giants destroy Cleveland in four straight, watching Dusty Rhodes belt pinch homers, watching Willie Mays make The Catch—the catch in which he did a passing imitation of my own over-the-shoulder style just as I crashed into the double garage doors. There is, however, something neurotic afoot here, because there were two baseball seasons in between, and the Dodgers won the pennant both times. Yet those seasons—Roger Kahn's seasons—have vanished from my memory. It is as if success has been taken for granted, success has left no trace; only the river of defeat has cut canyons in the landscape of my mind. True, the Brooks lost the series both years to the Yankees, but I have to pull *The Baseball Encyclopedia* off the shelf to look up in how many games, to rediscover what transpired.

Two consecutive Brooklyn pennants cast aside like unshaven bums, homeless in memory lane. This is something we must work on, Doctor. The cup is always half empty.

Like at the local racetrack the other day, opening day. I hit an exacta and two quinellas, modest ones. Then, in a two-year-old maiden race, I liked a colt named Whisky Willie. Last time out he had run four lengths behind the 9–5 favorite, a gelding named Hoistjose, a grandson of Boldnesian. Whisky Willie was 14–1, and a quinella combining the two made sense. But two other horses were getting lots of play, one a stakes loser, the other a first timer with good workouts. I didn't want to blow my winnings on a bunch of combinations. And I neglected to check the quinella odds. I just put my two bucks on Whisky Willie to win and relaxed. The bet had begun, after all, partly as a sentimental one. Willie is my dog, a bouncy black mutt built low and fast, named after Willie Shakespeare and Willie McGee.

Anyway, they break smartly out of the gate, Hoistjose in front, Whisky Willie second, and they circle the track that way, no one else in contention. They leave the field behind but Willie giving his all never is able to catch the leader. It's okay, I'm feeling no pain, I got my two bucks' worth, I can feel good about my handicapping. Till they post the quinella payoff: forty-four bucks! I go home a winner, but all I can think of, all night long, is how I blew the bet. Right there in front of me, so obvious. Forty-four bucks, and it churns away in my gut.

Go to sleep, schmuck, you won.

Woulda, coulda, shoulda.

As a ball fan, of course, it is them you blame, not yourself. *They* woulda. *They* coulda. *They* shoulda.

Which, all things considered, is probably healthier.

* * *

Last night I turned on ESPN to see if the Mets game was on. The picture that came onto the screen was black-and-white film footage of Ted Williams in his prime, in the 1940s, belting out solid base hits. The announcer in voice-over was recounting how in 1941, when Williams batted .406, he lost out in the Most Valuable Player balloting to Joe DiMaggio. The two men flashed onto the screen, young ballplayers near the batting cage, DiMaggio with his sharp nose, Williams with his navy flier's good looks, and a shock went through my system, followed by the onset of depression. From the solemn tone of the announcer's voice and his use of the past tense, it seemed apparent that Ted Williams had died.

Two minutes passed before the footage ended and I learned I had tuned in to the first of a new series about great players of the past. The film cut to tape of Williams, alive and well, being interviewed at his Florida home. I felt relieved, and surprised at how strong my initial reaction had been. I have reached that age in life when my own mortality has become of some concern, and Williams, this stranger, is twenty years older than I. Perhaps it was because, ever since childhood, we have heard of "the immortal Ted Williams." His likes are not supposed to confront us with our own fragility.

Though I never have rooted seriously for anyone but the Dodgers and the Mets, early in childhood I fixed on the Red Sox as my favorite American League team; it was they who had the best chance, year after year, of overtaking the hated Yankees. And Ted Williams became my favorite American League player; he was the only one who could at times overshadow the hated DiMaggio. Rooting for an American Leaguer was akin to choosing my favorite vegetable; but if the Dodgers were spaghetti and chocolate, Ted Williams at least was canned peas, not spinach or cauliflower. If an occasional visit to Yankee Stadium was deemed necessary, it was usually timed when the Red Sox were in town, when I could witness the sweet swing of Ted Williams, fluid history in gray flannel.

Sometimes I even put money on Williams. Except for recreational visits to the track, I do not bet on sports; that's not what they are *for*. Especially baseball. Betting Tom Seaver vs. Bob Gibson, or Dwight Gooden vs. Mike Scott, is like betting on sainthood. Ghandi 6–5 over Mother Teresa. My only exception to this rule was in high school, when we had a betting game that helped make school itself more tolerable. You chose three players and bet that they would collect at least six hits among them that day. If they did not, you lost a dime; if they did, you won big—a quarter or a dollar, I don't remember which. I never chose to be the bookie, I always preferred to bet. Four players were my main men, and I usually picked three of those four, depending on which pitchers they were facing that day. The four were Jackie Robinson, Stan Musial, Richie Ashburn, and Ted Williams. I won the bet a lot more often than I lost.

My allowance in those days was one dollar a week. The fact that I invested some of it in the skill of an American Leaguer may well be the highest accolade Ted Williams ever earned.

After Williams my next most-admired American Leaguer was Lou Boudreau, who led Cleveland to the pennant in 1948. Not only was Boudreau the shortstop, he was also the manager. Fascinated as I was by the intricacies of the game, I always believed that managing would be my calling when my playing days were through. And if my physical prowess—or lack thereof—conspired to keep me from the majors, I would become, along with Burt Shotton and Connie Mack, one of the few managers who had never played the game. But playing shortstop and managing at the same time, as Boudreau had done—that would be the kingdom of heaven on earth. As a player you would have the glory; as manager you would have the power. What more could a young boy desire?

Decades later, when I tried this in a men's softball league, I would discover what George Gershwin could have told me: It ain't necessarily so.

(That horror story we must save till later: till the children go to bed.)

Rare is the woman who does not begrudge the time her husband spends watching baseball. I have been very fortunate: I have married two of them. The city girl was an avid fan herself. The country girl is merely wise.

Baseball, for those who inhabit it fully, is no mere game; it is an alternate reality parallel to the "real" world; it is the seventh dimension, a separate warp of time and space that happens to be inhabited by many men and few women. In the realm of the spectator it is not exclusionary, but in the playing of the game it largely is; and it is the touch of the ball itself, usually at age seven, that opens through the palm of the hand the magic entry into this enclosed tunnel of time and history.

Inside this tunnel is a roster of hundreds of names that, when merely mentioned, send off sparks like an anvil properly struck. Christy Mathewson. Carl Hubbell. Hack Wilson. Eddie Collins. Joe Medwick. Arky Vaughan. Hugh Casey. The sparks explode like meteors traversing the night sky. Wins and losses, strikeouts, runs batted in, dishonor, hijinks, death. Death by drowning. Death by suicide. Sparks that ignite other sparks. John McGraw. Tony Lazzeri. Hank Greenberg. Joe Jackson. Enos Slaughter. Billy Cox. Jim Konstanty. And these, in turn, others—Connie Mack, Yogi Berra, Al Kaline, Buck Weaver, Red Schoendienst, Pie Traynor, Joe Page—on and on like a timeless ticking clock, in an infinite star-filled sky, a beautiful night sky without end.

This dimension La Donna does not inhabit. But she has her own parallel worlds. One in particular, though we have been together for ten years, I did not fully note until a month ago.

In a small space in the high desert, thirty miles to the south of our city, there is a plot of fertile ground called the Iris Ranch. Here, each May, a thousand different varieties of irises bloom in a carpet of crossbred hues that makes the term "riot of color" pale before its silky palette. The name given to each variety of iris is posted on a small marker beside it and is listed in a catalog; the ranch is an outdoor floral showroom, at which visitors can place orders for the kinds of bulbs they want sent to them in the summer, to plant in their own gardens, for blooms they will enjoy the following year.

La Donna had bought some bulbs there last year; they were blooming now in the garden behind our house, a garden she wrought four years ago out of a backyard of sand and rocks. The new Iris Ranch catalog had arrived a week or so ago, and she wanted to make a visit, to see what new breeds, what fierce color combines, might entice her eye this time. We set out early on a Thursday afternoon, a day of sunshine broken by intermittent clouds. As we drove down the highway, past the prison on state road 14, the clouds began to loom darker up ahead. La Donna was leafing through the catalog, reading hundreds of iris names and their descriptions. From time to time she mentioned aloud ones in which she might be interested. Coral Magic. Heather Blush. Windsor Rose. As we turned up a rocky dirt road that led to the ranch the smell of rain grew heavy in the air. Just as we parked the car the first few drops began to fall. I opened the trunk of the car, seeking protection, and was pleased to find still in there a white baseball cap and a royal-blue jacket, both marked SANTA FE SPRINGS. They were relics of my softball managing days, and had lain unworn in the trunk for several years. After La Donna declined their use I put them on, and we walked to the spreads of flowers, hundreds of different varieties of irises glowing bright under the gray and lowering sky. As we moved among the rows of flowers I read more names on the markers. Techny Chimes, Gene Buckles, Berry Wine. Quickly the rain grew harder. We could no longer enjoy ourselves or the flowers. We decided to leave, to come back the next day.

We both were disappointed, I more for her than for myself. *Game postponed on account of rain,* I thought. And then, as we climbed back into the car, as La Donna began to study the catalog again, I understood, for the first time. Gardening was La Donna's baseball. Precisely and exactly. All winter long, shut up in the house, she looks out the living-room window at the yellow or snow-covered grass, at the colorless borders, and waits with impatience till spring; till March, when the grass begins to green; till April, when the first blossoms open; waits with the same impatience that I await the crack of bat on ball, the infusion of daily box scores. She attends to the garden as I attend to the sport. She knows the names of the different irises, of all the different plants in her garden, as I know who played for the 1941 Dodgers, or the

1927 Yankees, or the 1948 Cleveland Indians. Gene Bearden certainly is a bearded iris. Heinie Manush too.

When we got home the rain had stopped. We went out back, we toured the garden. I have always made a point of doing this, to show my appreciation, to enjoy the gentle flowers. But now I looked with keener eyes; with the understanding that this garden is her Dodgers, her Mets; that it is *that* important. And I was flooded with a strong new love for her.

An hour later I returned to the garden to visit with her again. She was on her knees, planting a John F. Kennedy rosebush she had bought for ninety-nine cents the day before. She turned, and looked up at me. "The main difference between my obsession and yours," she said, "is that I get to buy my own players."

The next morning, over coffee, she was again studying the booklet from the iris ranch, learning which breeds had been introduced in which years. Yellows were the prizewinners in the thirties, she informed me. Blues in the forties. Poring over the stats. As we headed out again toward the ranch I put on my Brooklyn cap. It seemed appropriate.

In the weeks since, when I have seen her reading in the *Encyclopedia of Southwestern Plants,* as she often does, I smile inwardly. I have enjoyed the garden in the past, I try to be one who stops and smells the roses, but only now do I understand that while I am inhaling soft colors, absorbing gentle scents, La Donna is going far beyond that; she is making connections, setting off internal sparks, populating her own night sky. I have never begrudged the time she spends working in the garden. But only now do I understand that the beauty she has wrought, with nature's help, is a reflection of her own soul. Just as she understands—as she somehow always has—that baseball is not merely something that I love, but is who I am.

FOURTH

Walter O'Malley
Saves the World

Jorge Ramirez was born to a poor family in Chihuahua, Mexico. His parents were divorced when he was eight months old, and he grew up without a father. When he was six his mother moved to Juárez. It was there that he learned to play baseball, on rutted dirt fields, using bats thrown away by the older boys, sometimes using hats for gloves. The kids took their baseball seriously, and Jorge in those days was not very good. The other kids were tough on him when he struck out or dropped a fly ball.

Three of his mother's brothers crossed into the States and began to work in the construction business in New Mexico. When Jorge was nine years old the three uncles brought him across. For three years he did not play baseball; five days a week, after school, he worked with them, learning the construction trade. On weekends he picked up trash to earn extra money.

Later on he took up baseball again. Now Jorge has his own construction business in Santa Fe and plays first base on a men's softball team. He managed a Little League team last year and is thinking of doing so again next season. He also sponsors a Little League team, so that local kids can play ball on real fields with good bats and good gloves. He serves on the board of the league as equipment manager, purchasing $17,000 worth of bats and balls and uniforms each year.

Jorge's daughter, Nicole, is my daughter Amara's current best friend. Last Thursday, in early evening, I drove to Salvador Perez

Park to meet Jorge there and watch his team, Ramirez Construction, play against the Elks.

It was the last game of the season. Ramirez Construction was an expansion team, and they were mired in last place, with a record of two wins, eleven losses, one tie. The Elks had won eight games and lost five, and were battling for third in the nine-team division. It was not a crucial game, just one of thousands of Little League baseball games taking place across America on this warm June night, as inconsequential and as wondrous as fireflies.

When I arrive, the boys from Ramirez Construction are taking infield practice in their spiffy uniforms: blue shirts with white lettering, blue caps, gray pants. In the first-base dugout their manager, Melvin Chavez, is filling out his lineup card. Chavez is thirty-six years old, a maintenance worker for the city. Across the way the boys from the Elks, in green uniforms and green caps, are warming up in front of coach John Cunningham, a forty-five-year-old salesman who played Little League ball when he was young; his son Keith is the first baseman for the Elks, a potential All-Star. The home plate umpire, Pat Cordova, a thirty-eight-year-old security guard, is strapping third base to a spike in the ground. Also a former Little Leaguer, Cordova has been umpiring for twenty years. Jim Dickens, sixty-one, an investigator for the state attorney general's office, will be umpiring the bases.

In the small grandstand a scattering of parents has begun to gather. Behind the third-base fence a crowd of about twenty people is holding a picnic unrelated to the game; they are barbecuing hamburgers, and a westerly wind wafts the powerful smell of cooking burgers across the baseball field.

"Get two, get two," one of the Ramirez coaches, Will Knappen, shouts as he hits a grounder. Knappen, an art dealer, nods as his charges turn a warm-up double play. And again: "Get two. Make it two!"

A moment later the Elks take the field for their own infield practice. "Play's to first! Play's to first! Charge it, charge it!" I remember my brother dropping ball after ball in front of me in the concrete backyard in The Bronx in another era and endlessly yelling the same refrain.

As the game is about to start I look around for Jorge. He has been detained behind the stands by the president of the league; they are discussing the schedule for a forthcoming tournament, the purchasing of jackets for the league All-Stars, other administrative matters.

The Elks are the home team, and their pitcher, Robbie Bowen, a stocky blond kid, shows impressive form and a humming fastball. He, too, is an All-Star, who plays shortstop when he isn't pitching. Bowen strikes out the first batter for Ramirez Construction, Neil LeFever. He walks little Joshua Cummings. But when Jeremy Chato pops to short for the second out, Joshua takes off for second base and is easily doubled up. I wonder about the coaching he is getting; then realize that already I am falling victim to the fever that often grips Little League parents. I try to cool it: the kid is young, surely he has been taught better; perhaps he just got excited.

As the bottom of the first begins I fear it will be a long evening. The Ramirez pitcher does not throw the ball properly. He keeps his right foot perpendicular to the mound as he throws the ball, instead of turning it along the edge of the mound and pushing off. This causes him to flip the ball lamely across his body instead of firing it. I wonder, again, about the instruction, this time more seriously. I wonder if, next year, I should become a coach. Perhaps an assistant . . .

My fears of a blowout come true as the Elks score three runs in the first and four in the second. The score is 7–0 after two when Jorge Ramirez joins me in the stands. He introduces me to a slim, dark woman who is with him. Her name is Joanne.

I have heard of Joanne. She was once the best friend of Pam Ramirez, Jorge's former wife. In the months since Pam and Jorge went through a divorce, Jorge has been going out with Joanne. At the same time a fellow named Matt, who used to be one of Jorge's construction workers, has moved in with Pam. In the stands, too, they are playing hardball.

"It has been a frustrating season for the kids," Jorge says.

He is speaking of the kids on Ramirez Construction, of their lopsided losing season. But a private part of him may also be thinking of Nicole; of her brother Chris.

Chris used to play Little League ball, then Babe Ruth ball. The whole family—when it was a family—used to come out and cheer him on. This summer, for the first time in years, Chris has decided not to play baseball. He is riding a mountain bike instead, and playing the guitar, and hanging out with his friends. His father is deeply disappointed. Perhaps that is the point.

But Jorge is also hopeful. The other day, in the park, they saw two of Chris's former teammates in the Babe Ruth League hit balls over the fence during practice. For the first time Chris began to miss baseball. He asked his father if it was too late to rejoin the team next year. Jorge assured him it was not too late.

In the top of the third the boys from Ramirez score a run. In the bottom half of the inning the shortstop, a slim little kid named Danny Martinez, comes in to pitch. As soon as he begins to warm up I feel a new, serene pleasure. Danny knows what he is doing on the mound; he has the correct mechanics; and though he is tiny—a regular skinny-marink—his fastball has pop. The entire Ramirez team seems to get a lift from their new pitcher; they retire the Elks on fine plays by Neil LeFever, Raul Gallegos, and Patrick Marcus, on ground balls to short and second.

Ramirez cuts the lead to 7–2, and in the bottom of the fourth, fly balls to Josh Cummings in left and Jarred Sedillo in center, and a grounder to the pitcher, wrapped around a harmless single, are handled flawlessly; the Ramirez defense has tightened up. Danny Martinez has a ball club behind him now. I feel a hunger to be eleven years old again, to be out there in uniform, to fill in that gap in my life: born too soon for the Little League. The moment passes, though it will also never pass; the breeze again carries the pungent smell of burgers on a grill; a different kind of hunger takes hold.

Despite their tighter defense Ramirez cannot come back at the plate. The six-inning game ends with the score Elks 9, Ramirez Construction 2.

Another game will follow, and a bunch of kids in clean red-and-white-striped uniforms are lounging behind the fence, waiting. One of their mothers shows up carrying a large doughnut box. "Somebody's bringing Dunkin' Donuts for the next game," Jorge says. "That's what happens when you're in second place."

I leave to go home for dinner. In a small playground near the parking area a little girl in a blue dress is playing on a small jungle gym; she is being watched over by a man perhaps ten years younger than I, a man in a white baseball cap; he is sitting in a power-driven wheelchair. I can only imagine what he hungers for.

Three nights later Ramirez Construction played the first game of a postseason tournament against the last-place team in another division. The Ramirez boys lost; they would have to turn in their uniforms.

When you are eleven years old, next year is far away.

In 1953 baseball was still the national pastime. But the national malady was paranoia. Under chief witch-hunter Joe McCarthy the American people were being convinced that there was a red in every pot and two pinkos in every garage. In this climate, one spring afternoon, two FBI agents knocked on our door on Wilson Avenue. They told my mother she was an illegal alien—and quite possibly a Russian spy—and that she must report to Ellis Island to face deportation proceedings.

Needless to say, this put a crimp in our ensuing summer vacation.

My mother's best friend from childhood was Ruth Kaplan, whose husband, Lou, was a lawyer; my mother retained his services. Her four sisters rallied around her: when she went to Ellis Island, one of them would go with her. On each subsequent trip— and there were several—another sister went: to make sure my mother did not simply vanish, never to be heard from again. Anything seemed possible in that era of official insanity, of institutionalized cowardice.

My mother was a mother, primarily, and a part-time book-keeper for a local stationery firm. I had witnessed only two political acts by her in my life—if they can be called that. On April 12, 1945, a fellow named Marvin Stiglitz, who was my brother's friend, came running into our house from across the street, shouting that President Roosevelt was dead. My mother angrily told him that was nothing to joke about. When Marvin insisted it was true, my mother turned on the radio. She heard that FDR had, in fact, died. She sat down at the kitchen table, put her head in her hands, and wept. It was the only time in my life I would see her cry.

Seven years later, in 1952, she laughed a lot. Adlai Stevenson was the Democratic candidate for president against Dwight Eisenhower. My mother appreciated Stevenson's erudition, admired his wit; I remember watching his speeches with her on our new television set, both of us laughing at his clever sallies against the Republicans.

When the FBI came calling, neither of these acts seemed to me to be a criminal offense. But what did I know? I was only fourteen.

The government's case against my mother was this: They had somehow unearthed a form she had signed in 1930, when she and my father were returning to this country after a two-month honeymoon in Europe. On the form, where she had been asked to check a box indicating whether or not she was a U.S. citizen, she had checked that she was. But the government could find no record of her having been born in this country, which would automatically make her a citizen; and the government could find no record of her having been naturalized; therefore, she was not a citizen; therefore, she had lied when she reentered the country in 1930; therefore, she was not trustworthy, she had something to hide; and since her parents had emigrated here from Russia, she was most likely a Soviet spy.

This was in an era when computers with which to call up such information did not exist. The number of man-hours and tax dollars that went into these record searches boggles the mind. But no money must be spared, of course, in the defense of our country.

My mother, when she went to Ellis Island, told the immigration examiner that she had been born in London while her parents were emigrating here; that she was six months old when she arrived here; that her parents had become citizens, that all her brothers and sisters were citizens, and that she had always assumed that she was too. That was the reason she had so indicated on the form in 1930. It was possible, she conceded, that her father had not realized it was necessary to file naturalization papers for a babe-in-arms.

The examiner wanted proof that she had been born in London, and not in Russia.

The lawyers went to work. It turned out that during the bombing of London in the Second World War, many of the hospitals and record centers had been destroyed. Documentation of her birth could not be found.

The government smelled a minor league version of the Rosenbergs.

This madness went on for several months, during which time FBI agents were interviewing many of our neighbors to find evidence that my mother was a spy. Finally they gave up. They had found, of course, nothing. But there was still the matter of my mother's misstatement of fact upon her entry into this country in 1930, which somehow was considered in 1953 a major threat to the survival of the Republic. After several more consultations on Ellis Island the lawyers for my mother and the government worked out an agreement: she would leave the country; when she returned, she would state on the appropriate form that she was not a citizen. Then she could continue living in this country as an alien.

This charade was actually enforced. Early in 1954 my mother went to Canada for one day, with one of her sisters along to call the lawyer in case the government welshed on its agreement and refused to admit her. The next day, when they crossed back into upper New York State, she checked the box indicating she was not a U.S. citizen. The government's paperwork was now in order. And for the remainder of her life my mother had to file, every January, an alien registration form, letting the government know her address.

I am not certain if, at that point, she filed to become a naturalized citizen. She may have done so; or she may have been so angry at this government harassment that she did not. In any case, it is a moot point. To become a citizen she would have had to wait seven years. She died of cancer after six.

In recent years I have tried twice to obtain access, under the Freedom of Information Act, to the government's files on my mother, in the hope of discovering what madness lay behind this nonsense. Each time the Justice Department and the Department of Immigration have sent back only a form postcard, with the rubber-stamped response: INSUFFICIENT INFORMATION. The mystery remains unsolved.

If my mother technically never became a citizen, she did become a baseball fan. In our radio days she used to root for the Dodgers in an abstract sense, so that Saul and I would be happy, so that I would eat. Once a TV set took up residence in our living room, it was tuned in the summer months to the Dodgers whenever a game was on the air. Never a big TV watcher, except for the late-night shows of Steve Allen and Jack Paar, and Sunday afternoon's cultured *Omnibus*, my mother did not object to the Dodgers' commandeering the tube. She and my father both soon learned the rules of the game, in self-defense. This became important especially to my father, who in the years after my mother died spent many a long lonely evening, many a depressing weekend, being mercifully distracted by the Mets. His anger at a stupid move by Casey Stengel or Gil Hodges, at a bad throw by Charlie Neal or a bobbled grounder by Bud Harrelson, often would rival my own—though in his case, I believe, he was often redirecting a deeper anger at God, who had stolen away at a too-early age the only woman he loved.

For those who give themselves up to the game, baseball and love can run together like two streams that form a river. Other sports—basketball, football, hockey—have a prosaic sameness: up and down, back and forth, till time runs out. But baseball is timeless; it signifies. It is more like a startling form found in nature than the calculated creation of man. It is a complex crystal. It is the female form. What people who find baseball boring do not understand is that at the very moment they are most bored—when the pitcher is staring in at the catcher, in no hurry to throw the ball—a spider is at the center of its hexagonal web, tense, waiting. There is subtle strategy unraveling, of which the back-and-forth sports do not even dream.

Though they never ensnared my soul, I did form rooting interests in other sports. In what was surely a curious choice for a young Jewish boy in The Bronx, the first football team I rooted for was the Mustangs of Southern Methodist University, way off in Texas. This predilection was inspired by the well-publicized heroics of swivel-hipped halfback Doak Walker; perhaps I thought he was Dixie's other brother. When Kyle Rote, also of SMU, followed Walker into swivel-hipped prominence, my choice seemed inspired. In my sixth-grade autograph album, in which my classmates wrote such inspired quatrains as the following:

> *When you're in the country,*
> *Walking round the hedges*
> *You'll remember Ralph*
> *Who wrote around the edges.*

—and from whence I do remember Ralph, the class clown, whose full name was Ralph Waldo (I sometimes wonder if he is the Waldo that millions of children keep looking for, to no apparent purpose) in the front part of that album, where we were supposed to list our favorite color, song, et cetera, I listed as my favorite university "SMU." When my parents looked at my album, they asked me what SMU meant. "Southern Methodist University," I replied. At which point they immediately repaired to the kitchen, in which we used to light our Friday-night candles—the original Friday Night Lights—and sorrowfully asked an uncaring God just where it was that they had gone wrong.

Years later, in *The Universal Baseball Association*, I discovered the ditty that would have been much more appropriate in that antique sixth-grade keepsake:

> *Oh, when I die, jist bury me*
> *With my bat and a coupla balls,*
> *And jist tell 'em Verne struck out, boys,*
> *If anybody calls. . . .*

> —Robert "Bobby" Coover

Around the same time that Kyle Rote was chewing up the yardage in Texas, a fellow named Billy Vessels began to do the same at the University of Oklahoma, and the Sooners succeeded SMU as my favorite football team. In that choice an unseen providence may have had a hand. My rooting interest gave me a strong, positive feeling about that distant state of pecans, rednecks, and Bible-thumping Baptists, just around the time a certain country girl, whom I would not meet for thirty years, was sashaying toward Ada to be born.

It's a quiet Sunday afternoon, the Mets have just lost their third straight to the Pirates at Shea. La Donna needs some potting soil and I need to get out of the house. We drive out to Wal-Mart, get the soil, and on the way home we check out a new factory outlet store that just opened in De Vargas Center. Amid racks of T-shirts reduced to $3.99 I find a gray one lettered in orange and blue, very official looking, PROPERTY OF THE NEW YORK METS. The label says it's Irregular but I can't find anything wrong (unlike with the Mets themselves).

The next day I'm wearing my new Mets shirt for the first time. It fits perfectly, jock chic. I'm in the supermarket, waiting in line at the checkout counter with half a week's food in my basket—fresh tuna to grill tonight, chicken for chicken salad tomorrow, country-style ribs, the week's indulgence, that we'll smoke the day after. I don't notice the guy approaching, he is right beside me when he says: "I hate the Mets."

He's thin, with gray in his blond hair. I've never seen him before. He's got a frozen pizza, a few other items in a plastic Albertson's bag, which means he has already gone through the checkout line. I figure I'll bite.

"Why do you hate the Mets?"

"Because I used to be a Bum," the guy says.

"So was I," I tell him.

He looks surprised, I suppose because we are standing two thousand miles from Flatbush Avenue. "You know what a Bum is?" he asks.

"I do," I tell him. "That's why I like the Mets. I wouldn't root for the *Los Angeles* Dodgers."

"You know who I hate more than anyone else in the world?" he asks.

There's an edge to the guy, possibly a hinge loose, but I can't get a fix on it. He is being more or less rational, if obvious.

"Walter O'Malley," I say.

He looks at me as if I'm psychic. Then he starts to sing. Not real loud, he isn't making a terrible scene, but he sings quite clearly and with reasonable pitch, there in the middle of the supermarket, a song about Walter O'Malley. The song goes on and on, at least four verses, and every line rhymes with O'Malley, except the last, in which the cursed Walter finds himself burning in hell.

I nod in appreciation. It's my turn at the checkout counter. The lady starts ringing up my items. The bagger starts putting them into plastic bags; I don't have time to tell him I prefer paper. By now my new best friend is well into another song. This one is about the Duke and Pee Wee and Gil and the eternal joys of watching baseball at Ebbets Field, and it goes on even longer than the first. It sounds almost like an official Dodger anthem—like "We're Calling All Fans, All You Giant Ball Fans . . ."—and I'm surprised, because I have never heard it before.

"I wish I had copies of those," I say.

"Why?"

"I'm writing a book about baseball. About rooting for the Bums. I could put the songs in my book."

"I wrote them myself," the guy says.

"You would have to give me permission, then."

"They're copyrighted."

He pulls out a piece of paper and a pen. I write my name on the paper, and my address, and my phone number. "Give me a call," I say.

I pull out my wallet to pay for my groceries. The guy is standing at the end of the counter with his frozen pizza. "What part of Brooklyn are you from?" he asks.

"I'm not from Brooklyn, I'm from The Bronx. Near Yankee Stadium. But I was still a Dodger fan."

The guy studies me carefully. "I knew I'd seen you someplace before," he says.

"Where's that?"

Now he is shouting at me: "Behind the bars at the zoo!"

Then he is gone, out the door—with my name, address, and phone number in his fist.

For handing such information to a fruitcake I would ground my teenage daughter for a week.

For the first time I'm glad there are no extant copies of "Branca on the Mound." None that, unhinged by one sad fate or another, I might one day croon to strangers.

At home, putting the groceries away, I tell La Donna what happened. She suggests we go back to the factory outlet store, get me some different shirts to wear. "Different teams. See what happens."

"Maybe a Yankee shirt," I say. "Meet a better class of singer."

I am joking, of course. The Red Sox I could handle, perhaps; the Cardinals would be bearable, if strange. But I could never put on a Yankee shirt. I would not be able to breathe. My sense of integrity would wither. And after that, my soul.

I never intended to go to Southern Methodist University. I went instead to City College. Not bred to be a Mustang, I chose to become a Beaver. (It's all a matter of self-esteem.)

CCNY was situated smack in the middle of Harlem. This caused no racial tension back then, nor was crime in the streets a problem. Boys and girls alike, mostly white, we walked the eight blocks to and from the subway stops at 125th or 145th streets, even after midnight, with no fear and few incidents. If hostility was beginning to raise its head in the tenements and alleyways nearby, we were not yet aware of it. We even felt a certain moral superiority for going to school here rather than at some ivy-covered campus amid green lawns and snow-covered hills, far from the madding crowd; our surroundings, our daily rides on the overstuffed subways, helped us stay in touch with the world as it was. This did not prevent us from some serious self-mockery, however. Our favorite school song was a ditty called "Betty Coed." In the course of the lyrics Betty Coed indulges in every sexual practice imaginable—with the boys at Harvard, Princeton, Yale, even Brown—leading to the the final mournful couplet, always belted out at full throttle:

> Betty Coed goes to City College,
> But she's the whore of the Ivy League!

CCNY did not have a football team. A shortage of beef, as it were. But it did have one of the standout college soccer teams in the country, thanks to a large population of immigrants from Hungary, Lithuania, Yugoslavia, and assorted other points east. When, in my first semester, I became a sportswriter for one of the two college newspapers, I spent much time at Lewisohn Stadium, watching soccer, interviewing not swivel-hipped halfbacks but hardheaded goalies and center-forwards whose names all began with Wolfgang. It was not a bad start toward a liberal education, and in the meantime I learned to love another game.

The college's older section, called the North Campus, was a picturesque collection of old Gothic buildings in which the dark gray of the stones and the lighter gray of the surrounding pavement were the dominant motifs. That fall the school expanded for the first time into its newly acquired South Campus, which formerly had been a girls' religious school, the Manhattanville College of the Sacred Heart. Here the buildings were less picturesque, but green lawns offered the temporary semblance of a rural enclave in the heart of the city. The North Campus was devoted primarily to engineering and the sciences, the South Campus to the liberal arts. On the South Campus, too, was the Finley Student Center, which housed the college's various club activities, including the offices of the two newspapers. It was in these confines that I would while away most of the next four years.

Between 1947 and 1958, in every year except 1948, at least one and usually two of New York's three baseball teams were in the World Series. Because of this the school's newspapers, *The Campus* and *Observation Post*, were in the habit of hanging from their windows a makeshift scoreboard showing the inning-by-inning progress of each Series game—they were played in daylight back then—so the students passing below between classes could keep up with the action at Yankee Stadium or the Polo Grounds or Ebbets Field. It was off these cardboard scoreboards, between classes in history or English or hateful German, that in 1955 I followed the progress of the Dodgers as they once more extended the Yankees into the seventh game. For some reason, probably because I had just emerged from a required science class, I was standing amid the Gothic concrete of the North Campus, at the edge of a knot of students listening to a portable radio, when Johnny Podres completed a 2–0 shutout of the Yankees and gave the Brooklyn Dodgers their first World Series championship ever. Amid a mixture of cheers and groans that spread across the campus as the final Yankee out was made, I recall only a quiet exultation; it had been a long time in coming. And when it did, there were, for the first time, larger, more tumultuous claims in my life, not least among them how to distinguish which sexless nouns required *der, die,* or *das.* Worlds did not collide, pennies did not fall from heaven, Jane Russell did not melt into my arms. Not even Betty Coed. I remember only this: a quiet satisfaction: an inner peace.

In most aspects of human existence the somatic recollection of pain does not endure once the pain has gone; only pleasure can accurately be recalled. It may be that the Brooklyn Dodgers, ever perverse, are nature's one exception.

At fifty-three, he drives to the mall with his wife, and in a sporting-goods store he buys a blue-and-white Dodger baseball cap—the real woolen kind, not the plastic. It does not have a B on the front, it has an LA. The cap is a birthday present for Smith; the skinny-bolink is about to turn sixty.

At a small party on Saturday they give the cap to Smith, who is pleased. They dine on grilled salmon, beer, and birthday cake. He watches as the only small child at the party, a three-year-old girl, black haired, dark skinned, a mixture of Hispanic and Indian, throws a worn tennis ball to a dog. She wants the dog to fetch the ball, but it does not seem interested in playing. He gets up from the table, stoops for the ball, asks the little girl if she would like to play catch. She nods her head.

The child holds her small hands out in front of her. From about three feet away he tosses the ball, underhand, into her fists. She catches it, clutches it to her chest. She throws the ball back to him. He grabs it with one hand, holds it out toward her, tosses it gently. Again the child catches it, a broad toothy grin lighting her cherubic face, part Indian, part Hispanic, face of the child in a thousand Western paintings. Over and over he and the child do this. Sometimes she drops the ball; mostly she catches it, grinning every time. His pleasure, like hers, is powerful.

They play catch for several minutes, ignored by the others at the party. Then she begins to drop the ball more often. Her attention is wandering, she is losing interest. Finally she runs off.

As he watches her go he is clutching the tennis ball.

The child's name is Elizabeth. She is the daughter, adopted, of his former wife.

The skies were leaden and rain was falling intermittently one Saturday long ago as I took the bus to Van Cortlandt Park and watched the cross-country runners disappear over the rolling hills. When they came into view at the end of the long run, and sprinted to the finish line, and jogged to a stop to catch their breaths, I noticed that one of the fellows was from my neighborhood; he lived across the street from my cousin David. This gave me the courage, as a cub college sports reporter, to swallow my shyness and ask him what it was like to run all those miles in the rain. He gave me a good quote, which I incorporated into the story I wrote in longhand the next day and then typed out and turned in to the newspaper office Monday morning as a practice assignment. When *Observation Post* came out on Tuesday, the cross-country story had been written by the sports editor, Bert Rosenthal (who would go on to cover sports for the Associated Press for more than forty years). Midway through Bert's story he had appropriated the quote I had garnered, the quote about running in the rain. It was the first paragraph I'd ever written that appeared in print, and I was mighty proud—though the only words that were truly mine, placed discreetly in the middle of the quote, were "he said."

Thinking back, it could have been a disastrous day. Bert could have altered my "he said" to "he stated," or "he asserted," or "he exclaimed," or "he opined," or "he ejaculated"—any of those contrivances, so dear to said-o-phobics, which I learned early on to avoid, and by whose avoidance I often judge the writing of my betters. He even could have reversed the order, to the nauseating, if ubiquitous, "said he"—which might have driven me from the writing game right then, to no one's regret except perhaps my own.

After baseball my most ardent interest always had been journalism, for reasons I cannot explain. Neither my mother nor my father, as far as I knew, had ever written anything more passionate than business letters and shopping lists. In the sixth grade, when we all had to join a club, I chose the newspaper. Called the *PS 70 School Bee,* it was really a mimeographed newsletter, put out every other week by a teacher named Mr. Orange. At the first club meeting Mr. Orange, who had a bright round face that resembled his name, wrote a list of topics on the board. We were to choose one and write a short piece about it; or, if we were artistically inclined, we could draw a picture to illustrate one of the topics. Hating dentists, I chose to write about Dental Health Week; I have always had, I suppose, a certain morbid streak. Midway through the club period Mr. Orange asked us who had written on each topic. Fascination with tooth decay apparently was rampant that year, because no fewer than seven of us had chosen that subject on which to discourse. Mr. Orange called the magnificent seven to the front of the room with our masterpieces; we were each to read our work to the rest of the class; the group would vote on which was sufficiently insightful to include in the next edition of the *Bee.*

His democratic editing procedure—one punk, one vote—came as shocking news to this writer, who, ever since, has been a firm believer in autocracy in the newsroom. Not yet recovered from my recent attempt to coax "Home on the Range" out of my recalcitrant accordion in front of the entire school, I was in no shape to read my work aloud; my knees shook, my face flushed, my voice quavered. I think it was Stuart Kessler's article on the joy of brushing that garnered the most votes, but I didn't much care. I slunk back to my seat and, lacking any artistic talent whatever, spent the rest of the year drawing pictures, so I would not have to stand up in front of the group and read my work aloud. In the Halloween edition my traditional jack-o'-lantern made its way into print; that was the sum journalistic output of my first ten years.

It was downhill after that. In Junior High School 117 I also joined the newspaper. David Portman and I became sports coeditors. The major sport in junior high was intramural basketball, and Porky and I spent countless hours covering these games and writing them up. The trouble was, the *Wade Junior High School News*—I think that was the name—was published only once a year. When it finally appeared in June I turned the pages, eager with anticipation. I finally found a single column labeled "Sports." Under the title was a double byline: *By Robert Mayer and David Portman.* Below that was a single sentence, written by the faculty adviser. It said: "Following are the results of the intramural basketball games played this year." Then came a column-long list of scores; nothing more. All of our precious prose, all of our torrid descriptions, had vanished.

In retrospect, perhaps it was just as well.

With this discouraging background I kept my distance when I discovered that the so-called newspaper at Bronx Science was also a rag-paper annual intent only on glorifying the school and keeping any real news safely hidden. I flaunted my sperm cells and bided my time till college, where freedom would ring, where in four years I never once set eyes on our faculty adviser, where good, solid journalism would prevail, to the frequent regret of the academic powers-that-were. Where for two and a half years I would write about sports—fitting an occasional class in between—till I decided that the number of ways you could write that the Beaver baseball team had lost, 6–5, was somewhat limited and I would turn my attention to other parts of the paper, never quite sure if the skills I was acquiring were really a profession or merely an escape.

This glimpse of journalistic history has been included here for a single relevant reason: to account for the years, during and after, that I did not spend fielding grounders with well-scuffed balls on some poorly lighted, mosquito-infested Class D minor league field. More's the pity.

I am not a fan of pop psychology, but I awoke out of a deep sleep at four-thirty this morning with a theory in my head that is relevant to any discourse on baseball and men's lives. Call it mom-and-pop psychology.

All mammals, including homo sapiens of both genders, have a powerful rutting instinct. This instinct is the prime progenitor of marriage, babies (not necessarily in that order), infidelity, MTV, Cindy Crawford, beer commercials, and the survival of the species. My middle-of-the-night insight was that we also have a strong rooting instinct; that it appears to be more powerful in males than in females; and, most important, that the two instincts may well be inversely related—that rooting for a ball team appears to be fiercest during two ages of man: before rutting rears its hind quarters, and after rutting mellows out.

Most males become baseball fans around the age of seven. Physically, this is when they first become capable of catching a ball and hitting a ball with any regularity. It is also the age when they begin to reach out beyond their mothers' protective arms and seek a nonthreatening loyalty in the larger community. The selecting of a team to root for—Dodgers, Giants, Yankees, Cubs, Cardinals— is rather like a primitive tribal rite: like-minded rooters become tribal brothers; all other rooters become the enemy. It is during this prepubescent period, ages seven to thirteen or fourteen, that the fortunes of the selected team are taken most seriously—the time when I, for instance, was barely able to eat if the Dodgers lost.

In the early teenage years two things happen that alter the focus and intensity of this rooting interest. The first is the entry into high school, and then perhaps college. The rooting interest becomes bifurcated. Cheering for the Dodgers becomes diluted by cheering as well for De Witt Clinton or Bronx Science, for City College or Notre Dame. The member of the ball-team tribe is now also a member of the school tribe. With baseball loyalties siphoned off in part to the school football or basketball team, the ecstasy of a Dodger victory, and the agony of a Dodger defeat, both become less intense, and therefore less memorable.

This division of loyalties occurs precisely at the same time the second change occurs—the rutting instinct starts to kick in. Will you give up a Dodger victory in exchange for a come-hither smile from Felice? Suddenly, of course you will! This is a betrayal, a revision of the childhood order; shapely legs are now more interesting than base hits. Such a proposition would have been unthinkable a year or two before, but there it is; the rooting instinct has begun to succumb, at least temporarily, to the rutting game.

In my own case this theory would go far toward explaining why the Dodger pennants of 1947 and 1949, when I was eight and ten, are much more memorable than those of 1952 and 1953, when I was thirteen and fourteen: more memorable, even, than that first World Series victory in 1955, when, at sixteen, my loyalty had subdivided itself amoebalike into a rooting interest in the Beaver Booters, and my deep, dark eyes had begun to be distracted by the college girls in their autumn dresses.

The rutting interest of men, it has long been established, peaks at age eighteen, and then begins a long and gradual decline. I am not prepared to say that it is then replaced, again, by rooting. But the theory should give pause to those wives who chafe in irritation when their husbands watch a ball game on the tube. At that moment, though the men may not be giving full attention to their spouses—or be fixing the leaky toilet—they are not out leering at the blonde in the supermarket either.

I remember when I was a kid reading an article in *Life* magazine that presented an Oedipal interpretation of baseball. According to the author's theory the dark, flexible catcher's mitt represented the Mother. The pitcher, standing on his lofty mound, represented the Father, attempting with all his power to hurl his ball into the soft mitt of the mother. In between them, standing close to home, was the Son, menacingly swinging his phallic bat, trying desperately to prevent the father's ball from entering the mother's mitt. I dismissed the article at the time as nonsense; my mother bore no resemblance at all to Roy Campanella. I dismiss it still. More Jungian than Freudian in outlook, I think baseball is about myth and faith, not about sex.

Yet most of the things a man wants in a mate he wants in his ball club as well: loyalty, passion, intelligence, skill, soul. It is a connection I need to ponder in the bright light of day.

Out in La Donna's garden, perhaps.

Last game before the All-Star break, bottom of the eighth, Mets trailing Houston, 3–1. With Astros on first and second and two out, a bounding ground ball is hit toward the Mets' second baseman today, Chico Walker. Instantly as I watch on the tube my mind flares with the knowledge that Walker will commit an error on this play. I know it as an absolute certainty. A split second later the ball reaches him. He bobbles it, drops it; he picks it up and throws to first, too late. E-4. My blood turns electric—not with pride at having forecast the error, I do that often; I wish he had not committed it, the bases are now loaded, the game can be put out of reach. The electric chagrin is partly for him—if I knew he was doing something wrong, then he certainly should have known— but the reaction is also for this instinctive memory still stored inside my nerve-ends, as in a computer. I was not being psychic. The scoreboard of my brain merely had registered ERROR as soon as it did not recognize in Walker's movement the proper procedure with which to field the ball. Only a moment later, after he committed the bobble, did I make a conscious judgment of what he had done wrong. It was nothing very subtle or profound; the announcers already were explaining it to the viewing audience during the replay: Walker had failed to charge the ball; he had waited flat-footed, had let the ball play him. That will cause an error most times, and it had done so again. My brain had merely with lightning speed absorbed the potential problem and registered the likely effect before it happened, before it found words for the cause.

The other day La Donna smoked a brisket in the backyard and we had a few friends over for a barbecue. Our friend Mary called to say she and Randy would be late. When they arrived, I could not think of Mary's last name as I introduced her to the other guests. This despite the fact that I had known her for three years, had worked with her, had seen her twice in the past two weeks. This lapse in short-term memory happens with disconcerting frequency lately, especially with names. Yet the insistent message of my childhood—*Charge it, charge it!*—remains so ingrained in the baseball cortex that it fires off predictive, accurate judgments of errors prior to conscious analysis. This baseball instinct—partly acquired, but an instinct nevertheless—is an aspect of the game accessible only to those who have played it, who have practiced fielding grounders into the deepening dusk, who have felt in their breastbone the ignominy of the bobble. It is limited, in other words, primarily to men.

Sometimes with my wife, but more often with the teenage girl, I know an instant before I am about to say something that I should not say it; I have, by now, fielded enough of life's endless grounders to foresee in a flash the subtle consequences. If I proceed to say it anyway, which I sometimes do, out of pique or perversity, it causes the expected problem every time. In the box score of life, E-6.

At City College the start of the 1956 baseball season was overshadowed by the appearance of Millie Crotch. This was doubly surprising because Millie was a fictional creation.

It was the custom in those days for the newspaper appearing on April 1 to publish an April Fools' edition, satirizing college life. That year it was the turn of *The Campus*, whose editors, decades ahead of prevailing community standards, abandoned satire in favor of sex. What they wrought was deemed scandalous. (By current standards it was ludicrously tame, but what isn't?) Among the Club Notes, for instance, *The Campus* informed its readers that at its next meeting "the Industrial Arts Society will screw"; and that "the Debating Society will debate whether to join the Industrial Arts Society." Humor that was . . . collegiate. Where they broke into the big leagues was with the creation of Millie Crotch.

It was not a large headline, just a three-paragraph, one-column caption story on the bottom of the front page. The story informed readers that "Millie Crotch, the college's prostitute," was retiring, and that as a parting gesture that afternoon she would autograph balls in Lewisohn Stadium.

The original intent of the editors was to accompany the story with a picture of some bathing beauty or other. But late at night, at the print shop on the Lower East Side, someone had a better idea: if the college prostitute was retiring, it would be funnier to use the picture of an old lady. The boys scoured their photo drawers for an appropriate cut—metal photos on blocks of wood, which was the method of printing pictures in that not-so-distant era. When they could not find a suitable picture in their own files, they rifled those of the other college papers that printed at the same shop. Finally they found the perfect picture. It was a close-up of a gray-haired, elderly woman with a lined face appropriate to the situation. She was inserted into the story as "Millie Crotch."

If the picture of a bathing beauty had been used, the story, the entire newspaper, most likely would have raised some angry eyebrows on College President Buell Gallagher—"Cool Buell," we called him—whose eyebrows were notoriously thick in any case. But the gentle woman whose picture was used, who was passed off as Millie Crotch, college prostitute, turned out to be the oldest living alumna of Hunter College.

The sun had not yet set on April Fools' Day, as I recall, before the five senior editors of *The Campus* were kicked out of school for the semester.

Looking back, I consider this a salutary tale. The five seniors all found part-time jobs—one with a brassiere company—and returned to school after six months just a little bit older but a whole lot wiser. They earned their degrees and went on to become, respectively, the editor of a national newsmagazine, the dean of a college, a lawyer, an advertising man, and a magazine copy chief. Today they live on in the college's mythology as "the St. Nick Five," after St. Nicholas Avenue, which runs along the rear of the college. Millie Crotch, too, lives on unexpectedly in hallowed memory—like Lavagetto, like Gionfriddo—though the woman in question, under her Christian name, must surely in the intervening four decades have long since been interred in the earth.

A few months later the baseball season that began with Millie Crotch ended with Don Larsen, whose true identity also remains unknown.

One day in the autumn of 1957, in the fast-falling dark of our living room, I read on the front page of the *Times* that the Brooklyn Dodgers would be leaving Brooklyn; would be moving to Los Angeles, where they would play the following season and all seasons thereafter, presumably till the end of time. This was not something one ordinarily would believe; the Dodgers—Pee Wee, Jackie, Oisk—would just as soon move to Peking or Timbuctoo or Hoboken as to Los Angeles. But I was reading the good gray *Times*, and the *Times* didn't lie. As usual, however, despite its lofty motto, the *Times* did not tell the entire truth either. It was not mere greed that had lured Walter O'Malley to California. What the newspaper chose not to report was that the very sun itself was about to fall from the sky; that Jesus was being removed from the cross; that the oceans would soon dry up, and the fertile fields crack; that birds would die in flight, and tall buildings crumble; that the continent was out of whack, and that all these terrible occurrences had been revealed to Dodger owner Walter O'Malley in a dream. And O'Malley in his dream saw that to prevent these occurrences he must restore the balance of the continent, he must fill the last gaping void in manifest destiny, he must hitch the Dodgers to a covered wagon and drive them to California. No Johnny Appleseed he, to plant and nurture saplings on the coast. There was no time for that. This was a shriek of nature, and O'Malley its obedient servant. For no mortal would be capable of such a wrenching uprooting—leaving millions of his fellow humans twisting, bleeding, naked—in the paltry name of greed.

If all this had been reported in the *Times*, perhaps more people would have understood, would have forgiven. I think of the man in the Santa Fe supermarket who, thirty-five years later, sang to me of the Dodgers, sang of the cursed O'Malley. Perhaps it was on that very day, back then, that he became unhinged; perhaps there were dozens like him, hundreds, thousands. I do not think the phenomenon has been studied in the medical annals; it warrants scrutiny. As for my own reaction, the unspeakable has been deleted from memory. I only recall that, a junior in college, eighteen years old at the time, I fell to my metaphorical knees and thanked God—or the gods—that this had not happened when I was twelve; then I might not have survived it—not even as a half-mad wanderer in the aisles of canned fish, of feminine hygiene, of discontent.

From that day forth—from the day that, we must assume, Walter O'Malley saved the world—I was no longer a baseball fan. I cared not a whit for Los Angeles hits, San Francisco runs, Cardinal errors. If the Yankees had scarcely existed before, they vanished now altogether, to a place even farther than California. For the next four years I did not read the sports pages.

I noticed, as well, a subtle difference in the general nature of things. Hue and tint had vanished from the earth. Except for an occasional bright cartoon the newsreel of life now flickered in black and white.

It is in black and white that I see myself riding the Lexington Avenue subway at four o'clock in the morning the next two years, riding up from the print shop where we have just put the newspaper to bed—I'm on the staff of *The Campus* now—rising through the ranks to editor, wondering always if what I have discovered is really a profession or merely an escape. It is in black and white that I see red-haired Jack Schwartz and me at a student awards dinner the night my last issue is going to press, see us hear with astonishment the college president, the same Cool Buell, charging that the student government and the opposition newspaper were about to be taken over by Communists. The charge was absurd, but more important, it was the biggest news of the year. Furiously Jack and I scrawled black notes on white napkins, having neglected, reporters that we were, to carry pads with us, not expecting news that night. I ran to the nearest phone in the student center, dialed the print shop, and—the dream of a newsman's life—said, literally: "Stop the presses! Tear out the front page!" And they did, while Jack and I in black and white rode the D train downtown, writing in pencil on paper bags, and banged out stories on typewriters into the wee hours.

When at three in the morning I finished reading the proof of my last front page as editor—a full banner headline, going out with a bang—the lights in the print shop went out. I shrieked at whoever had done it to cut the crap. Instead, thirty candles moved in slowly, like a ship, on a large cake carried by the beautous Fran Pike—thirty being the symbol for "the end"—as Fran led into the print shop almost the entire staff of the newspaper, more than twenty fellow students, expecting to be home by midnight, who had waited patiently an additional three hours on a school night in a bar next door while we wrote, till they could bestow this touching tribute.

There. A touch of color was there, in the candles, in this happy cartoon. In the gleam in Franny's face.

A week later I ask her out on a date for the first time. And she accepts, this freshman-cum-sophomore. I will wear my new off-white, lightweight summer suit, and the night before the date I fantasize that Franny and I will be walking in the warm June air on Fifty-ninth Street, on Central Park South, and a faceless villain will emerge from the bushes with a knife in his hand, intent on raping Franny, and I, Robert Hero, will leap into the way, suffering a deep cut in my upper arm, blood staining my new white suit, as I overpower the villain and hold him for the police, and save my beauty's honor. This will become for a time my primal fantasy: rescuing a damsel in distress.

The following year, while in graduate school, I date the virtuous Franny every other Friday or Saturday night, feeling no pain, till I learn—in black and white again—that on the alternate Friday and Saturday nights she has been dating my three best friends. Fair enough, I tell myself (without believing it), till we learn the following summer that she has become engaged to someone else altogether, someone not even on the newspaper— marrying out of the faith, as it were—a premed student, of all things. Every Jewish mother's dream. A few years after that, this same college crowd, at a party, will hear that Franny, married to her predoctor now, living in Chicago, is pregnant. And Vic Ziegel, one of the other datees, paper cup of Dewar's in hand, will scream at the top of his voice: "What! You mean he fucked her!"

And I and the other nice Jewish boys will fall to the floor, gagging with rueful laughter on our drinks, on our unrequited memories.

It is in black and white that I ride the bus one summer night in 1960, from Washington, where I have taken a newspaper job in the real world, to New York, to visit my mother in the hospital, having received an emergency call that the end is near. "What are you doing here?" my mother asks weakly, seeing me, and then, no dummy, she understands. I lie, I tell her I just wanted to see her. She pretends to believe me. Whatever the truth, she astonishes the doctors, she rallies, she gains new strength.

The following Friday the same call comes again. I ride in the night the four hours on the bus and hurry to the hospital. This time my mother does not protest.

A few hours later, standing beside her bed, I see her die. There really is a death rattle; I heard it in my mother's throat. A moment later her eyes rolled back into her head. It was these terrible white eyes, not the glazed but normal eyes of victims in the movies, that the nurse came in and closed, and drew the sheet over. Each year since then, when on the appropriate day I have lighted a candle to her memory, I have looked heavenward with the certainty that she is looking down, content, no longer in pain. And yet, so brave and uncomplaining in life, my mother passed to me, involuntarily, in that white-eyed instant of death, a definite dread. What, in that final instant, had she seen?

I ponder now whether, in setting down this scene, I am invading her privacy with insufficient cause. I think not, if whatever it was that she saw awaits us all.

Two months later, having been awarded a traveling fellowship, I went abroad. Even Europe, in fall and winter, is black and white.

On the ship coming back, during a three-day snowstorm in the gray North Atlantic in January, most of the crew of the *Queen Mary* was throwing up.

I accepted a job in New York, to be nearer to my father, who had taken my mother's death badly. I liked *Newsday;* tabloid in size yet intelligent in content, it was revolutionary. And its blacks and whites were always bold.

A year later, in April of 1962, I was given a small but coveted assignment. A new major league baseball team, a National League team, the New York Mets—rhymes with Jets, shorthand for Metropolitans—would be starting its season at the Polo Grounds. I was assigned to go to the opening game, to write about the crowd, to describe this phenomenon.

The Polo Grounds was gray that day. The lineup of the Mets was drab. The faces in the crowd were varied and uncertain.

The startling change occurred in an early inning, when a visiting batter hit a pop fly into short right center. Richie Ashburn, the Mets' center fielder, the best player they had acquired in the draft, raced toward the ball. Gus Bell, the Mets' right fielder, the second-best player they had acquired in the draft, also raced toward the ball. At precisely the same moment these two major leaguers stopped, and looked at one another. As they did, the ball fell gently to the ground between them, while opposing runners circled the bases. I do not recall which one it was—Ashburn or Bell—who finally picked up the ball. But of this I am positive: when the shiny ball was lifted from the grass, the grass was green.

As I drove out to the newspaper office on the Long Island Expressway after the game, in my beige Chevrolet Corvair, the first sentence of my story was laid in my lap by a passing breeze.

The next day my byline, my all-time favorite among many hundreds, read as follows:

By Robert Mayer
(*Former Dodger Fan*)

Beneath it began my story:

The lost souls of the baseball world found a home yesterday.

So it had been written.
So it would be.

Fathers and Sons

On the day that color and truth returned to the universe, the New York Mets lost their first baseball game. They would lose their next eight as well, and a total of 120 out of 160 that year, constructing a pyramid of ineptitude that has not been equaled before or since. We pilgrims, we aberrant souls, hovered beside their blue and orange NY caps like hummingbirds and suffered their losses gladly.

Now, thirty years later, during this season of discontent, they boast far better players and are performing almost as badly. They have been hurt by injuries, yes—but also by a lack of hitting, fielding, and intelligent base-running, which, given the largest payroll in the game, is a disappointing riddle. In mid-July their pennant hopes are fading. I no longer suffer their losses gladly. But I suffer them nonetheless.

I do not think the children of today—the children of expansion, the children of malls, mayhem, and MTV—are as steadfast in their loyalties.

For forty-four consecutive years my friend Jerry Ortiz y Pino, a social worker and trenchant humanitarian down in Albuquerque, has picked the Cleveland Indians to win the pennant. For forty-three of those years they have not. Next year he will pick them again, with equal certainty, and root for them with all his humane heart, from the fresh breezes of April to October's setting sun.

Born in Santa Fe, Jerry as a young boy listened to the radio in 1948 as Cleveland defeated the Boston Braves in the World Series.

He became a Cleveland fan. Congenitally on the side of the under-dog against the oppressor, he developed, as I was doing half a continent away—as much of America was doing in those years—an abiding hatred for the Yankees. Year after year Cleveland seemed in his view the best bet to beat the New Yorkers, and so he remained an Indians fan. He watched on television in 1954 as his beloveds lost the World Series to the Giants in four straight. He has been waiting patiently for their next Series appearance ever since.

Jerry has been to Cleveland only once, for a professional confer-ence. He asked the organizer if he could get him tickets to a ball game. "You really want to see the Indians?" the man asked.

Turned out they were playing in Texas that week.

Another time he scheduled his family's vacation in San Fran-cisco for a week in which the Indians would be playing across the bay in Oakland. They arrived in town by train, Jerry eager to see his team in the flesh—and learned that, on that very day, the major league ballplayers had gone on strike. No game today—or any day for a while.

More recently Jerry took his son to Texas to see the Indians play the Rangers. When Jerry was a kid, the Indians held spring train-ing in Arizona, and they would play an occasional exhibition game in Albuquerque when they broke camp. Jerry would go then. But this game in Irving would be the first time in his life he had seen his team in the flesh in a game that counted. The Indians won, he recalls, on a home run by Joe Carter. Which makes Jerry Ortiz y Pino the only serious fan I know who has never seen his ball club lose.

Discussing all this, I asked Jerry if, after forty-four years of rooting for the Indians through newspaper box scores, he expects to remain a Cleveland fan. "Of course," he said. "I think they've finally turned the corner."

My friend Tom Collins, Jr., who hails from Chicago, still roots for the White Sox, as he did thirty years ago when his father, also a lifetime Sox fan, used to take him to the old Comiskey Park. Tom, an art writer, itinerant thinker, and father of a teenage boy, has given some thought to being a White Sox fan in general, and to the younger generation in particular.

"My son, Mike, is not a White Sox fan," Tom said. "He has always laughed at my White Sox fandom. 'You gotta be kidding,' he'd say. He was born and grew up in New Mexico. He's one of these new fans that doesn't have a loyalty born of growing up in a city. He grows up with WTBS and WGN and stuff like that. The global village has come to baseball.

"He actually became a Houston Astros fan, of all things. Because when he was very young we watched a baseball game on WGN here in Taos, the Astros versus the Cubs, and he loved their uniforms. Those terrible orange shirts. . . . He used to like the A's, but he hates them now. At least he has that old White Sox Yankee-hating blood in him. The strongest opinions he holds, or prejudices, are ones of dislike. Like his father. He hates the Cubs, which is good.

"Cub fans don't take their losing seriously. Kind of like Red Sox fans. Anybody who doesn't take losing seriously is not really in it for the real meat of the scene, the meat of the conflict. You gotta really hurt. Even when they lost in '69 to the Mets, there was this sense of, 'Well, it's okay, because they're our Cubbies. And, you know, we expect this from them anyway in a kind of cute way.' There's not that kind of morbid fatalism about being a Cub fan that there is about being a Sox fan. They're cute, ya know? Not serious."

Tom recalls a particular game to which he took his son, the one game when Mike finally understood what it was like to be a White Sox fan. The Sox were nursing a 2–0 lead over the hated Yankees into the eighth. With one out the Sox pitcher walked a batter. This was followed quickly by a pinch double, and a home run by Dan Pasqua.

"He hit a ball into the right field stands faster than I could say Rumpelstiltskin," Collins recalls. "The Sox lost, 3–2. I saw the look on Mike's face: *How could this happen?* Well, I could see that rap coming when ball four was thrown to the guy. That was a very memorable game. Having the White Sox show me they were still the White Sox. To me it was a metaphor for the entire history of the Chicago White Sox from 1919 on. Complete failure. But not just complete failure—I mean, excruciating failure. Gene Shepherd, the raconteur, once said if he were in a suicide mission to attack a pillbox, he would pick five Chicago White Sox fans. Because they've stared into the face of death every day."

There can be, in the quiet contemplation of an individual baseball game, a triumph over Self, a penetration into a cosmic connection—an experience akin to Zen. (This has been made much more difficult, in the American League, by the designated-hitter rule.) But in the long-suffering acceptance of its genuine fans—even a Gene Smith, a Jerry Ortiz y Pino, a Tom Collins, Jr.—there is something of the Jewish faith. Its essence is this abiding loyalty, in bad times even more than in good. *Thou shalt have no other gods before me.* I have asked men wearing baseball caps how they came to root for the team they did, and have been told such things as: "I used to root for the Cubs, then the Oakland A's. But this year I think I'll go with Milwaukee." Whatever other merits such men might possess, they are not baseball fans.

The Mets have taken three straight from the Giants at Shea. Friday night David Cone tossed a 1–0 shutout and struck out 13. Saturday night Sid Fernandez, with some relief help after he threw 136 pitches, shut them out 3–0. Today, Schofield—who had knocked in only three runs in his last 42 games—knocked in three with a base-clearing double, then knocked in three more with a homer. Must have made old man Ducky proud. The Mets won the game, 8–4.

In the evening we barbecued hamburgers. Smith came over with his friend Patsy and some other folks. They admired La Donna's roses, her daisies, her gladiolas.

"What's wrong with the Mets?" Smith said.

"I know. Three straight! Do you think this is the first day of the rest of their lives?"

They are still in fourth place, but only one game out of second. Two games under .500 at 45 and 47. Six games behind the Pirates—but down from eight. Do I dare . . . do I dare to hope for a pennant race? And risk the disappointment?

Saberhagen is coming off the disabled list. That will help, if he's really healthy. But Doc Gooden, enduring his worst season, is going on it. I, too, miss Doc's being great.

Murray Kempton once wrote: "There was this moment when Willie Mays caught the last ball hit in the National League in 1962 and turned and laughed and threw it at the right field foul pole. It was his ball and he could do what he pleased with it. All of a sudden you remembered all the promises the rich have made to the poor for the last thirteen years and the only one they kept was the promise about Willie Mays. They told us then that he would be the greatest baseball player we would ever see, and he was."

What, I think now, twenty years later, of the promise of Doc Gooden? At twenty-two he appeared to be one of the best— maybe the best pitcher ever. Now, at twenty-seven, will he become a mere footnote? Will he become another me?

David Cone, their only consistent pitcher this year, beats the Dodgers. The Pirates lose to streaking Atlanta. Fernandez wins again. The Mets, back at .500, are only one game out of second, four games out of first. It's July 24, and we've got ourselves a pennant race!

Maybe.

In June of 1964 I took my father to a ball game at the new Shea Stadium. We had not been to a game together since the days when I was a kid and he took me to Ebbets Field. But he was alone now, my mother long gone, and I had been foresighted enough to get a pair of tickets for Father's Day. This repayment was long overdue.

The Mets were playing the Phillies that day. I do not remember who was pitching for the Mets. The Phillies hurler was Jim Bunning. The rest, as you probably know, is Hall of Fame history.

The truth is, a perfect game is boring, if it is being hurled against your own team. Three up, three down, inning after inning. If you knew in advance that you were watching a perfect game, there might be some excitement. But in baseball, as in life, you cannot predict—and if you could, perfection would be last on the list: even perfect ineptitude. So there was merely this petty pace from inning to inning, until seven innings had been completed. Then, suddenly, you knew it was possible. You knew you might be watching a perfect game. And then this terrible thing happens. This moral conundrum. Do you continue to root for a seven-run Met rally, which is highly unlikely? Or do you find yourself, for the first time in your life, rooting against your own team; rooting for the enemy; rooting for the perfect game to remain intact, so you will be able, for the rest of your natural life, to say you had been there when?

In my case that's what I did. I became a traitor to my team. I rooted for the perfect game. My only consolation was that most in the crowd seemed to be doing the same. And God heeded—*He would!*—and the perfect game remained perfect, and as we streamed with fifty thousand other Father's Day fans towards the exits we knew we had witnessed one of baseball's rarest events.

Though he would live for sixteen more years, that was the last ball game to which I took my father. I don't recall why; perhaps he preferred to stay at home; perhaps I was too absorbed in other things. As for Jim Bunning's perfect game, my witness has not, through the years, made for much of an anecdote. "I was there" is all I can say. The ladies do not swoon at my feet. The men do not appear jealous.

Kempton, the wise man, knew this long before. On the day of Don Larsen's perfect game Kempton chose to write his column about Sal Maglie, who pitched for the Dodgers that day.

Perhaps it would have been different if it had been the Mets who'd shown perfection. *I was there when . . . !*

I think not. Among human beings, as with all the other beasts of the field, the shared experience, not the idle boast, is the tie that binds.

In the autumn we will be going to New York, our first visit to the city in five years. I went to a travel agent the other day to book low-fare tickets in advance. While my own agent fiddled with her computer, I overheard a man at the next desk. He was about my age, but dressed like a cowboy, in leather boots. He was an outfitter, it turned out, who took people on hunting trips. He was planning a trip to either San Diego or Houston, he told the agent, and he wanted to know how much the lowest fares would be. He also asked her to find out the next time the Pittsburgh Pirates would be playing in those cities. He said (I thought) that his son was a Pittsburgh fan, that his son's birthday was coming up, that he wanted to fly his son to a game.

The travel agent telephoned for the baseball schedules. Then she asked if the second passenger was over sixty-five, because if he was he could get a reduced fare. It turned out that I had misunderstood. It was the cowboy's father who was the Pittsburgh fan. He had been a Pittsburgh fan all his life, and in two weeks he would turn eighty-four, and he had never been to a major league game. The cowboy wanted to take him to see the Pirates.

When my own business was done I left them in midconversation. I envisioned the elderly man in front of the television set in a darkened room, and then seeing for the first time a major league park in person, seeing the black and orange of his league-leading Pirates under the bright sun or the even brighter lights, this vision he would one day take to the grave.

A week later air fares were reduced significantly. I went back to the travel agency to have my tickets rewritten. I asked the agent about the cowboy and his father: were they going to see the Pirates in San Diego? In Houston?

"It didn't work out," the agent said. "The Pirates were not in San Diego when he could go. And Houston was too expensive. He never came back."

It's possible the cowboy took his business to another travel agent. But there was no discernible reason for that. More likely it was just one of those good ideas that, like a sixteen-point buck, got away. Perhaps next year, when the old man is eighty-five, he will get to go.

Fervently, I hope that he does. Between fathers and sons even a perfect game is better than no game at all.

Under a late-morning sun that is baking the dirt infield, Jaime Dean trots into the empty dugout, looks for a plastic cup he has stashed somewhere, finds it, adjusts it into the pants of his gray uniform—number 14 of the Toledo Mudhens, the Triple-A farm team of the Detroit Tigers. Jaime's mother, Seva Dubuar, had bought him the uniform not long before, for his sixteenth birthday, a real uniform that had been worn in games by a Toledo player. We shake hands beside the dugout. I tell Jaime I will watch for a while before we talk—that they should go on with their practice as usual.

Protective cup in place, Jaime trots out to first base with his mitt. His friend Dave Sanchez, a lefty in a red hat, slashes a grounder at Jaime over the hard bleached earth. Jaime backhands it, turns, and fires to Jeff Dailey, who is covering second base. It is summer, school is out, and they are the only three players on the Santa Fe High School field. The coach has given them a key to the gate; three days a week Jaime, Dave, and Jeff come here to practice on their own, from nine-thirty in the morning to noon.

I do not have a son, to whom to hit grounders into the night. If I did, he would in my imagining be very much like Jaime Dean. I know this—I have long intuited this—although Jaime and I have never met, have talked on the phone only once, two nights before, to arrange an interview.

As I watch the infield practice—errors, wild throws, fine pickups—I select a bat from several that are stacked like a teepee against the chain link fence beside the dugout. The old sensual feel of the handle inflames my fingers, my palms, the muscles in my arms. I wave the thin-handled bat through the air, slowly, several times. Then a wee bit harder. I am tempted to join the practice, to offer to hit out fungoes to a three-man infield. But I know that if I do I will wreck my ribs, where there is still some kind of unhealed injury from a softball game a few years back. I resume my seat on the dugout bench, holding the bat, choking up, as I always did, making a few slow passes. When I pause, silent, a solitary lizard scampers across the shaded floor.

Jaime is still making pickups, pivoting—a right-handed first baseman—to make the throw to second. Impatient to be one of them, I stand, step out into the sun, take a few easy swings left-handed. I feel a slight popping strain in my left wrist, and I cease. It has been too many years since I have done this thing that I will never do again.

Jaime trots in toward the plate to take his turn with the bat. His spikes crunch on the baked earth as in a fine and distant dream. "Good grab, good grab," Dave is yelling to Jeff. They do not seem to notice the heat, which on the field must be nearing one hundred degrees by now.

When he is finished hitting Jaime walks to the dugout. He peels off his Mudhen shirt. Beneath it he is wearing a black plastic undershirt, to make himself sweat even more than normal. He explains that Brian Traxler, the chunky first baseman of the Albuquerque Dukes, the nearest minor league team, wears one of these plastic shirts. "He attributes all his hitting this year to it," Jaime says. "So I figured I try it."

He takes off the plastic undershirt, buttons his uniform shirt again, and walks down to the bullpen to pitch. I stand behind a wire cage, watch, listen to fifteen minutes of fastballs, and just a few curves, popping into the catcher's mitt. I wonder if I could stand in the batter's box today against such a fastball exploding; I wonder if I could have back then, punchballer, softballer that I was.

"I didn't have it today," Jaime says as we walk back to the dugout. He is a shade or two taller than I am.

"Looked like a pretty good fastball to me," I say.

"It was up," he says. "They'd have belted the heck out of it."

A perfectionism that echoes through the long-gone chambers of my youth.

Jaime has been playing on the high-school junior varsity. A junior when the new term begins, he hopes to make the varsity next spring.

"If you didn't play first base, would you want to pitch?" I ask.

"Sure," he says. "But short relief. So I could get in there every day."

He is the same age as my stepdaughter; in the semester just ended they shared a chemistry class.

Or is he, in fact, my son?

I think, mistakenly, that the boys are finished for the day, that now we will sit and talk.

"We're going to do a little bit of running," Jaime says.

I imagine they will jog a few turns around the outfield. Instead they exit the field. Behind the fence along the left-field foul line is a steep and rocky hill, the angle at least forty-five degrees. The three boys race to the top, a rutted uphill churn of about fifty yards. Slowly they walk down. Then they race up the rocky slope again. And again. This third time, at the top, they have to wait and catch their breaths. They are human after all. I pick up a ball, toss it into a glove. Punchball, I think, was not like this.

But it was; in its fanaticism, it was.

They return to the dugout and gather their equipment. They lock the gate behind them. Jaime is going to drive the others home. We agree to meet afterward at a nearby restaurant to have lunch; to talk some baseball.

I have been acquainted with Jaime's mother, Seva, for years. She used to own a good Italian restaurant; when that failed, she became a butcher in a supermarket. I do not know his father. Seva raised her son while a single mother, and for a number of years the man in her life was O'Brien, a globe-trotting photojournalist who is, after Smith, my closest compadre. From O'Brien I used to hear when the boy was eight or nine years old about the wonders of Jaime Dean, baseball fan. As I waited for him now in a corner booth of the restaurant, I knew he had become a Tigers fan because of his grandfather, who had lived in Detroit. I knew that he collected baseball cards with a certain seriousness, and that—this in particular intrigued me—he specialized in minor leaguers.

Jaime slid into the booth. When the waitress came I ordered a tuna melt, and he a cheeseburger; dishes clinked loudly around us. I placed a small tape recorder on the table, to free my hands for eating, and turned it on. What would strike me most as we talked was how pragmatic he was about his talents—an owl's cry from my own wishful dreams—and how persistent in his quirky pursuits.

I began by asking if he hoped to play professional baseball one day. "Anybody will say, well, I want to play pro ball," Jaime said. "But only one in twenty-seven hundred that are drafted play major league ball. I know I'll play at least Rookie League ball. Try

Class A. If that doesn't work out I'll try to play in Puerto Rico, Japan, Italy. They've got a league in Italy now. When you're playing there in Single A you have to have another occupation; those guys only make twelve thousand a year. You can't live on that. So I have to go to college. I can't sign out of high school."

Right now, he said, he was studying horticulture. But he might like to get into architecture, specialize in designing new ballparks, like Camden Yards.

He talked about his career in T-ball, Little League, Babe Ruth League. He was not playing Babe Ruth League this summer.

"I had a bad experience," he said. "I had a coach who abused my arm. He'd bring other coaches to our practices, and he'd have me throw curve balls for an hour and a half. To show off or something. My arm was hanging there. Finally I told him I can't keep this up, my arm is hanging as it is. He told me, 'You pitch or you don't play.' My grandfather is a doctor, and he said I had tendinitis. For that you need at least six weeks' rest. I told the coach I could play first base, I could play any other position. But I can't pitch. He said fine, but I won't put you on the ballot for All-Stars. I hit, like, .470; best defensive first baseman in the league; and I missed out going to Pine Bluff, Arkansas."

We laugh. Together. "It's not that bad," Jaime says.

I ask him if that particular coach is still coaching. He assures me that he is.

"Now I can't last more than three or four innings at a time," Jaime says.

The subject turns to baseball cards; I ask Jaime how he got into that. He tells me that, when he was eight years old, a dishwasher who was working for his mom and was going away to college gave Jaime a coffee can filled with baseball, football, and Star Wars cards. It was 1985 or so. Jaime was watching a television program that did a segment on the increasing value of baseball cards. "I went through them and I had a Darryl Strawberry rookie that was worth seven dollars, and I got all excited. Now it's going for sixty or so. I just started buying more cards, till now it's like an addiction."

A fellow in my neighborhood, hearing I was writing a book about baseball, had told me a few weeks earlier that I should talk to his brother. "He's got the biggest collection of baseball cards in the state," the man said. "He's got a room filled with them. He's got twenty thousand cards."

I had been suitably impressed, but I had wanted to talk to Jaime first.

"How many cards do you have?" I ask Jaime.

"About a hundred and twenty thousand," Jaime says.

I repeat the number with appropriate awe, with an implied low whistle. "Where do you keep them?" I ask.

"Everywhere. My house is hell. It's filled with baseball cards." He keeps them in large boxes and in plastic sheets, he says. "Right now I'm trying to narrow it down. From '87 to '89 I'd buy anything I saw. Most of my cards are from that era. Now it's getting to the point where I need money for the truck, for my girlfriend, for whatever. I can't afford to spend sixty dollars a week on baseball cards."

I ask if he has a favorite card.

"I have Double-A sets from '86, where none of the guys made it to the majors. I've got three right now. An '86 Shreveport, an '86 Idaho Falls, and an '86 Visalia, Single A."

"Most people" I say, "would want major leaguers. Why are you proud of those?"

"Just because of that. Most people want Jose Canseco, Juan Gonzales's minor league cards. They don't want, you know, Skeeter Barnes."

This boy loves the images of the never-was. Of the never-to-be. An indefinable poetry has joined us in the booth.

I ask Jaime if he collects the cards because he likes them, or because they are valuable.

"I like them," he says. "Right now it's gotten to the point where you are never going to see cards go up in value the way they did ten years ago. Mickey Mantle's rookie card is worth fifty thousand dollars. They made a hundred thousand of them. But right now they are making five million of each card. Minor league cards they make anywhere from fifteen hundred to five thousand."

This is new territory to me, this minor league immortality. "They make all the way down to A ball?" I ask.

"Below that," Jaime says. "They even make Rookie League. That's Instructional League."

Jaime likes to get his cards signed by the players. This is much easier to do while they are still in the minor leagues, largely devoid of admirers. To do this he has a pair of season tickets to the Dukes—the Dodgers' Triple-A team—in Albuquerque, which is sixty miles away.

"My seats are right on the clubhouse walkway," he says. "The players have to walk right by me. Most people get major league cards signed. I've got their '87 Pocatello. Now they're in Triple-A. They see these and they're happy to sign. Some of the rookies, they've just been called up, and I give them six of their cards, from Single A on up, and they just go crazy."

I imagine myself in his place, a rookie ballplayer, lugging my weak bat. Seeing these cards from my anonymous past. . . .

"You should come to a Dukes game with me one of these days," Jaime says, "to see how I work it. I take a box of about two-hundred cards. I've got them in alphabetical tabs. I see these guys coming by, I take three cards and snap them on a clipboard. I hand them the stuff. Most of the guys know me by now. They say, 'Are you back again?' And they sign.

"I've got a guy in Des Moines who I trade with. He gets American Association Players, and I get Pacific Coast League players, and we trade back and forth, complete sets." Jaime and a friend advertised in *Baseball Weekly* to find this fellow. "There's a minor league company called Line Drive. They make a set of thirteen hundred cards. All Double A and Triple A players. So we trade them, get them signed for each other, and send them back. We got two answers to our ad, but one guy wasn't serious. This guy said, 'I've got season tickets, I go to every game, I use a Sharpie.' "

"A Sharpie?"

"It's a felt-tip marker, but it's really solid. It comes out with a nice, thick—not too thick—a nice solid line, and it's permanent. It's a permanent marker, and it dries easily. So you don't have any smearing. With a ballpoint, it presses into the card, and leaves edges."

Jaime reads two magazines, *Baseball Weekly* and *Baseball America,* that publish minor league statistics. He knows the major league affiliation of every minor league team. "Except maybe a few single A's," he allows.

He goes to the Dukes games with friends, or his girlfriend, or his mother, or his father. I ask him if he ever went with Tony O'Brien. "He took me to my first Dukes game," Jaime says. His pride is appropriate.

One year Jaime's mother took him to spring training in Phoenix and Tucson, where six teams train, to see exhibition games. He noticed people getting their baseball cards signed. The following year he went again, and took sixty cards with him. He got them all signed. The year after that, he took twelve hundred cards to spring training. He got six hundred of those signed.

He rattles on about the intricacies of collecting, about players whose Class C cards he has who are now hitting .310 in the majors—American Leaguers of whom I have never heard. He knows which cards have been given out in restaurant promotions, and thus been overproduced, and thus are not as valuable as others. I recall my own excitement at putting a penny into the card machine at Coney Island and obtaining two cards for one. A horse and buggy clops noisily down the narrow streets of my mind. My brother's knuckle hurts my shoulder.

I ask Jaime what his collection is worth.

"Eight, nine thousand dollars," he says.

For a moment I am disappointed. Four to five thousand of his 120,000 cards are signed. I thought they would be worth more. But he is only sixteen, has only been collecting these last eight years or so. His cards do not date back to the early fifties, to the late forties.

The inescapable moment has come. I prepare to tough out the news. "When I was a kid—this was way back in the 1940s . . ." I begin. And confess to him the sad story of my own card collection, and of what I did with it. Hesitantly, I ask him if he ever sees those kind of postcard-sized, sepia-colored cards around. Even more hesitantly, I ask him what they are worth.

The waitress is clearing our plates. The clink of dishes is very loud. He waits till she moves off.

"Actually, there is a big market for those right now," Jaime tells me.

I do not let him see me wince.

"It depends on the company who made them. The guys who are really into it know about this." *The guys who are really into it?* "You can get Mickey Mantles, depending on the company, for a hundred to five hundred dollars." *I had Mickey Mantle!* "A common guy might be ten dollars or so." *I had hundreds of common guys!* "The Mantles, the Marises, the Musials, those are up around three hundred, five hundred." *I had them all. Probably I had doubles of them all!*

I dare not do the arithmetic in my head. The arithmetic of all those one-cent investments, when I was seven years old, and eight, and nine.

It would not be enough, in any case, to buy a house.

A nice down-payment, maybe.

"I tossed them all," I say.

To prove I was a man.

We leave baseball cards. We talk of heroes. Jaime Dean's hero is Ty Cobb. Jaime hates Pete Rose for breaking Cobb's record.

"My great-grandfather was a Tigers fan," Jaime says. "I'd go talk to him a lot. He died when I was five, I think. He'd tell me about Ty Cobb. That's the only old ballplayer I've really thought about. He's always been my idol. I feel that he was the greatest ballplayer. Not just because of his stats, but because of what he did for the game. He wasn't in the home-run era, but he could hit them when he needed to. One day the Tigers were in Yankee Stadium—I think it was 1927, when Ruth went on his big tear, sixty home runs, and everyone was thinking, well, the home run is the way you play baseball. Ty Cobb comes to town and there's a big article in the *Times*, that he isn't the great ballplayer everyone says he is, because he can't hit a home run. That day he hit three home runs.

"I hate Pete Rose. Look at the stats. He was hitting .267. . . . The only reason he was still playing was to break the record. If you look at Ty Cobb—he retired in 1928, I think—the reason he quit was that he didn't think he was playing up to par. He felt that he wasn't doing his best. So he hung it up after hitting .308."

Actually, I discovered later, Cobb quit after hitting .323. Rose, the year he broke the record, hit .264.

His favorite contemporary player, Jaime says, is Alan Trammell, the Detroit shortstop.

I ask him about the most memorable play in his own career. He pauses, thinks. "I guess it's still coming," he says. Though he does recall fondly his first home run in Little League.

I have just one more question. I tell him of my belief that, though he is obviously an exception, most kids today are not the rabid baseball fans we used to be. Jaime agrees. I ask him what he thinks the reasons are.

"They've got more to do," Jaime says. "Back in the forties, fifties, and sixties you played ball. That's all. Now the parents don't even take the time to get their kids interested in it. During the late sixties and early seventies, I think, everyone started to go against that jock feeling. Soccer became the game where you could use your head, you didn't have to be aggressive. Especially around here, soccer is the main sport you'll see kids playing. Also, kids aren't thinking as much. And baseball is a thinking game. A lot of people say to me, 'Why do you like baseball? It's boring. All you do is hit a little ball.' That's what people who don't know the game think about the game. But it's more than that. Anything can happen. That's what I like about it. Anytime I go to a Dukes game I see something different. If not on the field, then in the dugout—I'll see a guy doing something I've never seen."

We pause. The tape spins silently. I click it off.

An identity of minds. This is unusual, perhaps startling, between one who has been on the planet for fifty-three years and one who has been aboard for sixteen. Of all sports only baseball can be that rarest of bridges, a suspension span across time itself.

Perhaps not just among sports. Perhaps among all human endeavors.

I pay the check and walk Jaime out to his truck. I watch as he climbs in. Perhaps one night not too far off we will go to a Dukes game together, as he has suggested. But I think not.

* * *

He is not my son.

He is I.

I am he.

The Bronx is far away, and the promises we have to keep are different.

This confusion mingles in the dust as he shifts gears loudly and drives away.

Detroit. I had always had a fondness for the city because Hank Greenberg was the only Jewish superstar I knew of when I was growing up; he made my major league dreams seem possible. Later, the combo of "Kaline and Kuenn" had rhythm. But I have visited the city only once, and it had nothing to do with the Tigers. It was in the summer of 1967, to cover as a journalist the deadliest inner-city riot in our history. For four days I prowled this combat zone in search of stories, filed them in the wee hours, got some sleep, then returned to the streets. I expected to fly home on Saturday, because things had calmed by then, and because the paper in those days did not have a Sunday edition. But my editor asked me to stay over, to file a story Sunday about church service in the ghetto.

Saturday, then, was a day of rest.

I bought one of the local newspapers and sat in the sun on a bench in a park across from my hotel. Soon a young man about my age—I was twenty-seven then—sat at the other end of the bench. He struck up a conversation. He was a male nurse. He invited me to his nearby apartment for a cup of coffee. Politely, I declined, and the man soon left. I had resumed reading the newspaper—120 pages of riot news and pictures, and nothing else—when a small, elderly man took the place of the nurse. He looked a bit like my father, and he, too, was clearly eager to start a conversation, but did not know how. Finally he summoned up his courage. He said: "So, what's the news from Israel?"

Hiding a smile as best I could, I told him there did not seem to be any; that the newspaper was filled with stories about the riot. The man did not seem overly concerned about the riot.

"Where are you from?" he asked.

"New York."

"You Jewish?"

I allowed that I was.

"Your parents, they live in New York?"

"My father does," I replied. "My mother is dead."

"Are you married?" the man asked.

"No."

"Do you live with your father?"

I wondered why he cared about all this. "No," I said. "I have my own apartment. In Greenwich Village."

For many long seconds he pondered that. I was about to turn back to my newspaper when the old man said: "Whatsametteh, a single boy like you, you can't live at home with your father till you're married?"

Apparently, that week in Detroit, with forty-three people shot dead by the National Guard, there was not enough local guilt to go around.

That night I went alone to a strip show. I drank vodka tonics and watched black women and white women take off all their clothes. I do not know if this was in tribute to the male nurse, or the Jewish mother, or the forty-three corpses lying in the ghetto.

On Sunday I went to church. On Monday I flew back to New York. I could have gone home to rest, but I liked the work I'd done in Detroit and I wanted to bask in office plaudits. There was also another reason. I was the shortstop on the Nightside Editorial team in the *Newsday* Softball League, and we had a game that night. If I was not really prepared to play—no sneakers, no glove, and not much energy—at least I could watch.

Soon after I arrived, Bill McIlwain, the managing editor, summoned me to his office. He'd hired me six years earlier, and I'd always been one of his fair-haired boys—even, I suspect, a kind of son figure. He closed the door behind us; he congratulated me on my coverage of the riot. I thanked him, and I waited; he did not have to close the door for that.

Finally, McIlwain, a soft-spoken North Carolinian, asked: "When do you want to start your column?"

During our first interview years before, he had asked me my long-range goal. I'd said I wanted to be a columnist—not so much to express my opinions as to have the freedom to write about what I chose. A moment before, when I'd entered his office, it was still my life's goal—and still long range.

I let his question sink in a moment. A lark took wing in my chest. I shrugged with a casual air I was not feeling. "Anytime," I said.

McIlwain picked up his telephone and dialed another office. A few minutes later we were joined by Bill Moyers, who had left the Lyndon Johnson White House a few months before to become the publisher of *Newsday*. They'd obviously discussed this column plan already; McIlwain, with typical grace, had wanted to give me the opportunity to decline in private, if decline I would.

Moyers told me, in confidence, that he had hired Pete Hamill away from the *New York Post*; that Hamill would be going to Washington in a month to write a full-page column for *Newsday* three days a week. They would like me to fill the same space on alternate days, with my own column from New York.

Thwack — rooooohr.

"How does September eleventh sound?" McIlwain said.

Of the softball game that evening I remember only the end. We were three runs behind Classified Advertising going into the bottom of the seventh. As I watched from the sidelines we scored twice. One run behind now, we had runners on second and third and two out—and our weakest hitter coming up. I was having a good year at the plate. The coach—I forget who it was that season—asked if I would pinch-hit. I looked down at my dress shoes. I thought: *All I have to do is get to first.*

I pulled off my tie, selected a bat, took a few practice swings. As I stepped into the box, the outfield was fairly deep. I decided to take a shot to right; a liner between first and second would win the game.

The first pitch floated in over the inside corner; it was a pitch I usually tried to pull inside the third-base bag for a double; but if the third baseman snared the grounder, I'd be an easy out at first in my oxblood Tru-Form 8D's with leather soles.

"Strike!" the umpire said.

I let a high pitch go by. Then I got what I wanted—a floater on the outside corner. I held back for just an instant, then slashed the ball toward right.

It was not exactly a line drive between first and second. It was more of a low pop fly, a chip shot, down the right field line. But it landed fair and spun away into foul territory. I was able to trot to first, a secret columnist, while both runners scored and the game was ours, and I knew for an instant that there really was a reason for which I had been put on this earth (though I still did not know what the reason was).

Tom Seaver is being inducted into the Hall of Fame today. I recall my next to last visit to Shea, in 1983. It was the day Seaver was going to make his first start for the Mets after returning to New York from Cincinnati, to whom they had obscenely traded him in 1977. I was visiting the city from New Mexico. Jon Richards, who still lived on the West Side, had wangled tickets from a friend at *Sports Illustrated*. We went to the game and sat on the first-base side and watched Seaver warming up in the bullpen during in-field practice. When he finished his warmups and strode in toward the Mets dugout for the first time in seven years, we stood and applauded. So did fifty thousand others. For five full minutes the throaty cheers, the applause, rolled in, a tidal wave of recognition for all he had done for the Mets—for all he had done for all of us—in years gone by. Chief architect of the Miracle of 1969, he was the best player the Mets ever had. If baseball is played for another millennium, he probably will still be the best player the Mets ever had.

On the day Tom Seaver is being inducted into the Hall of Fame, the Mets are playing at Shea, and the game is on the tube. Someone hits a looping fly ball down the right field line. After a long run Bobby Bonilla dives for it in foul territory and lands heavily on his chest. He is forced to leave the game. X rays reveal a broken rib. He will be out of action for several weeks.

On the same day the Mets have revealed that Howard Johnson has a broken wrist and that Bret Saberhagen's index finger is acting up and he has been returned to the disabled list. The Mets lose two quick ones to the Pirates. Suddenly they are 7 ½ games back, and fading fast.

Like many folks I know, forced out by high rents or lured to climates more serene, God in the nineties no longer keeps an apartment in New York.

Dog racing will never replace horse racing as my second-favorite sport.

Early in my tenure at the newspaper Richie Kwartler and I decided to go on vacation together to Miami. We'd been class-mates in journalism at Columbia and were now working together. Richie was considering getting married for the second time and wanted to get away to think. It was a cold December, and I just wanted to get away.

Richie's girlfriend, Sheila, drove us to Kennedy Airport one Friday night, and decided to wait with us till our plane took off; neither she nor Richie was crazy about flying. As boarding time approached, fog began to roll in over the airport. Some incoming planes were put in holding patterns; some outbound planes, in-cluding ours, were delayed.

Suddenly, in the fog outside, we began to hear sirens; we began to see the halos of revolving red lights. Soon after, newsmen and television crews began to race through the terminal. At first the authorities would not say what had happened. Then the news came out. An incoming flight had crashed in the fog.

We debated briefly whether to call the newspaper. We decided not to. They probably knew already. We were on vacation. We did not want to be told to go to work.

The fog outside grew thicker. The rescue operations were too far away to see. Rumor had it that many on the plane had been killed.

Our flight remained delayed, but not canceled.

As time passed, many of the passengers grew restive; nobody was in much of a mood to take off in this fog just now. For several hours the airline refused to cancel the flight. It did so, finally, only to keep a revolt of the passengers from getting ugly. The flight was rescheduled for the following afternoon.

Outside, in the parking lot, it was impossible to see a car length in front of your face. The headlights reflected off the fog and only made things worse. There was only one way to get to Richie's apartment in a nearby Long Island town. While Sheila inched the car forward, Richie and I walked in front of it, to lead her along the circling roads out of the airport—out, at last, of the fog.

It was two A.M. when we got to the apartment. Sheila pleaded with us not to go. I think Richie was tempted, but he did not want to ruin our vacation.

The next day broke bright and blue. We heard on the news that the crash the night before had left twenty-three dead. Over Sheila's misgivings we flew to Miami. Driving from the airport to Miami Beach, I recall, there were two lovely college girls in a white convertible with red leather interior, with whom we flirted at every stoplight for fifteen miles.

We had arranged to meet up in Miami with John Dumoga, an experienced journalist from Ghana. John had been one of our classmates at Columbia. Now he was back in the States on an exchange program as a guest of the U.S. government, spending time at American newspapers, doing some sightseeing. By coincidence he would be in Miami the same time we were going.

On the appointed day we telephoned John, who was a friendly, outgoing fellow, very short and very black. We invited him to join us for dinner. To our naive surprise John declined. But when we told him that after dinner we might go to the local dog track, he got very much enthused. In early evening we picked him up and drove to the track.

We parked the car and walked toward the entrance together. There we were stopped by a man in uniform. The two of us could go in, he said. But coloreds had to use the other entrance.

"We're together," I said. "We want to sit together."

"Can't do that," the guard said.

My temper began to rise. I could not believe what I was hearing. This was the 1960s. Jackie Robinson had integrated baseball fifteen years before. Brown vs. the Board of Education had come down nearly ten years before; separate was inherently unequal. But this dog track, in which brainless greyhounds chased a mechanical rabbit, still was whistling Dixie.

I understood why John had declined our invitation to dinner. The restaurant might cause a problem. Already he knew America better than we New Yorkers did.

We explained the situation to the guard. Dumoga, reluctantly, at my urging, produced his press credentials from Ghana and from the U.S. Department of State.

"Looks to me like he's still colored," the guard said.

I had never before encountered segregation firsthand. Reading about it in newspapers and books cannot convey its horror. Being its victim—even briefly—makes you burn with a painful flame. For we felt as victimized as John. We wanted to sit with him.

I demanded to see the manager of the track. The guard warned us it would do no good. When we insisted, he went to fetch him. I told the manager the situation, confident that he would understand.

The manager refused to let us in. "I don't make the rules," he said.

I tried to keep my voice calm. I chiseled every word. "Let me make the situation clear," I said. "This man is a foreign journalist. He is here as a guest of the United States State Department. If you don't let him in, he will go back home and write a blistering article about how blacks are treated in America. This will not win friends for America in Ghana, where we are fighting the Communists for influence. The State Department will read the article. They will not be happy with you or with your track. They could make trouble."

The man was adamant. "We have our rules," he said.

No fog is thicker, or more deadly, than the fog that clouds men's minds.

Kwartler and I were seething. We were ready to leave. But Dumoga wanted to stay. It was all right, he said; he would sit in the separate section.

As we moved off in different directions, I could already imagine the copy this would make one day in the Ghana Times.

We entered the grandstand through separate entrances, ours the one for white people, John's the one for "coloreds." We climbed the stairs separately, then walked toward the center of the bleachers. We found seats that were almost adjacent. But between

Kwartler and me on one side, and John Dumoga on the other, there was a thick wire mesh.

Dumoga looked at me through the cage, and I at him, and he smiled with what seemed like forgiveness. An observer would have been hard put to determine which was the man and which the uncivilized beast.

Florida, which already has won an expansion team, the Marlins, is attempting to lure the Giants from San Francisco. Traumatized by O'Malley and the Dodgers, I view the uprooting of established teams rather like the pulling of teeth. But with the team's desire to quit playing in Candlestick Park I fully sympathize. I saw a game there once. I have had better times in Dr. Pacheco's waiting room.

It was back in 1963. Ziegel and I took a summer vacation together. We flew to Las Vegas and gave some money to the blackjack tables and the slots. We drove to Tijuana and I saw my first bullfight. The blood ran red only during the first kill. For the next five kills it was not blood at all, but cadmium oil, liquid silk, scarlet nectar. The grace of shortstops has a genuine challenger in the grace of bullfighters, these Plisetskayas of the ring. For the bulls, I suppose, the blood remains real, but we have seen through history, throughout this century, worse cases of mass denial than that of the cheering crowds in the corrida.

Then we drove to San Francisco, and went to a night game at Candlestick Park. Here the denial was harder to accept. Some in the tortured throng were making believe they were having fun.

It was early August. We had heard that Candlestick gets chilly, so instead of going in shirtsleeves we wore our lightweight sport coats—the only jackets we had on this summer vacation. We knew we were in trouble when, having parked the rented car, we joined the crowd streaming toward the park. Men and women alike were wearing wool sweaters and carrying blankets and fleece-lined coats with hoods. Many were carrying Thermoses that I later learned did not contain coffee.

I have no memory of who the Giants were playing that night or what the outcome was. I seem to recall that Willie McCovey blasted a home run, but I may have been hallucinating; it may have been Lucy tossing a snowball at Charlie Brown. My brains cells get lazy at right around fifty below.

The precise temperature, like the score, I do not recall. I do recall that by the third inning we had buttoned the top buttons of our summer shirts—making a fashion statement decades ahead of our time—and we had buttoned our sport coats and turned up the collars, and warmed our hands and gullets with paper cups of steaming coffee, and were trying to recall if we had read anywhere that Alexander Cartwright—or even Abner Doubleday—had been an Eskimo. Candlestick is the only ballpark in America where the scoreboard lists runs, hits, and windchill factor.

All around us, fans wrapped in blankets, as at a wintry football game, were getting drunk on their Thermoses of coffee while we shivered the night away. We awoke the next morning with the sniffles. All things considered, I would rather have been watching dog racing.

And yet, four times now, the good people of San Francisco have refused to authorize a new ballpark. Apparently they think there are better ways to spend the money.

Perhaps because of the Candlestick experience Vic and I took our next vacation together in the winter, and we went someplace warm. The travel agent recommended Cozumel, which, in the mid-sixties, was just being built up as an island resort off the Yucatán. We had never heard of it, but we just wanted to lie in the sun and ogle girls in bikinis, with which, the travel agent assured us, our new hotel would be crawling.

On Cozumel the sun was warm and the sea a liquid turquoise. As for the rest, the hotel was empty except for Vic and me and a snuggling couple on their honeymoon. For entertainment we spent five days watching the hotel's pet anteater inhale.

On the fifth day we flew to Chichén Itzá. The single-engine propeller plane touched down on a narrow strip of asphalt in the jungle. The airport terminal was a thatched roof supported by four poles. A jeeplike vehicle carried us between the trees along two tire ruts that formed the main and only road from the airport. Parrots and monkeys screeched overhead. Suddenly we came to a clearing; in it stood a magnificent hotel, all stucco and orange roofs and wrought-iron railings and mango trees, with peacocks walking around and Humphrey Bogart, or a reasonable facsimile, drinking at the bar. Thus began my love affair with the Mayans.

The next day we toured the remnants of their culture: the temples and pyramids, the sacrificial well in which they tossed virgins as sacrifices to the great god Chac. (They had a better source, no doubt, than our hotel on Cozumel.) But most impressive of all was the Mayan ball field. It was a grassy plain longer and wider than a football field. Sheer stone walls flanked both sides, atop which were grassy slopes for the spectators. High up on each wall—about thirty-five feet up—protruding vertically, was a small stone loop. The object of the game was to get a hard rubber ball through the loop. The ball was not much smaller than the loop, and the players could not throw the ball through—they had to bat it through with sticks or parts of their body. This game, which the Mayans called *pok-a-tok,* was, in the last millennium, the national pastime of Indian cultures from Nicaragua to Arizona. The games, which had religious overtones, often went on for days, even though a single goal won. When a game ended, the captain of the winning team was made a nobleman on the spot. The captain of the losing team was beheaded.

(Our guide made no mention of arbitration.)

This ball field was the largest of seven such fields at Chichén Itzá. At one end of the huge field was a stone throne on which sat the *halach uinic*—the "true man," the Great Lord, the tribal chief. Atop a grassy slope at the other end of the field was a throne on which the *ah kin*—the high priest—sat. This was no domed stadium, yet the field was so perfectly constructed, according to the guide, that any discussion between the players and the referee—even in a low tone of voice—could be heard by the nobles at both ends, more than a hundred yards distant.

I have pondered this ball field many times since. I have pondered the Reeses and Rizzutos, the Mantles and the Musials of the Mayans—and, yes, the Strawberrys and the Cansecos too—putting their very heads on the line, as they moved up from the minor league fields to the bigs. I have pondered, as well, the gods they worshiped, like Chac, like Itzamná. If the gods were immortal—as all gods are—then what became of them when the Mayan civilization died? Do these gods still exist, free-floating in the universe, lonely and depressed, in search of new idolators? In search of new ball games to watch?

And I have wondered how a civilization perished that could construct such grand and clever ball fields, while five hundred years later enlightened San Franciscans shiver in Candlestick Park.

Hear me, O City by the Bay, for I have communed with Chac. If you build it, he will come.

Knowing your situation, he won't even insist on a virgin.

She comes into the room where he is working. She holds out a trowel with which she has been digging in the garden. The metal blade is hanging loose, at a right angle to the wooden handle.

"I broke my bat," she says.

Celebration

It was at eight forty-four P.M. Mountain Daylight Time on the sixth day of August, 1992, that the blasphemous thought first broke into my consciousness.

I was watching the Mets against the Cubs, on the Chicago station. The battered Mets were losing 5–1 in the eighth. They were about to drop into fourth place, eight games behind Pittsburgh. Steve Stone was talking about the fine job Cub shortstop Rey Sanchez was doing filling in for the injured Shawon Dunston: how he had done so well, the Cubs probably would have to protect him on their fifteen-man roster.

What Stone was talking about was the fifteen men they will be able to protect when the Florida Marlins and the Colorado Rockies, the new kids on the block, draft their first batch of players in the fall, much as the Mets did thirty years ago. I knew about the theoretical existence of the Rockies, of course, just as one knows about black holes. But I had never seen one.

Now, for the first time, my mind began to take seriously the notion of a team in Denver. I began to wonder who the Mets will protect and who they might lose. I had been under the impression they could protect more than fifteen. They would protect Doc Gooden, of course. And Howard Johnson. And a number of others easily named. But, except for Doc and Hojo, few had been with the Mets very long. These were not Keith Hernandez or Gary Carter, who somehow, with the passing seasons, had grown old. They were not Lenny Dykstra and Roger McDowell, personality boys whom the Mets had dealt away for Juan Samuel in the worst trade in their history. (Tom Collins, who is not even a Mets fan, suggested a rhyming bumper sticker the day after that disaster was consummated. It said: WHO THE HELL IS JUAN SAMUEL?) I began to realize that it did not matter very much whom the Mets lost in the draft: as poorly as they were doing, it would make little difference.

I began to wonder whom the Rockies would choose. Denver is only 370 miles from Santa Fe. The new team will be our nearest major league franchise by far. A one-hour flight. A seven-hour drive. I have been a Mets fan for thirty-one years, the last twenty years from a distance of two thousand miles. Is it time, I thought, for a change? Is it possible I will want to start over—as I was forced to do in '62—and root for the Colorado Rockies?

No black lightning shoots down from the heavens at this unthinkable notion, no moving finger writes my name in flame (at least not so's I notice.) But the notion still seems strange, otherworldly—enough so that I look at the clock on my desk to note the red-digit moment of its occurrence, and wonder if at this electric instant some distant comet, baseball shaped, is being born in an invisible galaxy, is beginning to speed like a fastball toward the earth, trailing a fiery tail. The notion of abandoning the Mets, who are the spiritual descendants of the beloved Dodgers, is unthinkable (again: that seems to be the only word), and yet I have just thought it. Which makes it not unthinkable. Merely undoable.

Or is it?

If God no longer keeps an apartment in New York, must I?

In the ensuing days I ponder the concept of loyalty. If I am disloyal to my wife and she discovers this, she will be badly hurt; I do not want to hurt her. It might put my marriage in jeopardy, and then I, too, might suffer. Not to mention the inner turmoil; the guilt. But what of disloyalty to the Mets? In the past two decades, living so far away, I have purchased tickets to Shea Stadium just twice. So they will not be harmed at the box office, even if that were my concern. Though I root for them from afar, I root as desperately as any fan in Queens or Brooklyn or Hempstead. But do the Mets know this, any more than my dog knows it, or the sun? Do the distant Mets care? They have never heard of me. If my loyalty flickers and dies in Santa Fe, it will be like the dying of a dim star in an unseen universe. They could hardly care—they would not even know.

I imagine a computer at Shea lighting up the message board with the awful news: Bobby Mayer, out in New Mexico, has abandoned us! And the Mets officials falling to the floor in prostration, in grief. And one of them staggering to the telephone and calling me long distance, like a credit-card company, to beg me to return; to beg for another chance.

It will not happen that way. My credit-card companies care more.

And if that is the case, to whom would I be disloyal?

To myself?

Rooting for a team, I suddenly understand, is rather like believing in God. Our belief doesn't comfort Him; He doesn't care, He doesn't know we exist. But it sorely comforts us.

Applying this logic to the Mets, I feel a terrible isolation. It is supposed to matter! I think of all those moments in the past when I won games for Pee Wee and Jackie, and later for Cleon and Gil— won games for them by not uncrossing my legs, by not scratching an itch, by not getting up to use the bathroom. It does matter! It does!

Or it did. In this slowly evolving world, it did.

What of the napkin, the toothpick, just a few weeks ago?

I recall buying, when I was eight years old, a gold coin, a good-luck charm, for Pisces, astral sign of my February birth. Engraved on the back of the coin I found these words: *You are sensitive and loyal.* I wondered how they knew.

Men, women, who switch baseball allegiances every year are not, as I have said, true fans. Suffering is part of the game; I have nothing against suffering. (Sometimes, lacking a middle name, that is the one I choose.) But boredom is another matter. Boredom I do not suffer well. And the Mets, this year, I force myself to admit, are absentminded, are the walking-snoozing, are playing on a downhill slope just inches from the Plain of Boredom.

But switching to the Colorado Rockies? Is it possible?

Like a cosmetic company I seek out laboratory rabbits. I test the idea on Jon Richards, Mets fan. "Absolutely not," he says. With nary a blink.

I test the same notion on Smith; his Dodgers are doing even worse than my Mets. Like me he is growing cuddly in his dotage. "It's a thought," he says.

The dawn of a new baseball era has begun to gleam, ever so lightly, on the northern horizon. And with it the hint of subliminal excitement, as fraught with psychic danger as a new flirtation.

Married to the Mets. But for how long?

On the night that Marilyn Monroe died, in August of 1962, he emerged from a Manhattan movie theater with a girl named Rosalyn and saw the screaming headline on the front page of the Daily News. *He wondered why, as a boy, he had preferred Jane Russell. He remembered being desperate, as a boy, to see* The Outlaw.

He still cannot imagine Joe DiMaggio making love to Marilyn Monroe. A stork and a swan. It is as difficult for him to picture as to visualize his parents making love.

He has, at fifty-three, still not seen The Outlaw.

When John F. Kennedy was shot he was driving to work. At the office a dozen reporters and editors were pressed around the wire-service machines. He rolled up his sleeves, sat at his desk, and began to bang out a story for an extra edition, a story about the attempted assassination of President Kennedy. While he typed, Bill McIlwain leaned over his shoulder to read the first paragraph. The editor crossed out the word at-tempted.

In the employee magazine a few weeks later there was a picture of the Newsday *staff at work on the day of the assassination. He is prominent in the foreground, in the act of rolling up his sleeves. He cut out the picture, placed it under the glass of his desk at home, planned to treasure it always. Somewhere, during the years, it disappeared. Evaporated inexplicably into the ether of the past. (Unlike the baseball cards he killed so cruelly, in cold blood.)*

He was asleep when Lee Harvey Oswald was silenced. A phone call from his brother awakened him. He staggered down the stairs of his father's house and saw the first of the instant replays of the murder. And the second, and the third, and the fourth. He drank coffee, dressed, went back to work.

When National Guardsmen shot down dozens of black rioters in Detroit one summer, he drove from the newspaper office directly to the airport and caught a five A.M. flight out of Kennedy. He had not slept, but on the plane he felt exhilarated, a soldier going off to war. That night in Detroit there was a curfew. As he walked the midnight streets, shielded by his press pass, he watched the streetlights turning from green to red, from red to green, from green to red again, with no traffic visible anywhere, with no one to see the changing lights, with no one to obey them except the darkness and the silence, and he wondered if he existed at all. He saw an orange curtain flicker in an open window, and he wondered if there was a rifle behind it, loaded, the bolt clicking into place.

During the first march on the Pentagon to protest the war in Vietnam, he drove upstate with a pretty woman friend, and they walked among the autumn colors, red, brown, ochre, and kicked playfully at the crunchy fallen leaves. When the sun went down they drove to an old country inn for dinner, but they were not allowed inside, because he was wearing a sweater instead of a sport coat. The Viet Cong, who were winning, were wearing black pajamas, he should have told the maître d'. He did not think of it then.

When the Reverend Martin Luther King, Jr., was killed, he went to Times Square, which he always considered the litmus test, the true center of the universe, and he watched black men come up out of the subways and punch white men they didn't know in the face. When Bobby Kennedy was shot he was asleep. Richard Kwartler phoned at six A.M. to ask if he had heard. He cursed Richie for joking about something like that—just as his mother had been sharp with Marvin Stiglitz for telling her that FDR was dead.

In his basement apartment in Greenwich Village, the windows barred to keep burglars out, he watched men walk on the moon, even as it was rising over the dark, swirling waters of Chappaquiddick. When the boys, the young men, came home from Vietnam in body bags, he went to their funerals sometimes, and he wrote about them, so the people out in the *suburbs could not walk away from it. His editors told him he was writing about the war too much.*

Through all of this, when his unreliable back was not acting up, he played shortstop in the newspaper's softball league. His final season, going into the final game, he was batting .571, second in the standings, and had a chance to win the batting title. The opposing team that day—the other editorial team, his friends—aware of the limits of his power, knowing he was a singles hitter, brought the outfield in about fifty feet behind the infield. He slashed four line drives in four at bats that day, and every one was caught by the drawn-in outfield, and he dropped to third in the final standings. With such friends he did not need enemies—which, in general, was how the sixties were.

Through all of this the New York Mets remained almost as inept as they had been that moment in their first game in 1962 when the soft pop fly dropped between Ashburn and Bell. Seven lean years later, in 1968, they still were finishing ninth in a ten-team league. But oh, how he loved them! How all the former Dodger fans, and all the former Giant fans, loved them! He loved them wholly and without judgment. He loved them for just being.

The best nights, someone once wrote, are the nights when nothing happens. Even in the frantic sixties there were a few such nights, nights when there was nothing to do but sip your beer or Scotch and talk. One night, in a Manhattan pub, five bachelors talked about socks.

The discussion began innocently enough when someone mentioned that, along with rents and restaurant meals, the price of doing laundry was going up again.

"I wouldn't mind the price so much," Ronnie said, "if they would give me back all the single socks they steal."

When the murmurs of agreement died away, I made what I thought was a singular confession. "I don't mind that so much," I said. "The thing that kills me is the socks that don't match. Every time I buy socks, by the second washing they come back different shades. I have a whole drawer full of socks, and not one of them matches any other."

There was a pregnant pause. The other four men looked at me. Then their words tumbled out.

"And you spend ten minutes every morning trying to find a pair that matches," Vic said.

"And you hold them up to the light to see better, but that doesn't help," Jared said.

"And then you hold them by the window, in the daylight, but that only makes the different shades look even farther apart," Ronnie added.

"And one day you get so disgusted, you decide that from now on you will buy nothing but black socks," Lennie said.

"Yes," I cried. "Yes yes yes yes yes. So I went out and bought nothing but black socks. And now I have a whole drawer of black socks. And none of them matches! I never knew there were so many different shades of black."

We paused to drink our drinks, but more important, to absorb what had just happened. I had always thought I was alone, in those groggy first moments of wakefulness, padding barefoot over to the dresser, turning on the lamp, fishing out the socks, holding them up to the light, seeking a perfect pair of matching socks, finally settling for the closest hue, the closest intensity, but always settling, never really satisfied with my choice. And now this! The sudden discovery that all my friends had been going through the same secret ordeal. The discovery that Mother Nature herself seems to abhor matching socks.

"I always thought it was just me, because I have trouble with my eyes," Ronnie said.

"Forty pairs of socks!" Lennie said. "One day I got disgusted and went out and bought forty pairs of black socks. And now I don't have one pair that matches."

A mild exultation settled over the table. Alienation melted away. At that moment we all felt a new kinship. Some of us had known each other for ten years without disclosing such intimate details. We did not seem to want to let the moment drop. There was beauty in it.

"The way I've tried to solve the problem," Ronnie said, "is to cultivate the image of an unpredictable character. So when I walk into a room, people will just say, 'Here comes Ronnie, with his socks that don't match.' "

A fresh idea leapt into my brain. "Why don't we have a black socks party?" I said. "We'll all bring all our socks, and make trades. Some of my socks just have to match some of your socks."

"Party, hell," Vic said. "Let's rent the New York Coliseum, and let the whole town in on it. Everybody will bring their socks. The first annual New York Black Socks Exchange."

"We can call it the Black Socks Scandal," I said.

We never did hold our exchange. But the next night I met Ronnie at a dinner party, and he asked me, "Who did you think of when you were putting on your socks this morning?"

I replied, "You and Lennie and Jared and Vic."

And Ronnie said, "Me too."

Absent the pounding of Indian drums, I do not know if that qualifies as male bonding. The conversation has been included here to explain why men usually talk baseball.

On the opening day of the 1969 baseball season I went to Shea Stadium and saw the Mets get beat, 11–10. This was disturbing mainly because their opponents were the Montreal Expos, a new expansion team, playing their first baseball game. This was like losing an arm-wrestling match to your kid sister.

But God that summer looked down from His New York apartment (it was later ascertained) and decided to write the eleventh commandment: The Next-to-Last Shall Be First. And the Mets, that summer and fall, with a profound young pitching staff and otherwise as motley an assortment of major league ball players as has ever been put together, went on to become the Miracle Mets. To fulfill The Impossible Dream. To create all these marvelous Instant Clichés. *Joy in Mudville,* George Vecsey happily titled his book about the season. The taxicabs in New York were yellower that summer, and the buildings were taller. The pictures in the museums were more magnificent, the ballet was lovelier, the girls were prettier, the rain smelled like the country. Strangers talked to one another. Sometimes they even smiled. Other cities have rallied around other ball clubs, but there is only one New York. You had to be there.

I was there, a white-hot witness.

The day after the Mets clinched the eastern division championship, a man stepped slowly onto a subway train in Times Square. He was old, and he was black. He turned to the conductor. "Does this train go to Shea Stadium?" he asked.

He was told that it did. He sat down by himself in the almost empty car. His black suit was wrinkled, his flannel shirt was faded. On his head was a battered black hat. In his hand was an unlighted cigarette.

The train shook and rattled its way out of Manhattan and into the gray overcast of Queens. The city fled by in the windows: the upper floors of apartment buildings, underwear hanging on clotheslines, rooftop forests of television antennas, an American flag in a bedroom window, an undertaking parlor, a church. The old man saw none of this. His eyes were cast down into his lap.

The train stopped at a station marked BLISS STREET. The old man did not notice. He was going way past Bliss.

Finally the train reached Shea, and the man got off. He walked slowly across a ramp, dragging his right leg. He walked down the stairs even more slowly, pausing to put both feet on each step, a pace made necessary by whatever was wrong with the leg. He paused on a landing to rest, and he looked out at the stadium where the Mets, the lowly Mets, had clinched their first championship the night before. He looked at the blue and orange panels on the outside of the stadium and at the outfield grass visible through a fence. Then he spoke, for the first time since Times Square, only one sentence, aloud, to himself, or to nobody, or to the universe.

"Next year," he said, "I'm gonna be playin' with this club."

He stood there for a moment, and then he began to walk around the outside of the stadium, alone, past all the locked gates—for there was no game scheduled that day—dragging his bad leg and his dreams.

I did not think there could be in all of New York a more dedicated fan than me. But there he was, a crippled black Icarus flying toward the sun.

I did not forget the old man. The following spring I checked the roster. The Mets had signed no codger with a bad right leg. I could only conclude the old man didn't make it.

Unless he knew some powerful magic with which I am unfamiliar.

A week or two later the Mets beat Atlanta in the play-offs and won their first National League pennant. Many people crowded that night into Mr. Laff's, a bar on the Upper East Side that was owned by a former Met, Phil Linz. It might be a good night to see some ballplayers. It was a Monday but the place was as crowded with East Side singles as on any lustful Friday. The bar was four deep with people. Others were crunched in the spaces between the tables in the back. The air was heavy with noise and smoke; a too-loud jukebox was blasting away with—what else, back then?—"The Age of Aquarius."

Two of the Mets were, indeed, there. One of them, Ken Boswell, the second baseman, was standing way in the back, deep in conversation with a blonde, obviously too busy to be disturbed. The other, Wayne Garrett, the third baseman, was standing among the knots of people. He was wearing an open shirt and a red sweater that clashed with his rust-colored hair and his rust-colored freckles. Wayne Garrett was twenty-one and looked sixteen; he looked, in the words of my friend Stan Isaacs, as if he should be dating Rebecca of Sunnybrook Farm.

Garrett had smote the home run that afternoon that put the Mets in front to stay. The young men and women in Mr. Laff's were looking at him with appropriate admiration. Soon Wayne Garrett had his arm around the waist of a cute young dark-haired girl, and she had her arm around him. They were standing in the middle of the crush, trying to talk amid the blare of the jukebox. He leaned over and kissed her, and they talked some more, and she reached up and kissed him back. It was not at all indiscreet in the crowded, noisy bar, but lots of guys kept stealing glances at them, and it was not hard to guess what they were thinking: *If I had hit the home run that just won the pennant, I could have any girl in the place too.*

The noise continued and the young men thought their thoughts and Wayne Garrett and the girl kept their arms around each other's waist. Then somebody nearby mentioned baseball. The sweet young thing drowsily opened her dark brown eyes on Garrett.

"Do you play ball?" she asked.

"Uh-huh," Garrett said.

"Who with?" the girl asked.

I hope they had a fine old time.

A week later still the Miracle Mets won the World Series. Tommie Agee made two sparkling catches in center field, and in right field a lug named Ron Swoboda, who on most days was as graceful as Nikita Khrushchev, made a swan dive with the bases loaded, caught a line drive an inch above the grass, taking away a surefire triple, and the Mets beat the Baltimores in five. Some dreams do come true.

In those days I used to spend some of my time in a dark bar on Christopher Street called the Lion's Head, talking with other newspapermen about politics and baseball and socks. One of the waitresses at the bar was a painter, a petite brunette named Carol, who had grown up fatherless within cheering distance of Ebbets Field, and who had become as devoted a Dodger fan as I was. Like me she had been forced by circumstance and Walter O'Malley to switch her allegiance from the Dodgers to the Mets. Like me she had been known to grow despondent over so much as the loss of a spring exhibition game. She knew baseball better than any woman I had ever met, or was ever likely to meet. For two years, while she dated other men, while she painted in her railroad apartment by day and waited tables at night, Carol and I were friends. Though she lived only two blocks from me, we saw each other only at the bar, where she would set her cigarette on my table while carrying plates, where she would sit during her breaks, where we would discuss baseball and art and literature and baseball again, and such personal concerns as whether, if a psychologist cured your neuroses, you would lose your creativity. We never went out on a date.

The day the World Series ended I was in Washington, D.C., where I had been covering a protest march against the war in Vietnam. I watched the final game of the Series on television in my hotel room, then caught the shuttle flight back to New York. Quickly I banged out my column for the next day's paper. Then I hurried to the Lion's Head with malice aforethought, with definite salacious intent. I had decided I was going to take Carol home with me that night, to celebrate the victory of the Mets together in the best way I could imagine.

Carol had the same celebration in mind. Every five minutes that evening, she later confessed, she had looked toward the door of the bar, awaiting my arrival. We helped close the Lion's Head that night, with a bar full of other happy fans, and then we went home together for the very first time; perhaps it would be the only time; that would be all right. As it turned out, we stayed together the next night as well. And the next. And the night after that. We stayed together, in fact, for the next twelve and a half years, which must surely be the longest winning streak in the history of the National League.

Like all streaks, that one eventually came to an end. My second and present wife, La Donna, another petite brunette, is not, as I have indicated, a baseball fan. She grew up surrounded by boys in a small town in Oklahoma, and was allowed to play second base only when the boys were short a player, which was not very often. Most of the time she sat in the branches of a tree across from center field, reading books and eating oranges and disdainfully throwing the orange peels onto the grass below. Though this country girl does not share my passion for baseball, she knows many things that most women don't. Among them she knows that when a man is watching a baseball game, as when he is playing with his dog, something important is going on.

She doesn't even throw orange peels anymore.

Sometimes I wonder what would have happened if Ron Swoboda, no swift fielder, diving to make that catch with the bases loaded, had come up an inch short. If he had, three runs would have scored, and the Orioles might have won that game; might have gone on to win the Series. Would I, depressed, have taken the despondent city girl home that night? Would I then, years later and far away, have met the country girl, and helped raise her daughter as my own? If not, how would the daughter's young life be different—and the younger lives that she may one day create?

So there is Swoboda, suspended in midflight, about to make the catch of his life—the catch of my life. Is there a chance that he will miss the ball? Or was all of this preordained?

We shall never be certain. Only God knows if He's a gambler, or if He marks the cards.

The Lion's Head in those days was Baseball Central for the Village crowd. Journalists, authors, poets, folksingers, came to drink Dewar's or draft beer and spout opinions. It was a no-frills bar—no peanuts, no pretzels, no jukebox, no television set. Just talk. Friendships were formed of years' duration whose members had never been to one another's homes. The men felt they were wise and witty, such women as wandered in felt ignored, and the women most certainly were right. A cute young thing in a miniskirt dangling her legs from one of the high stools was, in this bar, no competition for a red-hot argument over whether Art Shamsky was half the hitter that Gene Hermanski had been. In the parallel reality such considerations carry great weight.

Discussions of literature ran a close second to baseball talk in the Head. It would be unkind to suggest that the patrons had large egos, but when the owner had the men's room painted, covering up a maze of graffiti, he was accused of book-burning.

One day, shortly after the noon opening time, novelist David Markson, the resident expert on baseball statistics, showed up at the Lion's Head and found it padlocked. A notice posted on the door by the Internal Revenue Service informed all and sundry that the bar had been seized for nonpayment of taxes. Panic spread through the Village over the telephone lines, from one regular to another, from Markson to poet Joel Oppenheimer to photographer Billy Powers to newsman Timothy Lee to sportswriter Vic Ziegel. Life without the Lion's Head was, to some, inconceivable. Markson sent a telegram to Pete Hamill, who was vacationing in London. It read: LION'S HEAD SEIZED BY INTERNAL REVENUE SERVICE STOP THIS IS NO JOKE STOP PLEASE ADVISE STOP REPEAT THIS IS NO JOKE STOP. What advice was expected, or received, from the British Isles I do not know. I do know Vic Ziegel's reaction. "It's one of the two events in my life that wouldn't sink in," he said. "The Dodgers and Giants leaving town, and the closing of the Lion's Head."

About two weeks later the tax matter was settled; the Lion's Head came back to life. Unlike Vic's Giants, my Dodgers.

Literature and baseball merged in the Head that summer of '69. Pitcher Jim Bouton, one of the smartest and funniest ballplayers in the game, was collaborating on a book with Leonard Shecter of the *Post*. Every night in his hotel room after a game, Bouton would talk the intimate secrets of major league baseball into a tape machine. Periodically he would send a batch of tapes to Shecter. Lennie was a cheerful fellow with a twinkle in his eye, and there was a twinkle in his step as well every time he received a new batch of tapes from Bouton and came into the Head to tell us how good they were, how funny Bouton was in describing his attempts to prolong his career by mastering the knuckleball. We could not know then that together they were creating possibly the best baseball book ever written.

One evening Shecter asked a bunch of us at the bar to suggest titles for the book-in-progress. One after another baseball phrases were tossed into the air like infield flies, only to fall to the ground untouched, with faint thuds. Sipping my beer, I strained my brain. I wanted to name this book. Gradually I focused on the fact that Bouton was a pitcher. *"Three and Two,"* I suggested. There were a few faint murmurs of possible assent, but no great outcry of hosannas. Then the only woman in the crowd—I think her name was Ellen, I think she was someone's date—took it the next logical step. "*Ball Four*," she said. The silence suddenly was tense. Immediately, we knew. "*Ball Four*," Shecter repeated, tasting the sound, the delicious morsel, on his tongue.

Though I would write, and name, my own books later, I would never again come that close: one pitch away from a best-seller.

· The night after the Mets won the series the mood of celebration still was rampant in the Head. Someone said we ought to have a victory party, and I thought that was a great idea and said it would be at my place on Saturday night. My apartment was small, just two rooms and a sleeping alcove, but with the party only two nights away there would not be too much of a crowd.

Saturday night at nine no one had shown up yet. I was beginning to think I'd made a bad mistake. By nine-thirty there were a few people sitting on my couch, none of whom I knew. But by ten o'clock the place was jammed, steady flocks of people arriving from the Village and uptown and Long Island. By eleven o'clock nearly a hundred people were crammed into the two rooms and spilling out both ends, into the front hallway and out into the small rear yard. People brought beer and wine and booze and genuine high spirits. Music was pulsing on the stereo and somebody literally rolled up the rug and turned the living room into a dance floor, and dozens of couples were making the place rock. (Luckily, I had warned the neighbors, and invited them.) Those who wanted to talk crowded into the oversized kitchen and jabbered over the music with animated glee. Two amply endowed girls from uptown were wearing see-through blouses and nothing but smooth skin underneath, and the men from Long Island wished they were single again. Hamill, whom I knew only slightly, showed up with a huge vat of homemade Texas chili. By midnight the throng was hungry. By one in the morning the chili was gone, but the music and the dancing and the laughter continued through most of the night, till at five A.M. the last remnants of us staggered out into the predawn dark to find a deli that would serve us breakfast.

That was the best party I've been to in my life, and I was proud that it was mine—mine and the Mets'—and I think it was so good because unlike New Year's Eve or someone getting another year older, everyone was truly celebrating an event, an occurrence with meaning, something deep within themselves, this secret place where the Mets lived and where the Mets had proved that anything was possible, that you didn't have to wallow in the pain.

Seaver, Koosman, Gentry, and Grote, Kranepool, Boswell, Weis, and Charles, Jones, Agee, Swoboda—we owed them all. And we owed the manager, Gil Hodges, an original Met, a hero of the hallowed Dodgers: blood-link to the Biblical past.

Like Jackie Robinson, Jim Gilliam, and Gil Hodges, too many of the Lion's Head regulars, in the years that followed, died too young: Leonard Shecter, Joe Flaherty, Joel Oppenheimer. They, too, were the boys of summer.

The August twilight creeps in earlier every evening. And night has fallen for the Mets. Dave Magadan and Willie Randolph have joined the others on the disabled list. The team has seven broken bones, which is more, I think, than it has complete games. They have lost 13 out of 15, are in fifth place, 14 games out. The team they are fielding might well lose in Triple A. Their season, for all but occasional aesthetic purposes, is over.

Bonilla comes back, hits five home runs in his first six games. The Mets sweep three in San Francisco, an aberration.

It's Thursday afternoon when the phone rings. Jon Richards is calling.

"I thought you were leaving for New York today," I say. "Don't you have tickets for a double-header tomorrow night?"

"We're leaving tomorrow morning. But it's supposed to be rained out. I guess we'll go to a movie or something. Anyway, I just got a call from Tad." Tad is Jon's brother in New York, the one who can't kill himself during the baseball season. "I thought I would be the first to pass along news of the Mets' latest trade."

I can tell from Jon's voice that this is not going to be good.

"Who? I don't think I want to hear this."

"They traded David Cone to Toronto. For two prospects."

"Cone?"

A feeling of nausea—Sartre's kind of nausea—is beginning to fill my chest. David Cone has been their only reliable pitcher this season. He is about to lead the league in strikeouts for the third straight year. No one has done that since Warren Spahn.

Cone will be a free agent at the end of the year. They don't want to pay him what he will ask. So they trade him to get something—instead of the nothing they will get at the end of the season. But two prospects? David Cone is one of the best pitchers in the game.

"They just won three straight," I say, weakly. "I guess they couldn't stand the success."

Jon says, "How are the Colorado Rockies looking?"

During the first weeks after Carol moved into my apartment—painter, waitress, baseball fan—she would sometimes answer the phone and then hand it to me, and it would be my father. He never once asked who it was that had answered the phone; he seemed to assume I had hired a live-in secretary. Finally I called and told him about Carol—that we were living together.

"Are you planning to marry her?" my father asked.

I told him no—at least not anytime soon. We just were living together.

My father asked, with old-world anxiety, with old-world sweetness: "Does the girl know?"

I assured him the girl knew. I invited him to drive down from The Bronx to meet her. He came the next day, and as we chatted over coffee, my father asked Carol what she did. "I'm a painter," she said.

Thinking, no doubt, of the losing pitcher in front of the open locker, the small painting that still hung in his living room, the only painting I had ever done, my father said, "Robert paints too."

After an hour or so I had to leave for an appointment. As I walked my father to his car he asked where I was going. "To see Sam," I said. Sam was a psychologist I was seeing at the time, to help work out a few things.

"You didn't tell Carol about Sam!" my father said.

"Of course I did."

"Ach," he said in disgust. "You should never have told her that."

"Why not?"

My father said, "Nobody wants damaged goods."

In the streets of Greenwich Village one day back then, birds were chirping in the leafless trees of a spring that was late arriving. Old couples moved slowly on their Sunday walks, the men wearing hats, the women bundled in kerchiefs, gloved hands holding gloved hands. Middle-aged men were pulled along the streets by impatient beagles. Girls in miniskirts walked with their boyfriends, who showed their bravado by keeping their coats unbuttoned. And in a hole in the ground that used to be 18 West Eleventh Street—a few blocks from where Carol and I were living—firemen were digging for bodies and pieces of bodies.

(Bear with me; this is a story about a Boston Red Sox game.)

The town houses on the south side of the block smiled serenely at the blue winter sky. They were neat and even and gleaming, like the smile of Miss America. Except that one of the front teeth was missing. There was a wide gap, with nothing in it but a blackened stump.

The stump was the rear wall of a town house in which somebody's children had been making bombs, bombs with which to protest the bombs we were dropping on women and children in Vietnam. The bombs had exploded accidentally ten days before. Two women had been seen running naked from the exploded building. Others, perhaps young men, had not been so lucky.

"If we find any other bodies, I think it will be where they are digging now," a deputy battalion chief said.

The afternoon wore on. Feet grew numb in the cold. "We rotate the men every three hours," the chief said.

A fireman down below called to him. The chief climbed a ladder down into the pit that was all that remained of the house. He walked to the corner where the men were working. Two firemen were on their hands and knees, clearing dirt away. The other firemen stood around them in a semicircle, like surgeons around an operating table. One of them brought over a large piece of plastic wrapping. Carefully they dug out whatever they had found and placed it in the wrapping.

The chief climbed back up to the sidewalk. "It looks like a head," he said. "It looks like a head. You couldn't tell if it was male or female."

The digging continued for half an hour more. Nothing else was found. The search was halted for the day. The firemen climbed up out of the pit with their spades. The last man pulled the ladder up after him. If anything was still buried in the pit, it would not go away. The digging would resume in the morning.

This was the poetry of Amerika, as some called it back then, and to get away from it, that summer, Carol and I went in search of an older America. We rediscovered green mountains and rugged coastlines, babbling brooks and tall fields of corn. We marveled at houses in Vermont that looked like little boys with their earflaps down. We ate lobsters plucked live from Maine traps and tossed into boiling water. Then we stopped in New Hampshire, and discovered that you could not get away. Not even with something as simple as a baseball game.

The motel was nondescript, but quiet. In the back was a gentle lake. Up the road was a place that sold homemade ice cream. In one corner of our room was a television set. For two weeks we had ignored these sets as best we could, but on this night—perhaps because we would soon be heading home—we wondered about the baseball scores. We turned on the tube and picked up a Boston station televising a Red Sox game from Minnesota.

It was a quiet game. There was no score in the fourth inning. We noted, on the scoreboard, that the Mets were losing. We were about to turn off the set when suddenly we became mesmerized. A man in street clothes was on the field. An umpire was waving his arms. The game was being halted. An announcement was being made to the crowd in the ballpark over the public address system: Bloomington police had been warned by telephone that a bomb would explode in the ballpark at nine-thirty P.M. (It was then nine-fifteen.) The fans were urged to leave the stands immediately. The game would be resumed in half an hour if there was no explosion.

We watched as the fans filed out in an orderly manner. There was no panic. Most of the twenty thousand people just streamed outside to wait in the parking lot. The players from both teams huddled in the middle of the field, away from the stands. The people in the box seats were also allowed to huddle on the field.

A minute later the broadcasters switched audio control back to Boston; they abandoned their booth at the ballpark lest they fall victim to the bomber. The cameramen locked their cameras in position, focused on the field and on parts of the grandstand, and they, too, left the ballpark. The voice from Boston emphasized this. The cameras were no longer being manned, it said; they could not swing around or zoom in on any part of the field. What the voice meant was clear: If there is an explosion, we will not be able to show it to you, unless it occurs in one of the sections now being covered by our cameras.

So we sat there at night in a motel room in New Hampshire, hearing an anonymous voice from Boston, watching through automatic cameras a scene in Minnesota of thousands of people huddled in the middle of a ball field, prepared for an explosion. Them, us, the police, all helpless: watching, waiting. The minutes ticked by. Would a bomb rip apart the stadium? Would it be on camera? If not, would the people go back and watch the rest of the game? More minutes passed. We stared at the screen in fascination. I wondered what John R. Tunis, who lived in New England, would have made of this.

Clack-clack, clackety clack . . .

The appointed hour came and went, and there was no explosion. The game resumed. The people stayed. Not being American League fans, we snapped off the set and walked up the road for a hot fudge sundae. The Red Sox won, 1–0.

One August night we went to a Mets-Dodgers game at Shea. Our seats were behind the plate but way up under an overhanging tier, and all the heat and smoke of the evening congregated there as the game progressed. The score was tied 1–1 in the tenth inning when Tommie Agee stole home in freeze-frame and gave the Mets the victory.

Carol was not feeling well, and, not wanting to buck the crowds, we waited till the stadium emptied before heading for the train station. We caught the last special ball-game train leaving Shea that night. We were able to find seats. Seated right beside us were Dodgers manager Walter Alston and two buddies. We were this far from greatness—and we could not think of a thing to say to the man.

The fourth stop the train made that night was between stations. It stopped on the tracks and stayed there motionless in the dark and fetid night, with no explanation given to us passengers as to what was causing the delay or how long it would be. We sweated and fumed and cursed for more than an hour.

Walter Alston was no longer on the train. He and his pals had gotten off at the station before. Perhaps that is why the Dodgers renewed his contract twenty-two times.

The most intimate and embarrassing fact I shall reveal in this baseball memoir is that, in those early days, in the privacy of our own home, Carol and I actually referred to our team as "the Metsies."

One day in 1970 a baseball computer was being introduced at a press conference in midtown. The computer had spent the past six years analyzing, studying, and measuring the game. It was now being promoted as the manager's best friend, a dugout assistant designed to help him win more games.

On the way to the press conference I kept thinking of a verse by e.e. cummings:

> (*While you and i have lips and voices which*
> *are for kissing and to sing with*
> *who cares if some one eyed son of a bitch*
> *invents an instrument to measure Spring with?*)

The computer was not yet measuring the crocuses and the daffodils. But baseball? That was coming awfully close.

The inventor of the computer program was a twenty-one-year-old engineering student at Princeton named Larry Rafsky. He turned out to have two eyes (brown), and he seemed in every respect a perfect gentleman, of proper upbringing. His story, in fact, evoked a certain sympathy.

Rafsky, a baseball fan, grew up in Philadelphia. That evoked a certain sympathy right away, because the last time the Phillies had won a pennant was in 1950, the year after Rafsky was born. When he was a senior in high school, in 1964, the Phillies under manager Gene Mauch were finally about to win another pennant. Rafsky was taking a computer course, and he decided to feed baseball statistics into a computer to see what would happen.

What happened, in real life, was that the Phillies collapsed, lost ten games in a row in the last two weeks of the season, and blew the pennant. Heartsick, Rafsky played the season over on his computer. The Phillies lost. He replayed the season. They lost again. In one hundred replays of the 1964 season the Phillies won only six times. The Cardinals and the Reds won many more.

"The computer showed that the Phillies simply were not the best ball club," Rafsky said. "They had been playing over their heads, and it should not have been surprising that they collapsed."

After that Rafsky spent parts of six summers refining his computer, testing the program, tuning it, so that it would reflect baseball reality as nearly as possible. Every manner of available statistic could be programmed into the computer.

"One trouble we had is that nobody separates double plays resulting from ground balls, from double plays resulting from line drives," he said. "Those are two separate events, with different effects on the movement of base runners."

He was that precise.

In the previous few weeks he had been studying the Mets. Among his conclusions: Joe Foy playing third base would yield the Mets .33 runs per game more than the 1969 third-base platooning of Ed Charles, Wayne Garrett, and Bobby Pfeil. Platooning Art

Shamsky and Ron Swoboda in right field would produce .35 more runs per ball game than playing Swoboda alone. Et cetera.

Rafsky said a computer printer hooked up in the dugout could help the manager in many ways. It would advise him of the most productive batting order; which pinch hitter to use against which pitcher; the percentage of trying to steal second with two out; the advisability of the sacrifice bunt.

"The computer won't replace the manager, but it will give him a lot of information that he can't possibly store in his head," Rafsky said.

One of those attending the press conference that day was a member of the Mets' front office, Joe McDonald. I asked him what he thought of the computer. McDonald toyed with the large, square New York Mets World Series ring on his left hand, and said, "I don't think Mr. Hodges would go for it."

Larry Rafsky was ahead of his time. I don't know if he ever got rich from his creation. Since then computers have invaded the game—if not the actual dugout—in many ways I do not care to investigate. When I think of the subject at all, I envision a one-eyed Mac Plus playing third base, and Ty Cobb hurtling toward it on the basepath, plowing into the screen in a cloud of dust, spikes high.

Gary Carter, curly hair and all, retired from baseball today.

When he was the catcher for the Mets, though he was not especially young, they called him "The Kid," because his enthusiasm gushed in youthful torrents. He was a springtime melody of a Met, but now, after brief codas with the Giants, the Dodgers, and the Expos, he has sounded the final note; he has succumbed to his catcher's aching knees.

From our seats in the dugout of real life we watch the baseball generations come and go. I have outlived Roy Campanella, Johnny Bench, Gary Carter. We await the promised blossoming of Todd Hundley. Cholesterol willing, I may outlive him as well.

This passing parade, this marching band, these tunes of glory, trumpet our bald but hopeless desire for immortality. Is that what baseball is? A toupee to cover my death?

* * *

In October of 1970, although the Mets did not repeat as champions, Carol and I decided to get married. We put a wedding together in two weeks. The rabbi, whom we had never met, concluded his peroration by saying: "May your marriage be as rich, as solid, and as enduring as the metal in this ring." I had to squeeze the bride's hand hard to stifle her giggles; the ring was a piece of tin she had picked up at F. W. Woolworth the day before for twenty-nine cents.

In October of 1971 the Mets again did not reach the play-offs. We left New York for good. This was not, however, cause and effect. There were other reasons, bad and sufficient.

We left out of fear. Fear of physical harm, and fear of what the new New York was doing to our psyches. We resisted the impulse to flee as long as we could. And then, born and bred New Yorkers, we fled.

We left because a fellow I knew was knifed in the belly as he walked through Times Square, minding his own business. He was in critical condition for many days before he recovered.

We left because a woman I knew was assaulted on the roof of her apartment building, a knife at her neck, and was lucky to escape with her life.

We left because my car was stolen and wrecked.

We left because a woman in my office was spat upon by a truck driver when she ignored his lewd remarks.

We left because a panhandler grabbed my camera as I walked in Washington Square Park, and threatened to smash it unless I gave him money.

We left because Carol could no longer go out alone after dark without shaking.

We left because one day, as I opened the elevator door in our building, a woman inside shrank back in terror, her face white, her eyes wide with fear. She was our next-door neighbor, but for a split second she had not recognized me, and thought I meant her harm. In that brief instant I had become the villain. I had victimized her.

We left because one Saturday night, while approaching our building, we saw a man standing in the street with a beer bottle in his hand. Instantly a plan of action formed in my mind. If he started trouble, my left hand would shove the Sunday *Times* I was carrying into his face. At the same moment my right fist would slam into his belly. That would stagger him enough so that we could run.

Nothing visible happened that night. The man ignored us. But the violence had already been done, in my own mind, to my own psyche. I had not had a fistfight since I was eleven. But I had been ready to punch a fellow man who had offered no provocation. I think it was that night I knew for certain we would have to get out of the city. Mets or no Mets.

We took a long vacation out West, seeking a place to live.

In Estes Park, Colorado, we saw an incredibly bright rainbow over the Rockies. I grabbed my camera and clicked off an entire roll of film, not knowing if you could photograph a rainbow. You can. I have the pictures still.

We stayed two days in the decaying railroad town of Salida, Colorado, eating pork chops in a rural diner. The crossing tracks of the old rail yard seemed to contain a mystery, an elusive truth yet to be unraveled.

In Santa Fe we were enchanted. We stayed a week. Carol took out her watercolors and began to paint in the astonishing afternoon light. From an Indian woman on the plaza I bought for four dollars a silver wedding band for myself, to go with the gold one Carol now wore. We knew at once that this might be the place.

In Gallup, New Mexico, a town of railroad cars and Navajo Indians, we watched girls playing softball. In Las Vegas, Nevada, amid the slot machines, Carol saw a woman carrying two paper cups filled with nickels, and mentioned to the woman how lucky she was. "Are you kidding?" the woman said. "I started the night with eight hundred dollars." On a highway beyond the Mojave Desert we were caught in a violent thunderstorm that reduced visibility to zero, and as tractor-trailer rigs hurtled by us on the two-lane blacktop we thought amid the flashes of lightning that here, now, most surely, we would die.

We made it to San Francisco and discovered, unexpectedly, in early September, a week of warmth and sunshine. We liked San

Francisco. But if we moved there, we knew we would still, one day, want to move to Santa Fe. And by then it might be ruined.

Bronx Boy, Brooklyn girl, Mets lovers, we left New York on the twenty-fifth of October, our first wedding anniversary, taking only what could fit in the trunk of the car. Carol would paint in New Mexico, and I would write. Beyond that we had no plans. Some of our friends applauded, even envied, this adventure; others bemoaned our foolhardiness, saying: You do not just walk away from a job of ten years. "I already had your plot picked out for you," a disappointed friend on Long Island said.

She meant a plot of land in her town, on which to build a house. I thought she meant a cemetery.

Leaving the city, we knew there would be much that we would miss, things we would not find in the West. We would miss Sunday-afternoon strolls in Central Park and the feeding of the sea lions. We would miss the musicians in Washington Square, the streaky black-and-white films at the New Yorker Theater, the click of heels on the marble floors of the Metropolitan Museum. We would miss the Hudson flowing beneath the George Washington Bridge as seen from a terrace at the Cloisters, the style of the girls on Madison Avenue, the urbane beauty of the Brooklyn Bridge, the ice skaters at Rockefeller Center, the department-store windows at Christmas. We would miss the laughing brunches and the baseball talk at the Lion's Head. And we would miss the people. Family and friends, yes, but not only them. We would miss people we had never met. The beautiful black girls with their Afro hairdos, the Puerto Rican man hurrying home to his family in East Harlem, the cop patrolling the subway train, the legless beggar rolling on wheels through Wall Street, the sullen old lady with her shopping bag, the other old lady with white hair and a kindly smile. All that infinite variety of faces, craggy and smooth, hawk noses and button noses, slant eyes and round eyes, weak chins and jutting jaws, sideburns and crew cuts, faces lined and marked and scarred by a thousand different acts of life. All this we knew we would miss. And we would miss the Mets.

Which is more significant to explore, to live among—the rural beauty of nature or the urban nature of man? That question would give me pause in the long nights ahead.

Our last day on the road we awoke in Amarillo, Texas, to find a thick fog covering the road. We drove very slowly. We had gone less than a mile when a terrible, ominous thumping sound—terrible, ominous at least to city boys, city girls—began to shake the car; we had a flat tire. While the tire was being repaired at a service station, the fog became rain. For four hours we drove through rain and mist. Then, just as we left the highway at Santa Fe, the sun broke into the gray afternoon with a smile all its own. It lit up the city with a clarity of light that occurs, I think, nowhere else on earth. We took this flood of sunlight as an omen of welcome as we drove into the city, drove down the narrow, twisting streets awash in ghosts and history.

Santa Fe was much smaller then than it is now, and not nearly as chic. It resembled no place else in America. Most of the flat brown houses—limited by law to two stories—were made of earth, of adobe bricks. Still, it would be a long time before I understood precisely where we had moved.

We had moved to Mudville.

SEVENTH

Dice One Elk

There was, alas, no baseball in Mudville.

Well, very little.

In the spring, sometimes, we would go to Salvador Perez Park after an early dinner and watch Little League games in the twilight. Or, on Sunday afternoons, to Fort Marcy Field, to watch the high-school-age boys in the Babe Ruth League. That first summer we drove one night to Albuquerque to see the Dukes. They were playing the Tucson Toros. The visitors scored sixteen runs— maybe it was only fifteen—in the top of the first, and that was that. We knew we should give the Dukes another chance—their stadium is kind of cute, is even reminiscent, in its coziness, of Ebbets Field—but we never did. We didn't like the sixty-mile drive to Albuquerque, through the high desert, with no roadside help more useful than prairie dogs should the car misbehave. In such psychological ways we still were cowardly prisoners of the city.

We tried to break its hold, small vanguard as we were to the new American migration. For many months we did not get a telephone. For a year we did not buy a TV set. We were engrossed in the quiet life, in the challenge of our work. O Pioneers! When we finally did tune in, the only baseball available, in those days before cable and superstations, was the Saturday game of the week. It rarely was the Mets.

Most residents of Santa Fe back then were more interested in

164

hunting and fishing and hiking than in baseball. The first week that we moved into a renovated adobe apartment, complete with Indian fireplace, our landlord and neighbor, a Santa Fe native named Stan Evans, invited me to go hunting with him. I told him hesitantly that I did not care for hunting. Well, it would not really be hunting, he said; we would just drive up into the hills and see the beauty of the morning; in all likelihood we would not see any elk, he said, but he would take his rifle along just in case. Since we were starting a new life, I agree to give it a try. On Saturday I woke up at four-thirty A.M.—in New York that had been closer to my bedtime than my rising time—and pulled on two pairs of underwear and two pairs of socks, and boots, just as Stan had instructed. Over my ears I pulled a blue woolen cap. Stan brought a Thermos of coffee and we drank it black and hot as he drove south out of town in the predawn dark.

The snow-covered hills of Apache Canyon were everything that had been promised as the sky slowly brightened and the first rays of the sun cleared the hills and set the crunchy carpet of snow to gleaming like a multitude of colored diamonds. The shape of the rifle on a rack behind us in the bouncing Jeep was ominous—I did not really know this man. Did he know how to shoot that thing? Would I come back alive? This was a genuine, if exaggerated, concern.

Happily, Stan was as good as his word. We saw no elk that day, he never touched the rifle. Which was fine with me, because a couple of days later, in the local newspaper, I saw a recipe for elk stew. It began: "Dice one elk."

The newspaper carried baseball box scores during the season, but in truth, the local police notes were of greater interest in those days than the Mets. I began to treasure them. One reported that someone had broken into a house and stolen a stereo, and that, while there, "the burglar cooked and ate three eggs." Another reported that an apartment had been broken into but that "the only thing reported missing were several chocolate chips." In a third robbery a bathtub was stolen. The tub was described as "porcelain, about five feet long, white."

This was a distinct improvement over knives in the bellies of friends. I no longer lulled myself to sleep with the thought that the Dodgers, or the Mets, would win the pennant. Instead I lay awake at night, picturing some anonymous victim counting his or her chocolate chips. How did they know some were missing? Had they counted them beforehand? And then I would worry about our own chocolate chips.

His first birthday in the West he receives, as a gift from his wife—from the city girl—an ax. The handle is curved and sleek and varnished, the steel head has heft. In the living room is an Indian fireplace, in which thin logs must be burned vertically. Stacked against the wall behind their house is half a cord of lumber they have purchased, delivered in a pickup truck. His neighbor shows him how to use the ax. He stands a log on end, he swings the ax over his head, he brings it crashing down. He misses the standing log entirely, like a wild pitch. The momentum of the ax carries it forward and earthward till the ax head crashes into the gravelly ground right beside his foot. He has almost cut off a toe. But he perseveres, he spreads his legs wider, removing his feet from the line of jeopardy. He raises the ax again, pauses a moment at the top, the faintest hitch in his swing. This time the ax head crashes down squarely into the end of the log, which splits neat and clean, clean as a double down the third-base line.

He likes the warp of the muscles in his shoulders as he continues to split logs; he feels like a thirtysomething Abe Lincoln. Sometimes he is off center, occasionally he misses entirely. But mostly the logs split nicely. His Levi's, his wool sweater, begin to smell of piñon as he stacks the split logs, as he carries an armload inside to the fireplace. In the coming years he will do this whenever wood is needed, or, in warmer weather, when some pent-up aggression needs to be released through the swinging of the ax.

To the end, however, the ax will always feel a bit too smooth, a bit too varnished, a bit top heavy. In short, a bit unnatural. No matter how many times he wields it, it will not radiate its essence up his arms into his chest, into his inner self. It will never be truly sexy. It will never be a baseball bat.

In the West I began to write novels. The first one published was a spoof of comic-book heroes, and life in general, called *Superfolks*. One scene took place at an art-show opening in a New York gallery for a painter named Carol who was also a baseball fan.

I take the book down from a shelf in my office. It takes a minute to find the appropriate page, for this was written a long time ago. Among the exotic guests at the gallery opening, I discover, were:

Countess Felix Mantilla; the Duchess of Hoyt-Wilhelm; fashion designer Emil Verban; the much-publicized southern debutante Kirby Higbe; millionaire philanthropist Goody Rosen; porn-film queen Sandy Amoros and her leading man, Herb Score; the Most Rev. Luke Easter; pop artist Andy Pafko; jockey Eddie Gaedel; parapsychologist Ryne Duren; the recently remarried Bobo Holloman; the French ambassador, Claude Passeau; stripper Nellie Fox; Karl Spooner, the Jungian analyst; ballerina Tookie Gilbert; potato-chip magnate Al Gionfriddo; evangelist Enos Slaughter; Gene Hermanski, the film director; Washington hostess Choo Choo Coleman; *Playboy*'s Playmate of the Year, Tracy Stallard . . . Georgia heiress Peanuts Lowrey . . . and Bubba Church, gossip columnist for the *Catholic Yenta*.

The uses of baseball are many.

From time to time in succeeding years, while I published other books, I thought about writing a baseball novel. I had devised a format that intrigued me. The entire book would take place during one game at Shea Stadium in late August. It would be the second game of a doubleheader between the Mets and Cincinnati. The Mets would be tethered hopelessly in last place. The Big Red Machine would be well on its way to another pennant. A meaningless game, in other words. We would see it entirely through the eyes of the anonymous Mets shortstop.

The title of each chapter was to be the name of a player in the

Cincinnati batting order, which, in those days before free agency, remained the same from year to year: Rose, Griffey, Bench, Foster, Geronimo, Perez, Concepcion, Morgan, Gullett. There would be twenty-seven short chapters—we would go through the batting order three times. As each player batted we would be in the mind of the shortstop as his thoughts drifted away from this meaningless game toward some crisis in his personal life. Perhaps his marriage was in trouble; perhaps his wife was having an affair with the pitcher. . . .

As the game progressed, the story would unfold in the shortstop's head, while batter after batter was retired. Only toward the end would we realize that no one had gotten on base, that we were watching a perfect game. And he would realize it, too, and the last batter would hit a grounder to short. Would our hero make the play, complete the perfect game? Or would he boot it intentionally, mess up the perfect game for the pitcher who was screwing his wife? Or who, perhaps, he only thought was screwing his wife. Or would he try to make the play—and boot it accidentally—and have to live with that?

Perhaps the book would end as he moved toward the ball . . . and we would never know.

I loved the format. Many of the names of the players in the Cincinnati lineup seemed to resonate with literary possibilities. Rose. Concepcion. Morgan. Gullett. But I was never satisfied with the storyline. I never wrote the book.

The Anxiety of the Shortstop During the Perfect Game.

Maybe someday I will.

It is the first cold morning. The country girl is wearing a sweater, and socks beneath her sandals. He turns on the heat for the first time. A summer's worth of dust blasts from the forced-air vents.

The Dallas Cowboys will be playing Phoenix on the tube at two P.M. Dallas is his football team, he gets to see them on the tube every week, and this year seems promising. Already they are 2–0. Emmitt Smith is a joy to watch, and Troy Aikman is coming into his own.

But there is a Mets game on first, at eleven-thirty A.M. local time. Watching a baseball game and then a football game will be more hours than he can tolerate in front of the set. The choice should be an easy one. The Mets, playing Montreal, are 18 games out of first.

The choice *is* an easy one. He watches the Mets.

He watches the Mets lose. At night he hears on the news that Dallas has won.

He has no regrets. There is a time to swing and a time to punt, a time to steal and a time to go off-tackle. There is a clearly etched time for the changing of the seasons, forced air or no forced air. That time comes when baseball ends. This truth is unequivocal.

A few days later, warmth and sunshine having returned, he comes across, in the national edition of the *Times*, a column about advertising, by one Stuart Elliott, which he finds depressing. Mr. Elliott writes that major league baseball has hired a new advertising agency "to turn young people into baseball fans."

The notion at first seems ludicrous, a variant of science fiction: *See giant pods turned into humans! See young people turned into baseball fans!*

Has human genetics, he wonders, changed that much since his youth? Are young people—at least young men—no longer *born* as baseball fans? Is *that* what strontium 90 was all about?

Reading on, he discovers that the new advertising campaign "is intended to persuade younger Americans, primarily males aged eighteen to thirty-four, to add watching baseball on television to their lengthy list of leisure-time interests that includes watching sports like football and basketball, not to mention MTV, movies, music, travel, and cars.

"Although baseball remains enormously popular," Mr. Elliott continues, "there is a growing perception that its fans, while devoted, are aging. Underscoring that is the sport's intrinsic nostalgia. . . . But, as they say, nostalgia isn't what it used to be."

What does this development signify? he asks himself. Aside from the decline of America as a civilization.

Well, first of all, it is less about baseball than it is about economics. The eighteen-to-thirty-four age group, as the column points out, is the prime target of advertisers because that is the group that spends most of the money at the malls. So the purpose of this ad campaign is not to create more real baseball fans, but to get the ratings of televised games higher, so the sponsors will pay more to the networks for commercials, and the networks will pay more to the teams for TV rights. Everybody will be happy except those poor manipulated souls, eighteen to thirty-four, who will be bored stupid watching a game they don't really understand. Better they should be out at the mall, spending.

The new commercials will take an MTV approach, Mr. Elliott says. "Three initial spots, set to a slow rap tune, offer quick cuts of game footage interspersed with younger players and fans having fun. . . . In the latest two spots hip smart-alecks excitedly explain baseball's most dramatic moments to communicate that 'it's cool to think about strategy.' "

It's cool to think about strategy! The line seems to echo from *Citizen Kane*, his favorite film. *"You think it would be fun to run a newspaper!"*

He envisions having a catch with his cousin David on Townsend Avenue back in 1949, and his saying to David, "Isn't it cool to think about strategy?"

"Robert, David, time for supper," his mother calls out.

"Later, Mom. We're thinking about strategy."

Short of depicting Madonna having a ball in one of those domed-stadium bedrooms, the ad campaign is doomed to failure. Someone who is not a baseball fan by age eighteen is not going to switch from football to baseball the way he switches from Kents to Marlboros. And, frankly, who cares?

But there is a serious problem lurking here, and it merits a serious solution. You don't create baseball fans when they are eighteen or twenty-six or thirty-one. For the most part only immigrants become ball fans at advanced ages, in self-defense, as an attempt to fit in. You create baseball fans when they are six and seven and eight. Do it right and they will watch the game for a lifetime. If baseball fans are a precious resource—and they are— and if we are in danger of losing them—as we seem to be—then we need to address the problem early. If absent fathers are not doing the job, mothers can. If not, we need to start breeding new players—who will become new fans—in the Head Start programs, in kindergarten, in first and second grade. That is when the ball begins to fit so erotically into the palm, when the handle of the bat suggests power. That is the time to inculcate strategy.

It was a better world when little Jerry Ortiz y Pino in 1948 heard the Cleveland Indians playing the Boston Braves in the World Series and became, from sixteen hundred miles away, a fan for life. But absent that, we need some focusing. Not regimentation—not Big Brother of the Diamond, not Universal Little League—but just enough of an early updraft to allow the chicks to flap their wings. And learn to sing.

If you must, think of it this way: Kids playing baseball—or even watching it—are not out holding up liquor stores or mugging your daughter. In the soul's nasty neighborhoods baseball helps to brighten the negative space.

The water in New Mexico is heavy with calcium and other minerals. You can easily see the thick white buildup of crud in a white ring on the inner edge of Willie's water dish; it is building up, just as surely, in the invisible, dark recesses of the teakettle. Yesterday my daughter, just turned seventeen, came home from having coffee with a friend at Carlos's Gospel Café. A hot young dude behind the counter was swirling ice cubes inside a coffeepot. When they asked what he was doing, he said it loosened the calcium crud from the bottom. Then he told them a trick I had not heard of in my twenty years here.

"What you can do at home," my daughter said, quoting the dude, "is you wash a marble and put it in the teakettle. When the water bubbles and boils, the marble dances. The dancing marble keeps the yuckies from sticking to the bottom of the pot."

I pounced on the metaphor, the way Willie pounces on his favorite sock. That's baseball, I realized. For me, for millions of men, for a few women. Baseball is the dancing marble in our brains; it keeps the yuckies from sticking.

* * *

In the mid-seventies, with Carol painting full time, trying to capture the western landscape, we made the rounds of the Santa Fe art galleries often, to see what other painters were doing. One day, in the Artists' Co-op Gallery, we were surprised to find colorful, oversized acrylic paintings—about two feet by three feet—of baseball cards. There were stars such as Jackie Robinson and Mickey Mantle; there were lesser lights like Rip Repulski and Sibby Sisti. What Andy Warhol had done for the Campbell's Soup can, a fellow named Bill Forsyth was doing for bubble-gum art.

I did not have the money to buy one of the paintings; in time the paintings disappeared from the gallery; then the gallery disappeared; then Bill Forsyth, as far as I knew, disappeared. Till recently, when I saw one of his works—it was a Yogi Berra—for sale in a local baseball-card shop. The owner had some of Forsyth's business cards, and he gave me one. The artist was living in Albuquerque. His business card featured his signature against a red baseball diamond, and the notation: *Major-league quality paintings of baseball cards. Any subject available by commission.*

I called him to find out how his unusual art had evolved, and whether or not business was booming.

Forsyth was born in 1946 in Chappaqua, New York. Such baseball games as his father took him to were at Yankee Stadium, but Bill became a Dodger fan, for reasons he does not really understand. "The old underdog theory, I guess," he said. The refrain was familiar; the brute strength of the Yankees in those days created a whole generation of Dodger and Giant fans. Elementary physics: every action has an equal and opposite reaction.

Where Forsyth is different from most of us is that, although he amassed a serious collection of about three thousand baseball cards, he stopped being a fan at the age of fourteen. His favorite sport as of 1960, when he entered high school, became track and field. In 1965 he went to the University of New Mexico to join the track-and-field team there.

His card collection disappeared in 1960 or 1961. "I forget what I did with them," he said. "Maybe my mother burned them. I can't remember. I'm glad I can't."

Forsyth studied painting at UNM. He began to copy old masters and then add little whimsical twists. He copied Edvard Munch's *The Scream,* for instance—one of the Super-Meaningful paintings of my adolescence (maybe of everybody's adolescence)—but on the face he painted the little yellow Smile button. He copied Rembrandt's *The Jewish Bride,* but in place of the groom he painted a self-portrait—wearing an L.A. Dodgers cap. The paintings began to sell.

"In 1972 I went back to New York to get all my stuff and move it to New Mexico," Forsyth said. "I was cleaning out my room back there in my parents' house, and in the sock drawer I found one last surviving card, wedged in the corner of the drawer. It was amazing. It was a 1954 Bowman card of Max Surkont, the Pirates pitcher. The card just looked so pathetic. The guy had such a pathetic look on his face. The card looked like an old seventeenth-century portrait. I said, 'I gotta paint this.' So I put it right on the easel. I gave the painting to my brother as a Christmas present and wedding present. But somehow I got it back from him. Or maybe I borrowed it back, to show. And it sold. I felt kind of guilty about that. So I did them another painting, a copy of a Vermeer—a portrait of him and his wife as *The Officer and the Laughing Girl.* They still have that. One thing led to another. I did another baseball card when I came out here. It sold to the wife of a TV star. Another Pirate, Roberto Clemente. I got pretty prolific with them in the late seventies. I started shipping them to a sports art gallery in New York." The prices ranged from $400 to $1,100. "I did pretty well, for a while, until the mid-eighties."

Then sales dropped off. "Every year I would do one of the guys who got voted into the Hall of Fame," Forsyth said. "This guy had a show in Cooperstown during the induction weekend. Three years in a row I did one. I was hoping he'd get them autographed. I was never there, but he had them in the show. They didn't sell up there, and they didn't sell in the gallery. I just didn't do the publicity for it. I guess the artist is supposed to provide that. You gotta pay your dues. I didn't."

Around the same time he received an inheritance, which undercut his need to paint for money.

Bill Forsyth remains interested in baseball statistics, but he no longer roots for any team. He gave up rooting when his adult eyes noted that baseball was "just a business"; he follows track and field instead.

I should, I suppose, applaud his piety. Instead, I regret his loss.

The implication of his paintings far exceeded baseball cards; they proudly proclaimed baseball as the art form that it is, worthy of the living-room wall; worthy of the museum. But Forsyth no longer paints baseball cards, except by special request. That, too, I regret.

A few days after talking with Forsyth, I come across a short item in the local newspaper that is headlined: 'CRIME' CARD SALES MAKING A KILLING. The item begins: "They may never be worth as much as Pete Rose or a 1952 Mickey Mantle, but trading cards that feature the grim visages of Jeffrey Dahmer, Ted Bundy, and other notorious murderers are selling apace after months of action by parents and victims' rights groups to ban them."

The item says negative publicity is increasing sales of the cards. It concludes: "We've never sold anything this well in our lives,' said Catherine Yronwode, editor in chief of Eclipse Enterprises in Forestville, Calif. The company has sold about $1 million worth of the cards."

Eclipse Enterprises. A nice touch for cards of killers. I debate whether to forward the item to Forsyth. A whole new hagiarchy awaits his brush.

On Monday evening the local sportscaster informs us that Oakland has clinched the American League West. He says the other ball scores do not matter.

Do not matter! I am in a rage. Who is he to tell us what matters? I do not know how the Mets did in their doubleheader against the Phillies, which was not being televised here. I would like to know.

Tuesday morning, in the newspaper, I discover that the Mets lost in straight sets, 7–6, 7–6. I concede that perhaps this is not earthshaking news, till I look at the standings to see how far the

Mets have fallen. They are now 25 games behind the Pirates, who have already clinched.

I notice that the Phillies are only 26 games out, one game behind the Mets. That means their game tonight, which will be televised, will be a struggle to stay out of last place. If the Mets lose they will be tied for last with less than a week to go.

Suddenly, this game assumes huge proportions; if it is not the World Series, it *matters*. I plan my day around settling in at five-thirty (seven-thirty New York time) to watch this battle of the titans. For if the Mets, with the highest payroll in all of baseball this year, should finish last, it would be a sublime reverse perfection.

La Donna, who writes scripts, has been in a sublimating—which is to say a housework—mood today. When I tell her about the importance of the game, she goes to my office, unbidden, suitably impressed, and cleans the TV screen with Windex.

I listen to the introductory remarks by Ralph Kiner, whose droll sense of humor always surprises, and by Tim McCarver, who is as good as they come when he omits the sophomoric puns. They give the starting lineups, they talk of Bret Saberhagen on the mound. They seem to have overlooked that this is a battle for last place. It's an honest mistake, I think. There is no Met pride left to protect.

In their current losing streak the Mets have been staggering in their ineptitude. One game against the Cardinals was scoreless into the fourteenth inning. Jeff Kent, acquired in the Cone trade, hit a three-run homer in the top of the fourteenth. But the Mets gave up four in the bottom of the fourteenth, to lose, 4–3. A few days later they lost to the Pirates, 19–2; they were down 16–1 after four innings.

Now the last week of the regular season is about to begin, with this battle for the cellar.

Saberhagen retires the Phillies in order in the top of the first. The Mets go down as well.

In the second, after a walk and a double, center fielder Ryan Thompson, also acquired in the Cone trade, makes a brilliant catch in deep left-center while barely avoiding tripping over Vince Coleman. An unbelievable catch. He gets up limping. He may be the center fielder next year. Still, a run scores from third on the play. The Phillies lead, 1–0.

The Phillies have runners on first and third. Saberhagen tries that weird windmill move that almost never works, faking a throw to third base, then whirling and throwing to first. This time it works! The runner on first is picked off. He breaks for second. Eddie Murray throws to Schofield covering. Schofield begins to chase him back toward first. As he does, the runner on third breaks for the plate. Schofield fires home—too late. The run scores. And the runner on first moves down to second. Once every Halley's Comet this Rube Goldberg of a pickoff move works— and Saberhagen made it work—and the Mets turned it into a run for the Phillies. It's now 2–0.

Bottom of the second. Daryl Boston walks. Ryan Thompson slams the ball on one bounce off the left field wall for a double, scoring Boston. Phillies 2, Mets 1. A grounder by Todd Hundley moves the tying run to third with one out. Then there's a wild pitch, and Thompson scores from third. Tie game! A humming-bird's wings are beating in my chest, here in the third inning, 25 games out of first place with a week to go; with six months to go till spring.

Schofield, with two strikes on him, hits a home run, to put the Mets ahead, 3–2. It's only his fourth of the year.

The announcers finally admit this is a battle for last place. They call the homer "the shot heard around Queens," because they have been talking about Bobby Thomson's 1951 home run, the shot heard round the world. Thomson is at the game this night. Now they show the old, blurry film of Thomson's home run. They discuss the radio call of Russ Hodges, who kept screaming "The Giants win the pennant! The Giants win the pennant!" They say he said it about thirteen times in a row. I never bothered to count.

Now they will play the audiotape.

Spare me, O Lord! O Wilson, Glickman, and Lee!

When they play the tape, it turns out he only said it five or six times. It just seemed like thirteen, to me in my aunt Sarah's apart-ment, to Kiner and McCarver wherever they were that day.

The Mets game continues. Schofield makes a good backhand

play. He has made only 7 errors this season in about 600 chances. If he does not make an error in the remaining five games he will set the all-time National League fielding record for a shortstop, beating out Ozzie Smith. Something else on which to concentrate. The season ain't over till it's over.

Middle of the seventh. Saberhagen has settled down. It is still 3–2 Mets. He sets the Phils down one-two-three in the eighth, throwing mostly fastballs. The Mets hold their one-run lead going into the top of the ninth.

Saberhagen has thrown 110 pitches. They don't want to risk his troublesome finger. With John Franco on the disabled list, Anthony Young will pitch the ninth. Last month he ran off a good string of saves. Lately he has not done well.

Young walks the leadoff man. An ominous sign of trouble, gray rain headed this way. The next batter singles. Distant thunder, runners on first and second with nobody out. I glance at a Dick Francis book on my desk, which I had brought home from the library in the afternoon. I debate whether to turn off the set now and plunge into mystery, horse racing.

There is no way I can shut off a baseball game before it is over.

A pinch hitter bunts, to move the runners along. Young picks up the ball and fires toward third, trying for a force-out. But he throws it down the left field foul line. The deluge. The runner from second scores. The runner on first also scores. The batter reaches second. The Phillies have taken the lead, 4–3.

That is the kind of season it has been. The season from hell.

Young throws a wild pitch. The runner moves over to third with nobody out. Jeff Torborg comes out to the mound. Finally. Young out, Jeff Innis in. On the first pitch the batter hits a fly ball to center. The runner tags and scores. The Mets are down by two. The weak bullpen has struck again.

Innis finally retires the side.

Bottom of the ninth. The Phillies lead, 5–3. Crazy Mitch Williams coming in to pitch. His record is five and eight, but he's got 27 saves.

Kevin Bass, pinch-hitting for Boston in a righty-lefty switch, leads off with a double to left. That brings up Ryan Thompson, who after his earlier double has struck out twice. There are not many people in the stands on this cold night in New York, not more than a few thousand, but they are screaming now: "Let's Go Mets! Let's Go Mets!" I am reassured to discover my breed, tyrannosaurus Mets, is not extinct.

Thompson walks. The tying runs are on with nobody out. Pennant fever!

Todd Hundley, trying to sacrifice, bunts in the air. The ball is caught by Mariano Duncan, playing third. Oh, Randy, didn't you teach your boy?

Chico Walker, a switch-hitter, will bat for Schofield. He hits a slow grounder to short. The play is to first. Runners now on second and third. Two out—but a single will tie the game.

Dave Gallagher will bat for Innis. I look around wildly for a toothpick to move. A napkin. There is nothing in the room but imaginary rain.

Gallagher slams a sharp line drive to right-center. For an instant there is hope. But the ball is hauled in by the right fielder with graceful ease. The game is over. The Mets drop into a tie for last place. Technically, a tie for fifth, but losers can't be technical.

I go to the bathroom. A blue detergent not used in our house before has been added to the toilet. When I flush, the water rushes out in a deep turquoise color. Unlike the Mets, it is very pretty as it disappears down the drain.

Annie Dillard, while discovering magical visions in Tinker Creek, wrote: "When I see this way I see truly. As Thoreau says, I return to my senses. I am the man who watches the baseball game in silence in an empty stadium. I see the game purely; I'm abstracted and dazed. When it's all over and the white-suited players lope off the green field to their shadowed dugouts, I leap to my feet; I cheer and cheer."

Looking back at a marriage conceived in baseball, I expect to recall a myriad of diamond anecdotes, a trail as long as the Milky Way. Instead, I recall only a few. If there were others they have vanished, like ripples on Walden Pond.

I remember, on a brief return stay in New York, watching together in the fall of 1973 as the Mets, with a humdrum won-loss record, with no major miracles, with a second-division team but a brilliant pitching staff—Seaver, Koosman, Matlack, McGraw—stumbled to the eastern division championship. They managed to beat the Reds in the play-offs, three games to two, then extended a much better Oakland team to seven games before losing the World Series.

The other memories have little to do with the Mets, mired as the team was for most of the seventies in mediocrity.

I remember that, during the 1975 World Series, I was rooting for the National League team, as usual—for Cincinnati—and Carol was rooting for the Red Sox. That was the first time in our six years together we had been on opposite sides of a baseball game.

I remember watching the Atlanta Braves on *Monday Night Baseball* when Hank Aaron had a chance to hit his 715th career home run—a chance to pass Babe Ruth. He did not homer his first time up, and then the telephone rang in our Santa Fe apartment and it was Carol's cousin Lynn calling from New York to ask if we had seen Aaron's homer. Carol asked what Lynn was talking about, he had not hit a homer yet. And Lynn swore that he had, in his second at bat—and then, furious, we understood. The local station, without saying so, was broadcasting the game an hour late, on tape delay. The delicious suspense was gone when, next time up, Hank Aaron set the record.

Beyond that there is a vacancy of vision. From the distance of a decade I see only the shadowed dugouts, the empty stadium. No white-suited players lope across the green of a quiet desperation not then understood, not then even felt.

Red Barber, the maestro, died today. He was the composer, conductor, and crooner of the sweetest music of my youth. I find myself thinking of him tonight more than I did when certain uncles passed on. This is perhaps not surprising; the Ole Redhead was in my house a lot more often. He spoke of matters a lot more important.

I recall a snapshot Carol showed me early in our marriage. It was of herself, at about the age of two and a half. She was sitting in a stroller, waving to someone, her small fingers spread wide. I used to joke that she was waving hello to me. In fact, symbolically she could have been waving good-bye to her father, who left when she was that very age and never came back. Except that she would not have been smiling.

I recall that snapshot tonight, I think, because, in her early absorption with the Dodgers, Red Barber may have become her true father figure.

So long, Red. No more rhubarbs, no one sittin' in the catbird seat. Been a long time since the bases were FOB.

This he does not know about when it is happening in November of 1975. This he will be unaware of until it is described to him many years later:

The woman is sitting on a small stool inside a huge homemade loom, which fills most of the bedroom of a small basement apartment in the village of Glenville, West Virginia. She normally weighs about eighty-eight pounds but has gained fifty-two more; she is very pregnant. The baby is perhaps two weeks late. The doctor has told the woman the baby is dead; the woman knows it is not. She warps the loom, on which she plans to weave a rug, until she is tired, around midnight, then eases her unaccustomedly bulky body through the frame of the loom and goes to bed.

An hour later there are labor pains; an hour later there are more. The baby is born at four-fifteen in the morning, by candlelight, the young woman alone with her husband. He holds the baby and tells her it's a boy, and he places it on her belly. The baby, hungry already, crawls upward; it wants to nurse.

When dawn breaks, the excited father races out into the streets of the village. "It's a boy," he shouts, over and over, "it's a boy." He runs to the home of their best friends, to tell them the news. The names of the friends—this will seem coincidental only later—are Bob and Carol.

In the apartment mother and child are asleep. When the father returns, the mother asks him to change the diaper in which the baby is loosely wrapped. The father removes the diaper. As he does, a look of horror crosses his face.

"What is it?" the mother asks.

"It's—it's . . ." He can barely speak. For an instant he seems to think the infant's little penis has fallen off. Finally he finds his voice.
"It's a girl," he says.
Three days later they choose a name. They call her Amara.

They could not know then, mother and daughter—any more than I could know then—how, years later and far away, our lives would come together.

The Mets wind up next to last, with 72 wins and 90 losses. They had been favored by many, myself included, to win the pennant.

A few weeks after the season ends, the Colorado Rockies name their manager: Don Baylor. My feelings are mixed. I'm glad they chose a black; baseball is still largely racist above the player level, and this is a step in the right direction. But I am also disappointed—because they chose an American Leaguer. In large part because of the noxious designated-hitter rule, the game in the two leagues is very different: Jeff Torborg, successful with the White Sox, demonstrated many ghastly times in the season just ended that he did not know how to manage in the National League. My flirtation with the Rockies wavers slightly—till I finish reading the news story about Baylor's appointment. He told a news conference he had spent a sleepless night after being hired as the manager. "I remember thinking, at three or four in the morning, who was going to be my leadoff guy, and then I started to put my lineup together," he said. "And we don't even know who our players are yet."

To this I could relate. I had lain awake many a night creating my own lineups when I managed a softball team called the Santa Fe Springs. I pictured Baylor, lying in bed in the dark, putting together his best possible infield: *Will Clark, Ryne Sandberg, Barry Larkin, Wade Boggs.* I envisioned him rolling over, trying to get comfortable, fluffing his pillow, swinging his long legs out of bed to get a drink of water. I saw him put together another infield, in case the first was not available: *Tom Collins, Jr., Gene Smith, Bobby Mayer, Phil Spitzer.* But mostly I imagined him as he had described, putting together his lineup like a Zen master, with no players at all. The Lineup of the Invisible. That is definitely a National League concept. Don Baylor would do just fine.

This was confirmed in the succeeding days, when his coaches were announced: Larry Bearnarth; Amos Otis; Don Zimmer. All of them were onetime Mets. Zimmer had even been a Brooklyn Dodger! As far as I knew he still carried a metal plate in his head from the time he was beaned. Rather like toting the royal silver.

A large advertisement in the Sunday newspaper features the first local promotion for tickets to Rockies games—an opening week celebration. I think perhaps I should send away for tickets for Smith and me: go up there in April, decide once and for all how we feel about this new team. The first three major league games to be played in Denver will pit the Rockies against the Montreal Expos; the next four—three in a row at night—will be against the Mets.

We can drive or fly up there, watch the newborn Rockies play the Mets. See which way the emotional scales tip in the raw glare of combat. But when I suggest this to Smith, he is not enthusiastic. "Denver? At night, in April? We'll freeze our butts off. A day game, I'll go to. Or a night game later on, in June."

I realize he is right. Memories of icy Candlestick scuttle across my skin like water bugs. Then I realize that the Rockies-Expos games are in the daytime—only the Mets games are at night. Is it the Rockies I want to see, or is it really the Mets?

The question puzzles me. My budding attraction to Denver suddenly seems a fraud. Till I think again of Baylor. The Rockies have no players yet. No names, no faces, to which to offer my loyalty, my support. The Lineup of the Invisible, however literary—even religious—a concept, must be made flesh before I can react in truth.

They begin to occupy my house and my skull, floating, drifting. They are antighosts; they have not died; they are invisible because they do not yet exist, because their time has not yet come. But some unspeaking Fate already knows. . . .

In two days we all will know. On the day of the expansion draft. We agree to watch it together, Smith and I. The TV set will become a telescope. Like humble Galileos, balding of pate, we shall watch the birth of galaxies.

There has been much hand-wringing by sportswriters in recent days to the effect that, with its high salaries, its television contracts, its assorted dirty laundry, baseball now is just another aspect of real life—as if it is no longer part of the toy department, as if it is no longer a game. I see what those writers see, but I must differ. To do so I shall relate briefly the stories of four men. They came into my consciousness in February of 1980, while I was covering as a journalist the worst prison riot in the nation's history. It happened at the New Mexico State Penitentiary, just south of Santa Fe. Thirty-three men died in that rebellion, killed by fellow prisoners.

One of them was named Archie Martinez. He was half boy, half dog—or so his neighbors in the nearby village of Chimayo believed. He grew up much too poor in that ancient village, a place of superstition and miracles and faith. And so he became a thief, a burglar of houses.

He was an excellent burglar. When he broke into homes, he always got away. He was so good that the villagers, who had no police force, banded together to stop him. They created a system. Anyone whose home was burgled would call a volunteer fireman. The fireman would turn on his siren. The entire volunteer fire department would converge on the house, surround it, trap the burglar in the area.

Archie always managed to slip away through the underbrush. That's how he earned his nickname: the Dog Boy of Chimayo.

But skill and magic both sometimes fail. One day the Dog Boy was caught. He was convicted of his crimes, sent to the state penitentiary, put in a cage like all the others. He escaped even from there. But he was caught again and penned again.

Then came February 2, 1980. The prison exploded, murder and madness ruled. And Archie the Dog Boy was slain, on Groundhog Day.

I watched as the dead were removed from the prison in trucks that day. They passed police cars marked K-9 PATROL, which were parked at the entrance to the prison. Inside the cars, as Archie's body passed, the police dogs began to bark.

One of the men was named Robert Mosley. He was twenty-one years old. He, too, was in prison for burglary. When the inmates took over that day, he was grabbed by fellow inmates. He was tied up in the fetal position. A hood was placed over his head. Then he was raped, over and over again. He counted ten times before he passed out.

When he revived he heard the screams of others. Others were in the same room. The same thing was happening to them.

When it was over, when the National Guard reclaimed the prison, Robert Mosley met with reporters, a cross on a gold chain around his neck. He gave his name, he told what had happened to him.

"We don't print the names of rape victims," one reporter said.

Robert Mosley insisted that his name be used, that the entire truth be told: how this goes on all the time, riot or no riot—how young inmates are raped every day in prisons across America, until they turn into zombies.

"Print my story," Robert Mosley said, "so the public will be enlightened."

One of the men was named Paulina Paul. People always said he was crazy, and maybe he was. Never mind that his name was Paulina and maybe his mama had wanted a girl. That wouldn't explain his brother, who took a gun into a movie theater in Vietnam and shot five of his fellow GIs to death. That was crazy, man. And it wouldn't explain his other brother, who shot a cop in Albuquerque. And it wouldn't explain his sister, who killed her own three-year-old child. Around that family dinner table, how sane was Paulina Paul likely to be?

He held up a hotel. He was caught and brought to trial. At his trial they had to tie him to a chair because he kept making loud animal noises, in between spouting religious chants.

He was convicted and sent to prison. The prison said he was

crazy and sent him to the state mental hospital. After a time the hospital sent him back, though no one could say why. In the prison he rarely left his cell. Mostly he liked to lie naked on the cold cement floor, bothering nobody.

During the prison riot Paulina Paul was murdered. But that was not enough. His mind had long ago been severed from his body. On this day his head was too.

It was paraded through the prison on display.

And people said *he* was crazy.

The name of the fourth man is lost to history. He was a child-molester. Even in prisons, where every imaginable crime has been committed by the inmates, the child-molesters are considered the lowest of the low.

One day this man was stabbed by a fellow inmate. He complained to the authorities; he agreed to testify against his assailant. That made him the only thing in prison that is lower than a child-molester. That made him a snitch.

He was placed in protective custody to save him from the other prisoners. There he was relatively safe—until the inmates took over the asylum. Somewhere they found a blowtorch. They came to his protective-custody cell. They began to cut through the bars with the torch; to melt them like butter.

"Say your prayers," they told him through the bars. And they told him what they were going to do to him with the blowtorch when they got inside.

His screams must surely hang over the prison even now. Because when they got inside, they did what they said they would.

I do not know if any of these men, the victims or the killers, were baseball fans. It hardly matters, of course. I only know they were children of God, on a day there was no God. I also know that, once you have written about such events, you gain a certain perspective. You understand that baseball's high salaries, TV contracts, assorted dirty laundry, are unimportant, a pale blemish on the craggy face of reality. Baseball only matters between the foul lines—and there it is still a game.

* * *

For the past sixteen months I have been seeing Jayne.

It is not an affair. Jayne is a physical therapist. Last year a problem in my lower back was causing sharp jolts of pain near my hip. My doctor sent me to Jayne for a program of stretching exercises. Thirty years of writing, first on typewriters and then on a computer, compounded by a lack of exercise due to back and shoulder trouble, had tightened my muscles like a mummy's wrap. I was a Rodin of adhesions.

Jayne worked wonders, pulling my legs in directions they did not care to go. In a few weeks the pain disappeared. My whole body was loosening up, thanks to her thrice-weekly tortures and a milder exercise program at home. She went to work on my shoulder. She pressed her pointy elbow deep into my back and ran it along tracks of hidden tissue like a freight train loaded with bricks. She chipped away the years as if they were barnacles. At the beginning of the summer I set a goal: to play tennis by the fall; or at least to toss a baseball around with Smith, using my rejuvenated right shoulder.

But my insurance coverage ran out. Paying the bill myself, I had to reduce our assignations to once a week. Now it is more a maintenance program; the tennis, the ball-tossing, will have to wait.

When I came home from Jayne's today I bumped into the shade of a lamp on a table in a narrow passageway. I grabbed the lamp before it fell, but a number of framed photographs on the small table were jostled, and some toppled over. I replaced them upright: small graduation pictures of my brother and myself, Amara as a child, my parents, La Donna's, La Donna as a girl of about two—the equivalent of Carol's good-bye shot, though nobody is leaving. But apparently I did not replace them precisely where they had been, because just now, as I was eating dinner—white bean chili and corn bread—I found myself staring at myself. The largest photo on the table—about six inches high—had moved to the front, a photograph of me in my baseball uniform, aged nine, in the backyard on Townsend Avenue, crouched slightly in a concrete batter's box, my brown bat held high, my elbow high and tight to my body, waiting for the unseen pitcher to deliver his best. Studying the picture, I could find no fault with the batting stance after all these years. My face was in shadow under the peak of the cap—the picture must have been snapped at high noon—but my steady form was flawless.

As I ate the chili I watched, I stared. In the photo I did not twitch a muscle, I did not wiggle the bat. Patiently, intently, I waited—waited for Jayne to finish her work, so that the eternal unseen pitcher at last could pitch.

Tomorrow I will be waiting still. Though she is good, Jayne is not *that* good.

November 17. The expansion draft is upon us. Gene picks up hamburgers, French fries, fried onion rings, at Bert's Burger Bowl, which has the best fast food in town. ONE LOCATION WORLDWIDE, their T-shirts boast. Jayne or no Jayne, today is no day for health food.

We settle in to watch; to see the Lineup of the Invisible made plain. We are keenly aware that this is no inconsequential matter: we could be meeting the imaginary friends of our second childhoods.

Gene, who rarely drinks, whom I have never seen drink in the daytime, asks for a beer. Perhaps he is feeling more tension than he shows. I take a Pepsi for myself; some challenges you need to meet cold sober.

The draft will be televised for seven hours. This sounds astonishing, till we realize it only allows five minutes per pick.

As the announcers talk, we discuss how, thus far, no New Mexico station has signed to televise the Rockies. That will be a problem to deal with later, should we choose to become Colorado fans. At a minimum, however, most of their games with the Braves, the Cubs, and the Mets will be available here on the superstations.

Finally the preliminaries are over. The draft begins. The Rockies, having won a coin toss, get first choice. I wonder in what order God created the animals, back in Eden Park. We lean forward, as if to wrench the name out of the set with our hands, bloody, bare-assed, and bawling.

The Rockies select for their first pick (the word made flesh) David Nied, a promising pitcher with Atlanta. This apparently was expected, though in my media-poor western innocence I have never heard of him. The announcers discuss his impressive minor league numbers, his 3–0 record with the Braves.

"Way to go," Smith says. "We've got an opening-day pitcher. Let's go Rockies!"

The Marlins go for Nigel Wilson, an outfielder with the Toronto chain. A hot prospect, apparently.

Colorado chooses Charlie Hayes, the regular third baseman of the Yankees. The announcers seem surprised that Hayes was left unprotected and that the Rockies have steered away from youth. I am distressed that they have chosen a Yankee. My distress deepens when the Marlins' next selection is Jose Martinez, a promising young pitcher from the Mets organization. I seem to want Colorado to be choosing Mets players. This suggests a definite confusion in my loyalties.

When the Rockies take a Milwaukee pitcher, Darren Holmes, Smith says: "So far, I like this team better than the Dodgers." But after three more rounds of picks, in which the Marlins go for promising youth and the Rockies go for mediocre major leaguers, his view has begun to sour. "I must be a Rockies fan," he says, "because already I think the Marlins are doing a better job."

The afternoon wears on. Watching the Rockies and Marlins play God seems not to be as fascinating as watching God play God. In our enthusiasm we had expected better.

"How many games do you think the Rockies will have to play," Smith asks, "before I hate Don Baylor?"

"One," I reply.

Few big-name players are being chosen, because their salaries are too high. Frustration, the Biblical creeping thing, enters the room. The Colorado choices seem uninspired.

"This is great," Smith says. "We're already mad. This is baseball!"

"Maybe we should become Marlins fans," I suggest.

"It would be more fun to go there for the games," Smith agrees. We envision the beaches of Miami. The girls in their bikinis.

"If the Rockies don't pick a good player in their next round," Smith says, "I'm going to become a Dodger fan."

So it goes. The draft elongates into a succession of strong young arms of whom we have never heard. When we turn off the set in late afternoon, Florida seems to have stocked a rookie league; their major league team is not discernible. But the Rockies already have chosen what could be their opening-day team. Only the future will tell which was the better strategy.

As Smith heads off into the quick-falling dark, we know that we have, indeed, witnessed the birth of two new galaxies. What we have not seen is any stars.

Like Don Baylor I select a starting lineup for the Rockies:

> *Alex Cole, center field*
> *Eric Young, second base*
> *Charlie Hayes, third base*
> *Andres Galarraga, first base*
> *Jerald Clark, left field*
> *Joe Girardi, catcher*
> *Fred Benavides, shortstop*
> *David Nied, pitcher.*

I realize I am short an outfielder. Some dealing will have to be done, perhaps in the free-agent market, which is how they signed Gallaraga the day before the draft.

I hope the Rockies, too, realize, before the season starts, that they are short an outfielder.

In 1979, when my father was seventy-seven years old, he hired a housekeeper. He told me this fifteen minutes into a long-distance telephone conversation one night. He had run into her on Tremont Avenue in The Bronx, a woman he had known many years before when she had been a bookkeeper for one of his best customers. The woman—her name was Anne, like my mother's—was a widow. She was cooking and cleaning for him, my father said. After another fifteen minutes of chatter he said she was doing this in return for room and board; she was a live-in housekeeper. Which explained why my father in this conversation sounded fifteen years younger than usual. This was the first real companionship he had had in nearly twenty years. Over and over he asked me if he had done the right thing; he wanted to make sure I had no problem with this arrangement. I assured him that I was thrilled for him, which I was. I was also thrilled for myself; his "housekeeper" helped assuage my guilt at living two thousand miles away.

I never got to meet Anne Williams. Three months later she required surgery for cancer; she died of a heart attack on the operating table. My father had been granted three months of happiness. No more.

Like Miniver Cheevy I cursed the Fates. My father did better; he decided to move to Florida, to a residence hotel, where there would be many companions his age. The following spring my brother, who lived in New Jersey, helped him sell his furniture and his house and move to Miami Beach.

Over the phone I could hear again that this new life he had not permitted himself for nineteen years was a genuine tonic. Within a short time he began going out to dinner frequently with a woman who lived in the hotel. Again he sounded happy.

Two weeks later I received a call from my aunt Rose, who lived down there. My father was in the hospital, she told me; he'd had a stroke.

I flew to Miami. From the airport I took a cab to his hotel, dropped off my bag in his room, then continued on to the hospital. My father did not smile upon seeing me. I don't know if he was capable of smiling, for I never saw him do so again. He could hardly speak, he could not move parts of his body. He had no desire to move the other parts. He made clear, in such words as he could spit through his depression, that he wanted to die.

I visited my aunt Rose and my uncle Ben. Rose showed me two gold wedding bands she had found in a drawer in my father's room. My father, she said, had been planning to marry in two weeks. The stroke had intervened.

The woman had been pressuring my father to marry, my aunt

said. I don't know if that is true. When I met her she seemed rather nice; she genuinely cared about him, even after the stroke; I would watch from behind the door of the hospital room as she mopped his brow, as she tried to get him to eat. But I did not enter the room while she was there, because I had seen the panic, the anger in his eyes the first time she came while I was there; angrily, he had tried to wave her away. He felt guilty about her existence, he felt she and I must be kept apart.

I knew then what had caused my father's stroke—if we can ever know such things. He had been torn apart. Getting married would have been a betrayal of my mother, a part of him believed, even after twenty years; that's why he hadn't told anyone about the plan. The stroke had been a brutal way out of the box in which he found himself, his body's way of canceling the nuptials.

The night I realized this, I went to a porno movie theater that was showing *Deep Throat* and *Behind the Green Door*. I am usually bored by such films, but these were supposed to be the best. I entered the theater and wallowed in this garbage with no enjoyment. Something obscene had been done to my father. In some obscure and pointless way this was my obscene response.

Tom Collins had a related response to similar circumstances a few months ago. He returned from Taos to Chicago because his mother, who had cancer, was dying. As she lay in the hospital, Tom, too, did the most obscene thing he could think of. He went for the first time to a baseball game at the new Comiskey Park— the park that had replaced the beloved ball field of his youth.

"I got there early so I could wander around," Tom said. "Old Comiskey had become a parking lot. There's the old home plate, embedded in black asphalt. They've put a batter's box and the foul lines there, so you can see where it was. It was an athletic, a historical, equivalent, to what was going on in my own mind at the time. It was death. It was not lost upon me, believe me. I wandered around remembering going to the old ballpark with my mom and dad. That's what life is all about, isn't it? Loss? Especially when you're a White Sox fan.

"I didn't like the new park. It's got blue plastic seats, golden boxes. I felt like I was too far removed. I think the average seat is sixty feet farther away from the playing field. It had a kind of airport-terminal feel. People seemed to be shopping more than watching baseball. People were wandering around as if it was a big event to be at the park, not to root for the White Sox. It had changed, it had become sort of a circus. At a key moment in the game, in the seventh inning, Kansas City had loaded the bases and Brett was up. It was incredible, George Brett, near the end of his career, twenty hits shy of three thousand. And people were wandering around buying souvenirs. I don't remember this happening before."

Before he went into the park, Collins struck up a conversation with a vendor outside. "He had never been inside the park in two years," Tom said. "He used to go to the old park as a kid. He grew up five blocks from the park. Black guy. He was selling hot dogs. I always buy hot dogs outside the park. I told him this was my first trip back, I asked him if he had been inside. He goes, 'No. It's a nice place to visit, but I don't wanna go in. Maybe next year.' *Maybe* next year, he says. He couldn't face it either. I had to go in. I had to check my reaction to the whole situation. It was disappointment. And depression."

Naturally, the White Sox lost that day, Tom said. By a run.

In the hospital in Miami, scores of beautiful young nurses, dark haired, large eyed, moved about, efficient and friendly; nursing was their ticket out of the Philippines, I learned, and Miami was the main port of entry. They seemed a willful counterpoint to the illness and death through which they moved. In the therapy rooms young American girls with light brown hair or blond, not as pretty but fiercely dedicated, pulled at my father's arms, his legs, determined to get him to walk again, to talk again, this little Jewish man they did not know; their patience was astonishing; in truth, it was greater than mine. But progress was slow. Soon I was informed that my father's permissible time in the hospital was running out; I would have to locate a nursing home to which he could be moved. This moment in life that every child fears was at hand; given my father's condition, there was no avoiding it.

That night I took Rose and Ben to dinner to thank them for their help. As we were getting up to leave the restaurant they met some friends of theirs, a couple who invited us to join them for coffee. When we were introduced, the name rang a distant bell, though it was common enough. A bit later on, when they began to talk of their grandchild, and then of their daughter-in-law, I knew who they were. Their son, the doctor, two decades before, had married Franny Pike; had stolen her from Our Gang. There had been the child—and then, I had heard, a divorce.

"I knew your daughter-in-law," I told them.

"You knew Franny?" the woman asked. "How?"

"I went to school with her. City College." I hesitated for the merest instant. "I used to go out with her."

The couple looked thunderstruck. They began to pale. My timing in the next moment would have been the envy of Jack Benny, Bob Newhart, Rita Rudner. Tick . . . tick . . . tick . . .

"So did all my friends."

The four elder faces looked at me, my aunt and uncle and this other couple, whose faces were growing paler still. I held the moment; there was power in it. After all these years I was taking revenge. I was striking a blow, not at Franny, who had done me no harm, but for Barry and Vic and Jack, for the me of my youth, for the innocence of the fifties in which we all had been mired, and maybe, most of all, for the shell that had become my father. It was only an instant, but it was sweet. Then I let them off the hook.

"It was okay," I said. "Nothing happened." They did not seem persuaded. "It was the fifties," I reminded them. "All you did was hold hands in the movies." They waited, uncertain. "A good-night kiss. That was it."

Slowly their color returned. They were not sure what to believe. Suddenly I didn't care. Franny might be the mother of their grandchild, but she was no longer married to their son. It hadn't worked out.

Heck. Me, Jack, Barry, Vic—any of us could have predicted that. She was much too good for him.

I found a clean, well-lighted nursing home that had room for my father. The night before he was moved, I lay in his narrow bed in the residence hotel and stared at the ceiling and wondered how much of him I had become. Now that he could barely speak, I thought of all the things that we had never talked about. I wanted to know what it had been like to cross the ocean in 1914, when you were twelve years old, to start a new life, in a new country, whose language you did not speak. What had it been like, *really*? I was a writer—I was a son!—and I had never asked. I had always believed his generation had been awesome, far more courageous than mine. We as children had baseball; they as children had life. But I had never told him that. Now I did not know if he could hear, I did not know if he would understand. And I doubted that it would matter.

The next morning I called the hospital; he had already been moved. I took a cab to the nursing home in another part of the city. I saw my father in his room, and then a nurse said she would bring him to the visiting lounge. A few minutes later she wheeled him out. There were no other visitors. I made one-way conversation, told him my brother, Saul, who had been away on vacation, unreachable, would be flying down the next day. As I stood beside the wheelchair, my father pressed his face into my belly. I put my arms around his thin shoulders. Neither of us moved. I thought he would pull away in a few moments, but he kept pressing his face into me, harder, with a strength I thought he no longer had. I dared not move. Neither of us spoke as minute after minute passed. I remembered the first time he took me to Ebbets Field, when I was nine years old. We sat in the upper deck behind third base, and at one point Harry (The Hat) Walker of the Phillies fouled a high pop in our direction and I thought I might get a souvenir. The ball was falling one row short and I wondered if it would be okay to reach down over the head of the man in front of me and grab the ball before he did. I had no chance to decide. The ball fell two rows short, and the man in front of me grabbed it away from the man in front of him. I remembered when I was about the same age overhearing my father fibbing to a customer on the phone about some merchandise that had not yet arrived. When he hung up I asked him why he had told a lie. "That's not lying," my father said, "that's business." These random thoughts of a lifetime flitted through my brain like gnats as I stood there, motionless, my back beginning to ache, my father's silent head pressed into my midsection. I'm not sure how long we remained that way, no word being spoken; in my mind it was forty-five minutes; perhaps it was less. We did not move till the nurse returned and said it was time to take him back to his room.

The next day I did not want to return to the nursing home. But I felt it was my duty. I hailed a cab and rode there. As I bent to get out of the backseat in front of the home, something sprung in my back. I could not straighten up. The pain was severe. The cabdriver drove off before I could stop him. Barely able to walk, I dragged myself to the front desk and asked them to call another taxi. My father was twenty yards away in his room but I could not see him like this. I returned to the hotel and went to bed. As I lay there in bed—his bed—my back in spasm, I understood. I understood that with his long, silent embrace the day before my father had said good-bye. I was not supposed to see him again. We were not supposed to speak again.

Two days later, my back still sore but loosening some, my brother drove me directly to the airport, and I returned to Santa Fe. Two weeks later my father died.

The funeral was a simple one. We watched his coffin lowered into the earth beside the grave of my mother. Immediately afterward Carol flew back to New Mexico to continue preparing for an art show she had coming up in a few weeks. I stayed with my brother for a week, receiving visitors, as was the custom. One night my sister-in-law mentioned a diary of my mother's that they had found when selling off my father's things the previous spring. She asked if I would like to have it, and I said I would. I took it to my room and spent the next few hours reading it. The diary was from 1922, when my mother was nineteen years old, five years before she met my father. There was nothing very personal, no startling revelations, just girlish items of the day, such as excitement over a coming New Year's Eve party. There was also a running sequence about how much she wanted a pair of ice skates she was saving for; I had not known my mother was a skater on ice. Typically, when she finally got the skates, she gave them as a gift to a younger sister.

She had also copied into the diary bits of literature and poetry she liked. One paragraph was from *Don Quixote*: "Think well about great things, and know that thought is the only reality in the world. Lift up nature to thine own stature, and let the whole universe be for thee no more than the reflection of thine own heroic soul."

Another line, unattributed, she had written large across an entire page. It said: "Earth's flowers of illusion are kept eternally fresh by death."

One day in 1973, as Carol and I were crossing Park Avenue, I had looked to the north, lined with apartment buildings as far as the eye could see, and I had looked to the south, lined with apartment buildings as far as the eye could see. Hundreds of thousands of people lived in those few visible blocks, and I had turned and said, "How do you think all those people feel, knowing that the world revolves around us?"

By the time we got home an idea had formed for a book. It would be an ironic novel about all those moments in a marriage that seem benign, even humorous, but which, little by little, begin to erode the psychic underpinnings. I jotted a title in a notebook: *Pee Wee and Prune on Good Intentions Street*.

That was another book I didn't write. Instead, in the ensuing years, we lived it, me and the city girl. Our faith in baseball was identical. So were our senses of humor. Our opinions about the movies we saw were invariably the same. We had the same favorite restaurants, we had similar tastes in art, in literature. Neither of us wanted children. We were very much like two peas in a pod.

And after twelve years the pod had become, for both of us, claustrophobic.

Late one afternoon, in May of 1982, in our four-room apartment in Santa Fe, someone said, "Do you think you would be happier if we lived apart for a while?" Carol insists it was I who said it; I am convinced it was she. Whatever the truth, we both felt a sudden exultation. The unspeakable—the unthinkable—had been spoken.

We drove to our favorite restaurant, the Guadalupe Café, to discuss this further. As we ate our juicy burgers we decided to see what it would feel like to take off our wedding bands. We did so simultaneously. Carol took off the gold band that had been made by a jeweler in Greenwich Village. I took off the silver band that had been made by an Indian in Santa Fe. We set them quietly on the table in front of us. When we were finished eating and got up to drive home, we did not put the rings back on.

It had taken more than ten years, but we had gotten the job done, there on Good Intentions Street. Together, we had diced the elk.

When, a few days later, I moved to my own apartment, I left the ax behind.

Wives and Lovers

The day before Thanksgiving I go to the mall to get a head start on Christmas shopping; it will enable me to avoid the crush later on. Strangers pass unseeing, unspeaking, like swimmers in underwater lanes. Outside a store called Sportsmania, I see through the window shelf upon shelf of major league baseball caps, folded one upon another, awaiting the fresh-scrubbed brains of little boys. Or little boys called men. A powerful sensation of want—what my teenage daughter calls *need*—springs up in my chest. There toward the lower right are the official Colorado Rockies caps: black wool with a purple *CR* on the front. My old Brooklyn Dodger cap is at home; I do not own a Mets cap, have for some reason never particularly wanted one. But now I am excited, my desire is becoming fierce, and it is for a Colorado Rockies cap.

I enter the store, move toward the corner, pull out a batch of the caps. Several are clearly too small. I try on a 7 ¼. It is a bit tight, I need a 7 ⅝. They do not seem to have any. I try on a 7 ¾; it is much too loose. I shuffle through the caps again, but cannot find my size. I put on the slightly small one, find a mirror; I like the look of it. The panache. I am not at all certain what is happening. The Lineup of the Invisible, made visible, was not all that inspiring; I had put it from my mind for a week. But now, this sudden fierce quest; this need.

The cap remains too tight. I find a clerk, ask if they have any other sizes. "Not till late February," the man says. "Not till spring training."

The tight cap is beginning to hurt my head. I put it back on the shelf. Directly across the mall I see another sports store. I try there. They are selling the same caps for three dollars more. I am no sucker, I will not pay that much—mainly because they, too, are out of my size.

I walk underwater through the mall, disappointed. I have made no conscious decision to be a Rockies fan; to abandon the Mets. But it has been a long time since I have wanted any material object more than this black wool cap. I want to wear it around town like a talisman. I want to be one of the first, a charter member. I want to show my support . . . for whom, exactly? For what?

I was there in the infancy of the Mets. Do the Rockies need me now? Is some long-suppressed paternal instinct coming out, some need to be a caregiver to these soon-to-be-borns? Or is this merely a baseball midlife crisis, a wimpy need to change athletic socks?

I telephone Collins, the lifelong White Sox fan, up in Taos. I ask if Tom, too, is experiencing this Rocky Mountain high. Tom emphatically is not; he speaks from behind the closed door of his office while out in the art gallery he is running, hundreds of blue-haired ladies mingle at a fund-raising party.

"Hell, no, it never crossed my mind to switch over," Collins says. "First of all, it's a National League team. Second of all, I'm a White Sox fan; there's nothing you can do about it. It's like being born Catholic or Jewish. Even if you become something else, you never will. You're saddled with it. I'm a White Sox fan. Even though Jerry Reinsdorf is the biggest asshole owner in baseball and was one of the prime movers in getting Fay Vincent fired. Just as my dad was a White Sox fan even though Charlie Comiskey owned the team. You just have to overlook these minor things. He'll die someday. The White Sox won't."

I agree with everything Collins has said. I would never have abandoned the Brooklyn Dodgers had they not abandoned me. But were the Brooklyns the one true faith, and the Mets—the Metsies—merely a substitute? It has never seemed so, these past thirty years.

Still, to the Christmas suggestion list posted on the bedroom door, I add: *Colorado Rockies cap, black, wool, size 7 ⅝.*

No other store in town carries these woolen caps. And I stopped believing in Santa Claus before I could turn a double play. There's no place the gang will find one; my request, aside from being blasphemous, is also impossible. Nevertheless, I write it down.

Philip Spitzer is my age minus six months. He has been my friend and my literary agent for twenty years. He's tall, lean, good looking, and smart, and I don't have to flatter him about any of it, it's all true.

If my own first marriage was born of a World Series, Philip's died of one.

As he looks back through the years, two brief scenes in his life stand tall and bronze and slightly tarnished, the Art Deco bookends of a love.

The first scene takes place in France in 1962. While taking courses in Dijon, Philip meets a nice French girl. The courtship is swift, the marriage delightful. The only thing Philip hates are the Parisian traffic jams. As he curses and fumes at the tie-ups and the other drivers, Anne-Marie, seated beside him, reads aloud to him the baseball news in the morning's *International Herald Tribune.* The only problem is that Anne-Marie does not speak English back then; she sounds out the words phonetically, in her French accent, not understanding a syllable she is pronouncing:

Dun Mue-ler boonted heem to thrid, ahnd Wee Lee Mays heet ze baul o-ver ze fance. . . .

Listening, Philip breaks up laughing; the tension of the traffic flows out from his body in a cooling stream of affection.

The second scene takes place in Forest Hills, thirteen years and three children later. It is October of 1975, the Red Sox and Cincinnati are playing in the World Series; Philip has lugged a TV set up to his attic office, he's sprawled on the floor watching the sixth game with the two younger children, a girl and a boy, aged eleven and ten. The game is a close one; it's one of the best World Series games ever. The score is tied when Anne-Marie yells up that there is school tomorrow, it's ten o'clock, the children must go to bed. Philip tells her to let them be, that the game is exciting. Anne-

Marie is adamant, obstinate; it's bedtime. She has never cared about baseball, has never comprehended the obvious truth that to her husband, *Wee Lee Mays heeting ze baul* is a passion. She marches the protesting children downstairs.

Philip already knew that something devious was happening in his marriage, something they would soon have to pluck out of the terrible silence and face. It had been on his mind for weeks. But now, hearing Anne-Marie shooing the kids off to bed, mindless of the baseball game, refusing to understand that some things are so important to a man that he wants to share them with his children—and that this particular World Series game is one of them—Philip grows sad and weary. He tries to perk up, sprawled alone on the floor, his kids gone to bed, when Carlton Fisk hits the classic home run down the left field line that ends the game in the twelfth inning, that sends the Series into a seventh game. But he knows that something more has happened this night. He knows that no amount of urgent body language can will his marriage from curving foul. He knows they will not deal with it. If his wife will not understand such a simple thing, then the marriage cannot be saved.

Two weeks later Anne-Marie announces that she is moving out. Nearly two decades later, wrapped though he is in the warm embrace of a happier match, the breakup still rankles, woven like a bloody wound into the fabric of the 1975 World Series, into the frantic waving arms of Carlton Fisk, into the merciless stare of the Big Green Monster of Fenway Park, into the merciless stare of the other green monster that dwells in us all.

Philip's parents were immigrants from France, with no knowledge of baseball, but they took him as a boy to ball games at the Polo Grounds, back in 1947, and at Yankee Stadium. On one opening day at the Stadium, with Eddie Lopat pitching, his mother earned the righteous wrath of the crowd; while the horsehide was being belted and Yankee runners circled the bases, she calmly ignored these All-American carryings-on and read a book. In French.

A Yankee fan at the start, Philip spent his childhood hoping he would not grow tall; he wanted to be like "Little Phil" Rizzuto. He did grow tall, however; and though a Yankee fan, the boy, apparently possessing as generous a soul then as he would grow up to demonstrate later, made of Jackie Robinson a higher hero. What turmoil there must have been in his gut when, at the age of eleven, under the influence of his best friend, who was three years older, he switched his allegiance to the Giants, with Little Phil still scooping grounders in The Bronx and Jackie Robinson stealing home in Brooklyn. It was a prescient move, however, this turning to the Giants, made as it was in the spring of 1951. . . .

For twenty years I have known him, known that his baseball fanaticism equals my own, and for twenty years I took it for granted that he rooted for the Red Sox in one league and the Mets in the other: the Red Sox because for ten consecutive years he traveled to Boston to meet up with his brother and one of his writer friends to go to opening day at Fenway Park; the Mets because when I met him and for many years thereafter he lived in Queens. Only this week did I discover that I was wrong twice over. The Red Sox games were a friendly ritual, not a rooting passion; and of the proximity of Shea to Forest Hills he was uncaring. Ever since Horace Stoneham stole his Giants west in 1957 to help the sainted O'Malley save the world, Philip has chosen a different team to root for every year—always an underdog, like feeding a mongrel cur in the street. This news astonished me, convinced as I have always been that true baseball fans are, above all, loyal. Yet here is Philip who every morning of his adult life has turned with his morning coffee to the sports pages first, to check the baseball scores in summer, to check the baseball deals in winter—here is Philip admitting to be a rooting dilettante. (That word is mine, not his.) Of all the proverbs and sayings that have been handed down to us by presumably wiser ancestors, the one I never understood was the frequent reference to "the exception that proves the rule." I saw no logic in that statement. Why does an exception prove anything? Still, there it is, and my cap is off, Philip: you are the exception that proves the rule.

And what kind of cap will yours be this coming season?

"I'm thinking about Baltimore," Philip says.

The underdog is ever his passion, be it unpublished writers whose literary works he hopefully drags from one prospective publisher to another, or kids in Harlem to whom he teaches writing when his frantic schedule permits. He remembers one night crowding onto his bed with his three kids to watch *The Jackie Robinson Story*, with its message that he felt every kid must learn. And he, the grown-up, crying throughout the film.

Like me, like so many, Philip endured a neighborhood nemesis during the stickball games of youth, a terrible old lady who would run out of her house and steal the ball every time it landed in her yard. My old lady, previously described, was Mrs. Newman; Philip's was Grace Kelly. (What can I tell you? Even then the lad was suave.) Eventually this particular Grace Kelly, who never moved to Monaco, wrote a blistering "anonymous" letter to Philip's parents with the general message that Frogs such as themselves ought to slither back across the ocean, from whence they had come. Philip's father, who was a lawyer and a linguist, calmly corrected the spelling and grammar mistakes and returned the letter to Mrs. Kelly.

From childhood on, the will to be a major league ballplayer burned in Philip on a low flame, never fully extinguished by the passing years, by the onset of manhood, by the birth of other careers. He was another son of immigrants who became an all-American boy—and an eternal boy. In his early thirties Philip underwent back surgery; this did not stop him, upon his recovery, from playing on a publisher's softball team in Central Park. He had moved by then from shortstop to third—advancing age will do that—and he made diving stops of an inordinate number of hard ground balls, because he could not bend over and field them more routinely. By his own admission many of the plays were sensational. An agent friend of Philip's developed a working relationship with the Pittsburgh Pirates by selling some of their players' biographies, and Philip, at the age of thirty-five, asked his friend if he could be invited to spring training: if he could get a tryout with the Pirates. The friend said that could be arranged;

Philip packed his bag and prepared to fly to Florida. He was sure he could beat out Richie Hebner for the third-base job.

"Really!" he insists.

At the last moment the Pirates decided their camp was over-crowded. The magic journey never took place. Philip had to settle again for softball in Central Park. As a kind of literary penance for his hubris, he has spent the eighteen years since reading manuscripts about guys who drive to Florida and talk their way into a tryout and make the major leagues, without ever having played organized ball before. Most of the manuscripts do not get published.

On the day he turned forty, Philip grew sad. It had little to do with intimations of mortality, with a midlife crisis. He grew sad because on that day, along with the candles on his cake, the flame blew out; on that day he knew for certain that he would never make it to the bigs. On his fortieth birthday, for him as for millions of men, his biological clock shut down. He was banished to the dugout forever.

Except . . . except in the realm of love's sweet charity.

Flash forward another ten years. It is the sixth day of August, 1989. It is Philip's fiftieth birthday. He has been married for two years to an actress named Mary Armstrong, whom he met while both were vacationing in Paris—again!—willing, seductive city of the sultry eyes. They are spending his birthday at a beach house on Long Island: Philip and Mary and his kids and a few friends. They loll on the beach, they swim in the Atlantic. Philip swims far out from shore, alone, then turns to head back, but there is a powerful undertow pulling him farther out, and for many seconds he makes no progress; his arms grow weary; he fears that today, on his fiftieth birthday, he will die. Finally, with a surge of strength and endurance, he beats the undertow, he swims with long, lean strokes back to shore.

As the sun begins to set they are all in the beach house, milling about, sipping drinks before they barbecue dinner. From across the room, where Mary is sitting with some of the others, he hears the sounds of a baseball announcer. It penetrates his consciousness only dimly at first. Someone waves him over, and he joins the group listening to the game on the radio. It appears to be a World Series game—here in August—it must be a replay of some sort, he thinks—the Giants are playing, it might be the 1954 series—but no, the players coming to bat are current ones. And the Giants are playing the Yankees, "who are two outs away from a champagne shower," the announcer says. Philip is not sure what is going on. He hears the crowd noises, the announcer saying it is the bottom of the ninth, last game of the series, the Giants trailing by a run. Dave Righetti has come in from the bullpen to face Kevin Mitchell. There's a man on first, one out, the Yankees leading 4–3. Mitchell is 0 for 4, the announcer says. He takes the first pitch for a strike. Brett Butler is leading off first. Mitchell hits a line smash to Sax at second, but Butler gets back to first before he can be doubled up. The Giants are down to their last out. Philip, still puzzled, listens to the announcer:

"Donell Nixon is being called back. That's Philip Spitzer at the bat rack, and he's coming up to bat. . . . Well, what a story this is. Roger Craig is betting the whole season on a seldom-used ball-player, who's shown he has power, but really hasn't had a taste of this kind of pressure. In just 162 at bats at Phoenix, Spitzer hit fifteen homers."

In the background the crowd is roaring. Philip Spitzer stands transfixed in Long Beach, listening with rising emotion, as Philip Spitzer comes to bat in the World Series in Candlestick Park, a continent away.

"But who'd ever think that a fifty-year-old teacher in a Harlem tutorial program, who owns his own literary agency, would be up here in this situation?" the announcer says. "It'll be Philip Spitzer, from Forest Hills, New York, with the world on his shoulders right now. . . . The first pitch from Righetti—in there, strike one, a breaking ball at the knees. Spitzer weighs about, oh, a hundred eighty pounds on a six-foot frame, he's got the perfect baseball build. And he's always wanted to play in the big leagues. He came up in August, hit .286 in just fourteen at bats. And that big pinch homer he belted last month—well, that's probably what stuck in

Craig's mind, and that's why he's up here now with the game on the line. Okay, Righetti's next pitch—low and away, the count even at one and one."

Moisture is forming in Philip Spitzer's eyes. *Do, it Philip, come on, you can do it.* Rooting himself on.

". . . Righetti goes to his stretch, looks the runner back to first, now delivers. Swung on! There's a deep drive to left, way back, way back, Barfield to the wall, but it's gone!" The crowd cheering wildly in the background now, the crowd going crazy. "The Giants win the World Series. Philip Spitzer's two-out, two-run homer to left off Dave Righetti does it. Well, this has to be one of the greatest moments in baseball history. Baseball has a brand-new hero as the Giants are mobbing Philip Spitzer as he crosses home. Now they're picking him up and carrying him off on their shoulders, while the Yankees are in shock in their dugout, some with tears in their eyes. Just an incredible finish, thanks to Philip Spitzer, as the San Francisco Giants win the World Series."

The crowd in Candlestick Park continues to roar. Like the Yankees, Philip Spitzer, fifty years old, standing among his friends in Long Beach, is crying over this dream home run . . . crying tears of thanks for Mary, who ordered the blessed tape . . . for lovely Mary, who understands.

Good-bye to 1975. Goodbye to Carlton Fisk. Good-bye to all that.

The Sunday after Thanksgiving, as I drove through town, I passed Canyon Road Park, a broad expanse of grass often deserted in cold weather. On the baseball field this day a man was pitching a baseball to a boy with a bat. Both were wearing winter clothing. The man could have been anywhere from thirty-five to fifty, the boy perhaps nine or ten. I saw the boy swing only once— and miss—as I drove by on Alameda. The sight of the two of them out there alone on this late fall afternoon was at once startling, joyous, and, in an unexpected way, momentarily depressing. I realized what a rare sight this is in the West, a father teaching his son to play ball (if that's what they were, father and son) instead of abandoning instruction to the organized ministrations of some

Little League. I felt gladdened too; it was like coming upon a bright yellow bird amid the snows of winter; and then, as I might with the summer bird, I pondered the why of it. I hoped neither had dragged the other, not father, not son, that this out-of-season workout, serious in its implications, was a mutual desire.

The following weekend it snowed. Thin hard flakes barely graduated from rain fell all day Saturday and into Saturday night, and on Sunday kept coming, now larger, like pillow feathers. By the time the snow quit there were fifteen inches on the picnic table in the backyard, on the cover of the grill, on all the visible world. That is a lot of snow for this city. There would be no more baseball in the park this winter. The weather remained cold all week, the snow remained on the ground, we took turns shuttling the child, now seventeen, to school and back, to her after-school job and back, because the car she drives does not handle well in snow nor on the icy patches that formed every night on the streets, that slicked black and invisible near stop signs. The following weekend, as if punching in on some new and furry wintertime clock, the snow worked its beauty and its misery again, eight inches this time, equally hazardous. Early December and already more snow than we get during most years. Between the two snows I followed in the newspapers the winter baseball meetings, bright bird in warm flight, held this year in Louisville, still the home of Pee Wee Reese. What transpired there reminded me of Jack Kennedy's remark after he hosted a group of Nobel Prize winners: "It was the greatest gathering of intellect at the White House since Thomas Jefferson dined alone."

In this era of free-agency a river of cash flowed green. Here is what happened in those two days of meetings between the winter snows: Barry Bonds, the National League's Most Valuable Player, went from the Pirates to the Giants; David Cone, the major league strikeout leader for three straight years, went from Toronto to Kansas City; Greg Maddux, the National League Cy Young Award winner, went from the Cubs to Atlanta; Andre Dawson went from the Cubs to the Red Sox; Randy Myers went from San Diego to the Cubs; Mark Gardner went from Montreal to Kansas City; Todd Worrell went from the Cardinals to the Dodgers; Dave Stewart went from Oakland to Toronto; Ivan Calderon went from Montreal to the Red Sox; Bob Ojeda went from the Dodgers to Cleveland; Dave Magadan went from the Mets to the Marlins. It was the greatest mass movement of baseball talent in a single week since the Red Sox traded Babe Ruth to the Yankees.

In the summer of '82, axless in Paradise, I sought the comfort of slow horses and fast women. Some days, such as the Fourth of July that year, the two got turned around.

I had published that spring my third novel, called *Midge & Decker*, about two underachievers who spent most of their time at Santa Fe Downs. To garner some joint publicity the track named a race after the book, scheduled it for Independence Day, and asked me to present the blanket to the winner. They tossed in a free box up in the Jockey Club.

My best bet at the time (as Raymond Chandler might have put it) was a twenty-six-year-old filly named Valorie, a sweet young lady with whom I'd shared a feed bag several times. I invited her to join me at the track along with David Hill, my frequent track companion, and David's wife, Susan. The "*Midge & Decker* Purse" would be run as the eighth race on the card. But this little tortured vignette is about the sixth.

A field of twelve cheap horses—$4,000 claimers—would be going seven furlongs. Poring over the *Daily Racing Form* the night before, I developed a strong interest in the one-horse, Gary's First. The *Racing Form* showed a series of past performances that ran from mediocre to stop-and-shop; Gary's First would be a longer shot than Walter Mondale. But he'd shown a bit of life his last outing. And they were switching to a girl jockey. For most of the crowd this would be further reason to stay off the horse, thus increasing the odds; for me it was an incentive to bet. In the loudly macho Southwest there is a strong prejudice against females in general and female jockeys in particular. Girl race riders had to ride like the fierce spring wind to get good mounts. They had to try harder, in every race. With a weak field such as this, I reasoned, getting the most out of a horse, even a walking glue factory like Gary's First, might be enough to bring him home in front.

While researching my novel I had spent two summers back-stretch at the track, amid the goats and roosters and illegal Mexican grooms, and I'd gotten a lot of colorful data from a dark-eyed, ponytailed, spunky race rider named Marie Irigaray. I'd also won big on the frequent occasions when she brought long shots home in front. I always followed the horses she rode, and usually bet on them. One day one of them, an improving brown filly named Magic Salrina, running in her first stakes race, was going off at odds listed on the tote board as 99–1, the highest the board could handle. The filly had been a late entry and Marie was off riding in Denver that day, but the *Racing Form* showed the filly had run her last race only a fifth of a second slower than the best clocking of the 6–5 favorite, who had won six straight. I put a ridiculously cautious two bucks on Magic Salrina, a stretch runner. The favorite tired in a speed duel, and Magic Salrina swept past the entire field in the stretch to win by several lengths, with the majesty of a grand slam. She paid a whopping $288.80 for my $2.00 bet, which at actual odds of 143–1 is still the highest win payoff in the history of the Downs.

Another day, in a trifecta race, there were two legitimate favorites and an otherwise hopeless field. A late rider change just before the race put my friend Marie on a terrible mount. There was no way the horse would win, but I figured Marie might just get her to outrun the other clunkers and come in third. I bet the trifecta that way, Marie did as I thought she might, and I tucked $113 into my wallet. The name of the horse she rode that day was Gary's First.

That had been a couple of years before. Marie Irigaray was no longer riding. But horseplayers, even two-dollar bettors, have memories as long as time. When I saw that once again, for the first time in two years, Gary's First would be getting a girl jockey—this one was named Harla Webb—I couldn't resist.

The track was crowded on the Fourth of July, the sun shone brightly, my young date was beautiful, the Sangre de Cristo—Blood of Christ—Mountains were shimmering like a mirage in the distance behind the paddock. I won enough to break even during the first few races. Then the sixth came around, the horses being saddled far below our grandstand box.

"Who do you like?" David asked.

"I like the one-horse," I said.

A bit sheepishly I explained my female-jock reasoning. David was aware of this emotional weakness of mine; a former teacher who'd explained James Joyce to college students, he preferred a more rational approach.

"I think the twelve should run away with it," he said.

Puzzled, I checked the *Form*; I hadn't seen a horse in this race that could run away with a carrot. Then I saw my mistake. There had been a scratch, and one of the also-eligibles had gotten in, a horse called Mean and Lean. I studied the past performances. Mean and Lean had been a consistent winner at this price. After a long layoff he had run the week before at a higher price, at a shorter distance. Clearly a prep race. Today he would clean up. I told David I agreed.

I looked at the tote board. Mean and Lean was the weak favorite at 3 to 1. Gary's First was 25 to 1. I decided to play both horses in an exacta. Five minutes before post time the 12–1 exacta was paying $800. I had my bet.

The race was a slow-motion unfolding of prescience and beauty that happens maybe once in a hundred races. Mean and Lean broke smartly out of the twelve hole and took the lead. At the quarter pole he was ahead by two lengths. At the half mile he had opened up four. Gary's First was ninth at the quarter, deep in the pack. At the half he was still ninth. But by the top of the stretch Harla Webb had moved him up to fifth. And now in the stretch he was flying along the rail—as fast as a $4,000 horse can fly—under Webb's urgent whipping. Right at the wire he leapt forward and got his nose down for second, half a length behind the tiring Mean and Lean, a head in front of the wobbly third horse.

Birds were singing in the eaves of the grandstand as I waited for the results of the photo; we were right on the finish line and my vision is 20-20; I knew I had won the exacta. When the board lit up OFFICIAL, the payoff had come down some, but the exacta still paid $532.20 for my $2 bet. I had never won more at the track, not even on Magic Salrina. I squeezed the knee of the gentle Valorie, whose admiring eyes looked even bigger and deeper than usual. I ordered a round of beers. Then I noticed that David was looking glum. David, it turned out, had played the twelve on top with a bunch of other horses—but he hadn't bought my logic about the one. Now he was destroying himself in the gut.

There was nothing I could do to console him. "I better cash this ticket before I lose it," I said, and I walked up to the cashier's window with the biggest win of my life.

At the window I couldn't find the ticket. Not in any of my pockets. Not in my wallet. Nowhere. Again and again I checked my clothing's every orifice, with mounting panic. I hurried back to our table and looked on the ground beneath the table, beneath my chair. Nothing. My friends were horrified, and helped me search the immediate area. Nothing. I retraced my steps from the window, back to the window, searching the floor. Nothing. A $532 ticket, and I had lost it. For ten minutes I looked for the ticket among a myriad of others on the floor. Finally, miserably, I gave up. It is bad enough to lose a winning ticket. It is impossible, I knew, to find one.

I felt sick to my stomach over the self-portrait I had painted—the proud and dashing bachelor author as mindless idiot. But I needed to preserve my pride in front of Valorie; I had friends with me, and a blanket to present two races later. I tried to focus on the positive side. The win would count in the betting records I kept with the accuracy of a prying conscience; I'd merely been mugged on the way home, that's all.

David left the table, still visibly upset at his own costly prudence, and stayed away for seven or eight minutes more. I thought he was merely feeling unsociable, that he needed to be alone, and I understood; I would have felt the same way myself. When finally he came back, he dropped a ticket on the table in front of me. The first bet on the ticket was a 12–1 exacta; that was followed by a few other combinations I had bet with Gary's First. I was astounded as I touched the silver-colored slip of grace, afraid it would disintegrate in my hand.

"There was a ticket on the floor near an old lady's foot," David explained. "I couldn't bend down, she would have thought I was being fresh. Finally, she moved, and I turned it over."

My emotions were careening. Midge, in my novel, was a down-and-outer who spent her days picking up tossed-away tickets at the Downs. This had been the real *Midge & Decker* Purse.

Carefully, I cashed the reborn ticket, carrying it to the window as cautiously as a hand grenade. I gave David a finder's fee. I bought a round of hamburgers. Valorie, the first postmarital conquest of my dreams, did not come home with me—never did, sweet thing, she had a boyfriend in Albuquerque—but all in all it was that rarest of racetrack events, one in which you take home not only the awful anecdote, but the hard cash too.

The scene is related here also as a metaphor. Only six months after my marriage was lost, I stumbled upon La Donna.

The Rockies have signed Daryl Boston to a one-year contract. This pleases me very much, because it gives the Colorado team a Met. That's not many, but it's one third the number of Mets the Mets have: theirs being Doc Gooden, Howard Johnson, and a questionable Sid Fernandez. (A mild case could be made for John Franco, but only because he's from Brooklyn.)

I am pleased, too, that the Rockies noticed they were short an outfielder.

A tale of He and She:

He goes for lunch, in the autumn of '82, to a place he used to frequent, a place he somehow has not been since his marriage broke up. The food is good, the long room bright and airy, with large windows, with open bins that hold all manner of cheeses, smoked meats, and other delicacies. He notices a waitress he has never seen before. She is slim and graceful, has long brown hair, gray eyes, a genuine smile she turns on customers. He hopes she will wait on him.

She does not wait on him. She does not look at him. He is not sitting in her station.

He watches her work as he eats his submarine sandwich. He decides that along with swift efficiency she displays the gentleness of a fawn. The next day he returns. He sits at one of the tables that she was waiting on the day before.

She does not wait on him. She waits on the table where he had been sitting yesterday. He does not know there are four stations in the restaurant, and that the waitresses rotate every day.

On the third day he peers through one of the large windows before he enters. He notes where she is working. He goes in and sits at a table in that region.

She does not wait on him. The stations are erratic, like a gerry-mandered district. He is one table off. She carries glasses of wine, plates of sandwiches, bowls of soup, cups of coffee, to tables all around him. But not to his.

He watches her move with smooth efficiency in the casual restaurant uniform of blue jeans and a white shirt. He thinks she looks very good in white. He can tell she really cares that her customers get good service. He sees her noticing no one who is not in her station.

She tells another waitress: "That geek keeps coming in and staring at me."

He listens for her name when the kitchen puts up food on the counter. He sees her respond to the call of "La Donna." He knows of only one other La Donna, the wife of the former senator from Oklahoma, La Donna Harris. He rolls the name on his tongue with his sandwich. La Donna. It is the prettiest name he has ever heard.

She makes a point of not returning his gaze.

He comes back another day. He does not see her. He feels a touch of panic, though he knows nothing of her, of her life. Perhaps this is only her day off. Still, he notes the depth of his disappointment.

She enters the restaurant, not in her work clothes. Holding her hand is a little girl, about six years old. The child is very cute, very pretty.

He thinks: *The child is surely hers. But what of the father? Is he still in the league?*

She picks up her paycheck and leaves with the child.

On Sunday the restaurant is closed. He goes to another place, alone, for brunch. The place is mobbed, every table is taken, but the wait should not be long, he is told. He waits. He then he sees her. At a table near the wall. Alone with the child.

He waits. He waits for a table to open up. There are more than fifty tables in the place, all filled.

The table that empties first is the table next to hers. They seat him there.

He orders his scrambled eggs, his French fries, his bagel, his coffee.

She is writing in a notebook, drinking coffee; the little girl is eating birthday cake.

His food arrives. He eats, glancing at her while she writes. He tries to think of a way to start a conversation.

She finishes her coffee.

He is afraid she will leave now. He tells himself: *God did ninety percent of the work. God opened up the table next to hers. Ten percent I have to do myself.*

She speaks with the child. He cannot hear their conversation. Only later—much later—will she tell him what the child said. The child said, "Mommy, that man is staring at us." And she replied to the child, "Don't look at him, he's a geek."

He doesn't know this then. He finishes his brunch. *It is now or never,* he thinks. He steels himself. He has an opening line precariously in mind. He stands, he approaches their table, a tremor of anxiety in his chest. "Excuse me," he says. "I've noticed you working in The Winery. I would like to ask you a question."

She says, "What's the question?"

He says: "What does a lady named La Donna name her daughter?"

She looks at him curiously. She answers: "Amara."

He replies, quick as a whip: "Huh?" Then he repeats the musical word as a question: "Amara?"

She says it again.

He looks at the child. "That's a very pretty name," he says.

The child says nothing. The child doesn't tell him her mommy called him a geek.

He manages, somehow, to string this into a conversation. For five minutes, perhaps ten, he stands beside the table as they talk.

She asks him, at last, to join them if he would like.

The child wonders why.

He brings over his chair, his cold coffee.

Years later—even a decade later—in moments of panic or nostalgia, he will relive this scene, and he will wonder: what would have happened if the child's name had been Joan? Or Susan? Or Barbara?

But it wasn't.

Two days later he goes to the restaurant. Focused as a laser beam, he locates, at last, her station.

She serves him his soup and sandwich.

He takes out a small piece of paper, he scrawls a one-sentence note to her. *If you are not attached,* he writes, *would you like to have dinner with me sometime?* Beneath the sentence he draws four small boxes, and he puts a word beside each:

Yes
No
Maybe
Drop dead

He hands her the folded note. He watches as she takes it behind the counter, as she opens it immediately, as she smiles slightly and chuckles; as she picks up a pen and makes a swift, bold mark. His heart leaps at her grin, at her swift, bold answer.

She approaches his table shyly, she hands him the folded note. Shyly she walks away.

His heart is lilting, tremulous, as he unfolds the paper.

He finds a strong, decisive check beside *Maybe*.

She is very busy, working two jobs to support her child; nearly two months pass before they go out on a date.

He takes her to a Brazilian movie, in Portuguese. He thinks the movie is awful; she seems to be enjoying it. Not till weeks later will she confess that she had not wanted to put her glasses on, could not read the subtitles, had no idea what the film was about. He tells her she did not miss much.

He takes her, after the film, to his apartment.

She tells him of the ghost with whom she is warring, ghost of the previous occupant of the house in which she lives—a biker who was murdered there. She tells him of the unicorns she wants to raise.

He plies her with Amaretto, with Billie Holiday.

She tells him she has decided to give up men in order to raise her child.

He kisses her good-night, softly, and in that softness he does not find deep resolve.

She drives off down the street in her red Datsun pickup, which backfires like a pistol shot.

He, who had expected he would be playing the amorous field for years, takes out a large pad and a dark brown crayon. He scrawls on the pad, in large, ominous letters: *This Is Big Trouble.*

When, by February, she has yet to see him bite the head off a live chicken, which technically is the defining talent of geeks, she is trusting enough to take him to one of her special places, a sloping mesa twenty miles from town, upon whose barren rocks ancient Indians carved the images of snakes, palms, wolves, forked lightning—all manner of rustic wisdom. Hand in hand they climb among the rocks beneath a sky of blue and the eye of only the sun, and when they emerge from a small secluded grotto of ancient boulders, brushing pale dirt from their clothing, he tells her that one day a towering ear of blue corn will grow there, will reach as high as the clouds, blue corn on which the ancient spirits will travel, will play, will make new visits, corn sprung from the warm commingled seed with which together they have watered the parched but thawing earth.

Every so often, they agree, they will come back to check it out.

A shortstop and a pitcher were two of the women with whom La Donna worked. They spent most of their days carving the meats and cheeses in the deli, while La Donna waited tables or tended bar. In slow moments in late afternoon there was often much laughter among the three of them. The place closed at six o'clock, and when spring arrived, the shortstop and the pitcher would hurry off to practice, and then to play, in the city's women's softball league, in which they had been fixtures for years. On warm or even windy evenings, of which there were many, La Donna and I began to drive to one city park or another to watch the pitcher and the shortstop play. To root them on.

Their team had a manager—a man—but no base coaches; the women who were not at bat took turns in the coaching boxes. Noticing this, I offered at the start of one game to coach first base. I was welcomed aboard, and for the next two seasons spent most games in the coaching box, while the pitcher, the shortstop, and their teammates battled for city trophies in front of cheering husbands and helter-skelter kids. It was my first active (more or less) role on a diamond in fifteen years; I waited with a forgotten anticipation for the games each week, though I was both a part of the team and not—not really. In one key game an opposing batter belted a long drive between the left and center fielders with two runners aboard; it was a triple, and gave the enemy the lead. I told the pitcher to put on an appeal play; I'd seen the batter miss first base. She hesitated, then threw to first, and the umpire called the batter out. The runs did not count, the victory was preserved. I basked in a secret pride. It was the first ball game I had won in many a year without superstitiously moving a napkin, a toothpick.

The pitcher was a quiet, soft-spoken woman whose teenage son played drums in a rock band. One night La Donna and I went to hear the band practice in an isolated garage far out in the desert; the boys thought La Donna might like to become their manager. Before they started to play, the band members offered us earplugs; we declined, of course: we were not sissies; and to accept would have been impolite. The band began to play, the music from their electronic instruments blasting from six-foot speakers a few feet from our faces. It was the loudest sustained sound I've ever heard outside a dentist's chair. When they were through playing, and we tried to tell them how much we liked their music, the band members first removed the earplugs they themselves had been using. I walked around deaf for two days.

The shortstop was a fun-loving woman who liked to joke and

laugh. She had an all-athlete family: a teenage daughter who played right field and later joined the Navy, a husband who played in a hardball league, a teenage son who also played hardball. She lived not far from one of the softball fields, and sometimes after a game a few of us would adjourn to the shortstop's house to laugh and drink some beer.

After two seasons the manager of the ladies' team left. The new manager brought with him a couple of inept nieces and their friends, and his blatant favoritism led to open dissension and hostility on the team. Tired of being ignored at first base by the newcomers, who willfully ran past my stop signs and got themselves thrown out at second base, or who stopped at first when I waved them on, I removed myself from the coaching box. Soon after, when a pigheaded new owner bought the restaurant and started running it into the ground, La Donna quit her job. We still went as often as possible to watch the pitcher and the shortstop play, but gradually, as happens, we began to lose touch with them.

A year or so later, late one afternoon, the shortstop and her husband needed to drive across town to pick up their daughter. Their son said he would wait at home. He was fifteen years old, a three-letter man in high school, including baseball, and when they returned home twenty minutes later, they discovered that he had taken a shotgun down from a closet and blown himself all over the front room. No one except the boy knew why.

That was years ago. No one knows why still—unless life, for reasons of its own, had decided it was time to wipe the bright smile off the face of the shortstop.

If that was the intent, life succeeded. Sometimes even the dancing marble meets its match.

One of the guys Philip Spitzer grew up with in South Jamaica, in Queens, N.Y., was a fellow named Richard Dreyer. It is Philip's recollection that Dreyer used to get beat up a lot by black kids; Philip mentions this only because, later in life, Dreyer would choose to become a Big Brother to a couple of black kids in East Harlem. It is Richard Dreyer's recollection that Philip got beat up more than he did. "I could run faster," Dreyer says. "When God gives you a gift you have to use it. I had the good legs."

At fifty-three Dreyer has been an insurance man in New York for thirty years. His life has been entwined with baseball as fan, player, and coach ever since his days in elementary school. A lifelong Yankee fan, he used to cry as a kid whenever Joe DiMaggio struck out.

"The first day I ever played hooky from school, it was in the second grade," Dreyer recalls. "My friend Skeet and I. It was Joe DiMaggio Day in Yankee Stadium. We hid in the bushes—I went to a Catholic school in Jamaica—we planned this, second graders or third graders. We went to school in the morning. At lunchtime we hid, because we were supposed to be walking back from lunch. We had saved money on the side. We walked about a mile, got on the subway, went to Yankee Stadium, got bleacher seats for sixty cents. Johnny Lindell hit a home run They played Boston. Dom DiMaggio was there. But Joe D. and the Yankees were our guys."

As for playing the game—well, let Dreyer continue.

"My baseball career is really tied around a guy by the name of Joe Austin. Joe Austin is a guy who worked nights for Piel's Brewery in Brooklyn. He used to coach teams in South Jamaica. He gave all the teams Irish names. He started right after World War Two. His first team was called the Celtics, and then there were the Gnomes, the Shamrocks, the Blarney Boys, and the Leprechauns. I was a Leprechaun.

"He started these teams at St. Monica's Church. They played basketball in the winter—he also had a girls' team called the Colleens—and in the summer he had baseball. All the kids in the neighborhood played. I started playing baseball with Joe when I was about twelve years old. I played a little bit before with kids in the neighborhood in the Police Athletic League, but my first real baseball on an organized basis for a whole summer was with Joe Austin."

"This was real baseball?" I ask. "Or softball?"

"I only talk about baseball in my life," Dreyer says. He sounds slightly insulted, probably with good reason.

"I played the outfield. Three teams older than me—which

would be Blarney Boys, Shamrocks, Gnomes—maybe the Gnomes—Mario Cuomo played. Mario lived around the corner from me. But he was older, I didn't really know him. I played baseball with Joe right through September of last year."

"What?" I ask. "Last year?"

"The first Sunday after Labor Day he has Old Timers' Day. He's now eighty-eight years old. Last year he coached about thirty or forty games. When he was eighty years old he had coached for fifty years. We had a big get-together. He went through every race, creed, religion, there could be. All my memories about baseball are from Joe. I last played for Joe when I was about seventeen years old. Then I played four years of college baseball, at St. Francis College in Brooklyn. I stayed in touch with Joe. For this Old Timer's game I went back to Jamaica High. I was two for three. Against a twenty-six-year-old. Two shots, let me tell you. But they've got aluminum bats now."

When Dreyer finished college he got an offer to go to a minor league camp with the Boston Braves. But he pulled a hamstring in his senior year, and the leg was bothering him. He accepted a job coaching baseball at Pace College in Manhattan, and he decided to stay there. He coached for five years.

"Tell him the story about . . ." That's his wife of eleven years, Lisa, speaking in the background.

"I got baseball stories coming out of my ears," Dreyer says. "I'll tell you two stories. One—there were a couple of kids who played in Queens for Joe. They played in the high school. And no one was really helping them go to college. A guy named John Smiley, who had played for Joe, told me about these kids, Danny Martinez and Joe Bucchari. I went over and talked to Danny. In his senior year, in a seven-inning game against Flushing High School, he struck out seventeen out of twenty-one batters. Everybody told me Danny was great. There was a guy I worked with who had gone to Delta State College in Cleveland, Mississippi. The coach there was Boo Ferriss, who was a Boston Braves guy."

"Red Sox?" I offer, politely.

"Red Sox, right. So I called Ferriss up, I told him I was a coach, I had these kids who could really play ball, would he be willing to take them. He said he couldn't offer a scholarship, but if they got down there he'd get them into school. So the kids went. I got letters from the guys, I got a call from the coach a year later. They won the little college World Series. And he said, 'You know, Coach'—he had a southern accent—he said, 'You know, Danny could pitch, he had like a one point three-four average—ERA— and of course John was MVP in the All-Star game. Joey is one grade down from them but he's a strong catcher. You got any more boys up in New York, you send them down.' They all got scholarships and continued on at Delta State."

(This was not the John Smiley who would later pitch in the majors.)

"A little later on, I was over at Danny's house, and I was talking to his mother. His mother was very excited about what had happened, and very happy about her kid going to school, and asked if she could do anything. 'What could we do for you?' I said, 'What you could do, as I told Danny, John and Joey, is just make sure that your sons continue doing what I did. I played with Joe Austin. And they played with Joe. We just keep trying to help each other. So why don't they just keep that in mind as they go through their lives—to help other kids?' Well, I got a letter back a few years later. And they had gotten seven kids into college. On scholarships.

"At this Old Timers' day I saw Danny. He's still pitching. He's forty-two, maybe forty-three, he's pitching in the Alliance League, which is a very good league. And Joe and John Smiley stayed down in Mississippi and are coaching baseball down there. This is twenty years after they got out of school."

The second story Richard Dreyer tells me is less civic minded, but a whole lot funnier—if you don't mind wooden-leg stories.

"Pace College, where I coached, was playing Queens College one day. It was the seventh inning, Pace was ahead by a run, there was one out, Queens College had the tying run on third. I had a right-handed pitcher named Jerry. The field was noisy, the Queens fans were yelling. There was two balls and a strike on the batter.

"Now, Jerry, the pitcher, had a wooden leg, from the knee joint down. He had a knee joint. And a slight stump underneath the knee joint. The wooden leg tied over the knee and up around the thigh, I think. It was all wood in those days. He had his spikes on, and you couldn't tell he had a wooden leg. Because his knee could bend. Anyway, he winds up—he's a righty. Now don't forget, you're coming off your left leg, your right leg comes around with your right hand—and he throws, and the ball goes in, and the leg rips right off. It was flying to the plate—halfway to the plate.

"Dead silence. The leg is lying halfway between home and the pitcher's mound. Dead silence. And Jerry standing on one leg. The whole place was shocked. Our team wasn't shocked, we knew about the leg. We had seen it come off a couple of times in practice.

"I didn't even move. No one ran to him. Now you see him standing there, just with his pants leg hanging down. In a minute—which seemed like an eternity—we all went out to the mound, and he just hopped around and got another leg. But I said to the umpire, 'What was it, a ball or a strike?' He had no idea."

The human nature part of the story is still to come.

"I told that story to a guy named Joe Labate," Dreyer says. "He was a scout for the Philadelphia Phillies. He always had a story. I was a young guy and he was in his seventies. A Brooklyn guy. He used to come around the ball field. Labate always had these stories about players in the minors. So I told him this story, figuring that he would not have another story to beat this. After I finished my story, he took out a picture of a pitcher in the Canadian League, on the mound—with no legs. No legs, on the mound, with a glove. I said, 'Labate, I'll never tell you another story in my life.' "

Dreyer did not play baseball after college except for Joe Austin's Old-Timers' Day games or those chance occasions when he saw a batting cage along the highway and could not resist taking a few whacks against a pitching machine. He could always hit the hell out of the ball. Then, for his fiftieth birthday, his wife, Lisa, gave him a special gift. If Philip Spitzer got from Mary a dramatic moment in the imaginary sun, Dreyer for his fiftieth birthday, in 1989, got an expensive week in the sun—a week at the Mets Dream Camp, where former athletes and would-be athletes and never-was athletes play on the Mets training fields under the direction of former Mets. Dreyer bought a new pair of cleats, borrowed a glove from his son, who played softball—he has three boys, all in their twenties—and he flew to Florida, to the Mets camp at Port St. Lucie.

"It was terrific," Dreyer said. "They run it as a minor league training camp. There were a hundred guys down. Mostly dentists from Brooklyn"—he laughs—"who had the time off and the dough. During the week they broke the hundred guys up into ten teams, ten guys apiece. Each day you played two six-inning games. On Saturday, at the end of the week, all ten teams played three-inning games against the '69 Mets. Ed Kranepool was there, Ed Charles, Wayne Garrett . . ."

I wonder about the girl in Mr. Laff's. She would be a woman now. . . .

". . . Duffy Dyer, Joe Pignatano. They were coaches during the week. Then on Saturday there were ten three-inning games against the Mets old-timers. When I got up I knew I was gonna hit the hell out of the ball. They didn't play too deep in the outfield. And I clocked a shot one bounce off the fence. But I couldn't run—my legs were so sore I only ran to first base. I hit good down there—nine for sixteen. I was always a good hitter.

"I lost ten pounds in a week. You get up at seven o'clock, you have breakfast, you go over and have calisthenics, you get dressed. They fine you—a dollar if your socks are down, or if you smoke on the field, or if you don't run out a hit. The trainers got the money. They had three trainers down for the week, in a brand-new training room—whirlpools, training tables, everything. The first day there weren't too many guys in there. By the third or fourth day there was a line to get in—with swollen arms, ice packs on the elbows.

"Everybody's old. Most guys were in their forties. There's a guy who was thirty-two, guys were going, 'What the hell is he here for, he's still playing ball.' The year before, there was a guy in his seventies.' "

At dream camp, in addition to a uniform, they gave him a Mets cap to keep. But Richard Dreyer doesn't wear it. He still wears Yankee caps, the kind he fell in love with in the days when he used run like hell from the tough black kids, and go home and cry when Joe DiMaggio struck out.

I tell him that I am a New York Mets fan. "But of course, we're getting the Colorado Rockies out here now."

"A very nice cap," Dreyer says.

Amara's blood is pouring out of her mouth, raining down like some sacrificial comment, turning the green grass brown beneath her blood-soaked screams.

Why? Why did she choose to come with us that day?

She was eleven years old. She did not like baseball. A straight-A student, very smart and very pretty, she liked to swim, to go tubing in the snow; she dreamed of learning to ski. But competitive sports were not on her agenda; she had rarely if ever touched a softball in her life. On this spring day, however, when some of the gang decided to go to Canyon Road Park to mess around with a bat and ball, Amara against all expectation decided to come along. Perhaps it was because La Donna had opted to stay home and clean house, and the child, no dummy, figured that even softball was preferable to vacuuming.

So she came with me in the car as we all met on the sprawling greensward, where the ball field was empty as usual. Jon's girls were there, too, India and Alex, and some other men and their wives. Nursing a bad back, I watched from behind first base as a small game was played, the wives and the girls doing their best, the men taking half swings or batting left handed, trotting around the bases. After perhaps half an hour of that the women had had enough and the men wanted some real-man practice. Butch Smith, Gene's brother, picked up a bat near home plate to hit some fungoes, and the men trotted out to the outfield. Amara, perhaps surprised that she was enjoying herself, took my glove and ran out after them. Butch is a strong, solid, two-hundred-pound man, recently retired after twenty years in the Navy. He hit some fly balls to left, to center, an occasional grounder off an overly ambitious swing. I was still watching from near first base when Butch belted a high and brutal line drive that began to sink in medium center field. Amara was standing a few steps away, glove on her left hand, and as the ball steadied like a cruise missile she began to move toward it, somehow guiding herself, like some precocious Andy Van Slyke, to exactly the place it would come, as if she had been judging fierce line drives through all of her eleven years, while from behind first base I saw the terrible truth beginning to happen, and I began to shout, "No! No!" I did not want her to try to catch that ball. But with the fierce determination with which she goes through life, she moved toward the approaching ball unstoppably—it was only a few steps—not hearing me or mishearing me—perhaps she heard, "Go, Go"—and just as the ball sunk to eleven-year-old level she put the glove in front of her face to catch the line drive. But the ball exploded behind it like a grenade, struck her square on the nose or square on the mouth, I could not tell which, and as I raced toward center field she fell to her knees as if shot, and stayed that way, facing the ground on her hands and knees, like a dog, blood gushing out of her face, blood pouring into the grass, turning the dirt to little driplets of mud. The others hurried toward her as well, and when I got there there was nothing I could do for her but drop to my knees and hold her around the waist, offering physical and moral support, while her cries and choking sobs intermingled with the blood that was pouring out. I pulled a handkerchief from my pocket, and Bonnie Knickerbocker Smith, Gene's wife back then, who had no children of her own and who at times acted the part of a flake, Bonnie in this moment of crisis took charge—perhaps some repressed maternal instinct vaulting out—and helped when the sobbing subsided slightly to wipe away the blood that quickly soaked my handkerchief to gluey red. Amara's nose was pouring blood but did not seem to be broken; most of the blood was coming from her mouth, where the ball had smashed her upper lip against her teeth. I prayed that no permanent damage had been done to the delicate face of this child, who wanted to be an actress, this child not truly mine but only lent to me, but just as precious, and as we hurried her to the car I thanked God that La Donna had not been there as witness. For that small favor I am grateful still.

At their house nearby Bonnie brought ice to where Amara, a trouper, sprawled quietly now despite her pain, and used it to stem the bleeding, first from the nose and then from the mouth. Already the child's upper lip had begun to thicken and swell like an aborigine's. Her nose looked fine, her teeth seemed all in place and still tight. The only damage we could find was the cut inside her mouth and the swelling caused by the blow. For half an hour I let her rest there, holding the pack of ice to her face. Then I brought her home to her mother.

La Donna paled when she saw her baby's face. But a mother's tears and many hours with the ice pack led to a surprisingly quick recovery for a kid who that day proved herself to be sturdier than she knew. Her mouth that seemed almost as large as a baseball had within twenty-four hours returned to normal. No disabled list for her, there was no lasting injury, although Amara, no ball fan before, seemed even less likely to be converted afterward. Not till she entered high school a few years later and had to play softball in her physical education class did I convince her to put on my glove again, to stand in the street as, from ten feet away, I lobbed some balls to her. Easy, underhand.

Ever since that bloody day in the park, whenever I hear an announcer repeat the cliché that baseball is a game of inches, I know that he is wrong. I see again Amara with too much grit moving in front of that ball—that Navy missile—and I know she had no business in center field at all, that I should have thought of that before Butch swung the bat, and I know that if it had struck her the merest fraction higher the ball would have smashed her pretty pug nose into splinters. And if it had struck her the merest fraction lower it would have knocked out half her teeth or broken her jaw. But a fraction of the power was absorbed by the edge of the glove, I think, and the rest she caught flush on the bony ridge just below her nose, just above her upper lip. And somehow, baby, the bony ridge held. And I have known ever since that baseball, and maybe life as well, is a game of quarter inches at most.

In the recesses of our lives the ball is bounding. The ball is bounding toward first. Mookie Wilson is streaking down the line. . . .

A few days before Christmas, in the supermarket, La Donna and I run into Carol. We have not seen one another since the summer; we chat rather pleasantly. I do not bring up baseball. Carol is the most dedicated Mets fan I know; she would not be able to fathom, I'm sure, this shame within me. This flirtation.

It is Carol who speaks the unspeakable. "Isn't it exciting about the Rockies!"

There amid the grapefruits, the bananas, the oranges, the bell peppers, the avocados: Isn't it exciting about the Rockies! She and Daniel have friends in Denver, they'll be going up for a game. . . .

Who would have thought it?

The ball skips down the line. Bill Buckner on bad legs tries to bend, suspended for all eternity back there in 1986. The parallel reality has its own hall of miracles: the ball squirts through his legs.

There are more ways than one to become immortal.

A few days before, we'd been burning up the phone lines house to house in the ninth inning, the thirteenth inning, the sixteenth inning of the sixth game of the play-off with Houston—the greatest professional baseball game ever played, in my prejudiced yet indisputable opinion. The sun would rise in the morning—but not Mike Scott.

And now this . . . the ball squirting, squirting between Buckner's shaky legs. The Mets win! The Mets win! The Mets win! Tomorrow, as Scarlett said, is another day! Or night.

The next night we are gathered around the set in our living room to watch the final game of the World Series together, to celebrate or mourn—me and La Donna, Gene and Bonnie, Jon and Claudia, Carol and Daniel. Very civilized. (Some people find it strange.)

The Mets do it again. Exquisite tension—and an 8–5 victory. There are joyous hugs and kisses all around.

The last time the Mets won the World Series was . . . 1969.

On Christmas morning there is no Rockies cap. This I already knew; there were none in town that fit.

Now it is the week of the Super Bowl. Carol invites Smith and me to watch it at her place: all rabid Dallas fans, here in the Southwest. With La Donna's blessing I go. At our house she will have a party for football widows.

"Where's Bob watching the game?" Julie asks.

"At his ex-wife's house," La Donna says.

Julie is astonished.

"It's all right," Fran says. "He'll come back."

La Donna, too, knows I'll come back.

"Can I bring something?" I ask Carol.

"No."

I ask her something else; her memory always has been better than mine. I ask if she remembers any good baseball moments from back in the late seventies.

"We weren't very good fans then," she says. "The Mets were lousy. And we were too depressed."

I do bring something to her house. One for her and one for Smith, all shiny in purple and black and white. On Super Bowl Sunday, the schedule of the Colorado Rockies, unfolding like an accordion.

The very best present. The promise of spring to come.

In March of 1988, after twenty years of riding the pines, I resumed my playing career. I was recruited by Smith, who always had an eye for talent.

The year before, Smith had joined a softball team in a city league. He was one of the few nonlawyers on a team of attorneys, and though he batted .667 and did not make an error in those games in which he roamed second base, he did not get much playing time. Fed up with what he perceived as legal discrimination, he decided the next year to form a team of his own. A wealthy friend who owned a mineral-water company agreed to put up the money for shirts and caps. Thus, in a league agrowl with macho types representing the police, the sheriff's department, liquor stores, and construction companies, I became a charter member of the Santa Fe Springs, in a cap of baby blue.

The first step in my return to the active list was to go to Wal-Mart and plunk down forty-eight dollars for a glove, the same mitt that graces my shelf today. I also bought a softball and a small can of 3-in-1 oil. The glove was large and stiff, but the smaller, softer models of my youth were no longer made. At home I oiled the glove, and day after day pounded a ball into it till it offered the perfect tactile sensation.

Uniformly out of shape, we began to work out a few times a week at Alto Park, just two blocks from my home. We took it easy at first, myself in particular, ever wary of my uncertain back. But my prowess on this team would also be otherwise limited. Chronic tendinitis in my shoulder—the same condition Jayne is still trying to cure today—prevented me from throwing the ball overhand. This effectively limited me to two positions: pitcher, where almost all the tosses would be underhand anyway, and first base, where I could catch pegs, field grounders, and get by without any overhand throws.

Annie Dillard, on some other softball team long ago and far away, played second base. "Second base is a Broadway, a Hollywood and Vine," she wrote. "But, oh, if I'm out in right field they can kiss me good-bye. As the sun sets, sundogs, which are mock suns—chunks of rainbow on either side of the sun but often very distant from it—appear over the pasture. . . . It might rain tomorrow, if those ice crystals find business. I have no idea how many outs there are; I luck through left-handers, staring at rainbows . . . everyone is running, and I can't hear a sound. The players look so thin on the green, and the shadows so long, and the ball a mystic thing, pale to invisibility. . . . I'm better off in the infield."

On the jacket of the book that contains those words there is a photo of the poet, showing short blondish hair, lovely clean features, slightly parted lips, eyes looking away at once determined, appealing—a gentle wild-woman waiting for release. I am a sucker for this image locked in time, this photo taken twenty years ago, much as twenty years ago I first fell for her poet's words, her intelligence fine and crisp as an apple's new skin. I am aware she is married, as I am married; I hope she is happy, as I am happy. I realize there must be wrinkles now, small crow's-feet, perhaps even a thickening of the middle; I choose to imagine otherwise. I am Fellini and she is Cardinale, locked in time's sweet spidery lace, every man's girl in white.

She is correct, of course, about second base. But first base and the pitcher's mound, too, are like Hollywood and Vine; little transpires without your taking part; they would do me just fine. Yet why is the ball, after all these years, a mystic thing still, I want to ask her—this insightful woman unknown, this pretty girl unmet—and the feel of the bat choked up, and the throw in the dirt neatly scooped, and the ball in the pocket of the glove? When I am writing I am wholly myself, and when I am playing ball. Only then. Why? And why do birds sing?

The poet offers no answers. Nor can I.

Those first days of practice my muscles became appropriately tight, appropriately sore. But with each new workout they eased up some. My problem back held, and that was all I asked of the softball gods. If I could not drive the ball over the heads of the outfielders—well, I never could. If I had lost more than a step in fielding grounders, if I could no longer bend low enough—well, certain tolls must be paid on the highway of life. But the mystery, the magic, the subtle exultation that transcends, still was there, on the green grass, in the warm sun, after all those years . . . all those years of a barely understood vacancy in the tenement of myself.

Two weeks before the season was to start, Smith scheduled a practice game against another team—the team of lawyers he'd abandoned the year before. I recall only two plays, I shall describe only those two plays—two plays which, together, spun my psyche quietly off in the direction of life's third act.

For reasons unknown to me, then or now, the name of the opposing team was the Bongo Straights. The cleanup-hitting Bongo was a tall, balding civil rights attorney who kept himself in good shape. I was pitching, and the cleanup Bongo waited me out, worked the count to three-and-two, waiting for just the pitch he wanted. Two of the pitches had been perfect strikes, three had not missed by all that much; the fellow was making a fool of himself, even to his own teammates, in this meaningless practice game. What I should have done was roll the last pitch to the plate, or loft it high over his head, give him his hard-earned walk, take the bat out of his hands. But I didn't think of that then. Instead I floated up a lovely arc. He swung from the heels, getting his full body strength into it, and he laced a screaming line drive right back at me. It was about four feet off the ground. It must have been traveling a hundred miles an hour. It had death written all over it. I had finished my pitching motion in good defensive position, my glove in front of me. In a reflex motion as fast and automatic as a hummingbird's wings, the glove came up in front of my chest as the ball exploded into the pocket with a resounding crunch that could be heard in center field, and which left the palm of my hand the color of boiled lobster. The Bongo batter stood there staring at me in disbelief. I conceded no sign of pain, nor of relief. It was the third out; I dropped the ball on the mound and walked toward the bench without a word, as if I always ate line drives for lunch. The batter remained at the plate, staring, staring, his hurt more exquisite than mine.

My first reaction was pleasure that my ultimate baseball instincts—not to say my digits—were intact. *Hey, Mom, I can goddamn field!* But I also knew before I reached the bench that—much as with Amara a few years earlier—if the line drive had been hit twelve inches higher I would be lying flat on the mound now, writhing with a broken jaw or a broken nose; my glove in the split second the ball exploded toward me would not have moved in front of my face. And I knew, conversely, that if the screaming shot had been hit about eighteen inches lower, my glove would not have protected me, could not have reached down and turned over in time. I would have been blasted in the testicles. All this I knew and chose not to know as I sat on the bench and basked in admiring glances, in unspoken praise.

The second play occurred an inning later. I was on first base after my first at bat, when the next batter lined a shot to left-center. I raced toward second, took the turn, and stepped up my dead-catcher's speed as I headed toward third. I made it standing up, if gasping, and was very pleased with myself at having gone from first to third on a base hit. I was less pleased, however, with the pain that had ripped through the left side of my rib cage midway between second and third. It hurt like hell as I stood on third base, catching the breath I had left behind at second; it burned with every step as I raced home on a ground ball. The pain would pass, I assured myself back on the bench. As crucifixions go, the wound was mild. I was a devoted softball postulant, and I'd just scored my first run in twenty years.

I don't remember who won the game: it didn't matter. But driving home afterward I was acutely aware again of the line drive hurtling toward me so fast as to be more sensed than seen, hurtling with a force I would not have been able to deter with my aging reflexes had it not been fired like a leather-seeking missile almost directly at my glove. I was aware of the pain that was stinging my side with every breath. I felt the muscles in every part of my body tightening from the extra exertion of a game— even a practice game—as opposed to the prior workouts. And I thought: *What the hell am I doing? I have no business playing a kid's game at the age of thirty-nine.*

I knew this was a mortal truth that must be faced.

I drove on for two more blocks, absorbing this thought, before I realized that I was forty-nine.

The knowledge hit my brain like a hammer. There had always been this disparity between my inner years and my actual years. A moment before, the unnoticed gap between my psychological age and what my birth certificate said had been a full decade. As if some inattentive nurse had made an error, a typo, in Bronx Hospital long ago. But now the truth was out, was running loose in my brain like a black dog long penned and suddenly let free. I was forty-nine years old. And there was nothing I could do about it.

Following that knowledge came a darker knowledge still: If I was already forty-nine, I was not going to make it to the majors. I would never play shortstop for the Dodgers or for the Mets. I would not be the next Pee Wee Reese. This truth that had been obvious to my brother when I was twelve years old had taken thirty-seven years more to root into my soul. But there it was, long delayed, in all its ruthless modesty. *I wasn't going to make it.*

When, a few minutes later, I pulled into the driveway and climbed out of the car, carrying my new glove, wearing my imposter's cap of baby blue, some unknown fabric torn apart in my chest, I was a different person than the one who had left the house only three hours earlier. I wondered, like a virgin deflowered, if anyone would know.

Apostles of maturity—there are many I could name—might smile unctuously and say that, with the death of my ludicrous dream, I had become a man at last. But I was not so sure. I tended to side with Robert (Bobby) Browning:

> . . . *a man's reach should exceed his grasp,*
> *Or what's a shortstop for?*

He and She (redux):

On the twenty-fourth day of February, 1989, a Friday—exactly on schedule—he was going to have another birthday. This would be a big one. The big five-oh.

A few weeks earlier she had burned up the telephone lines, called a bunch of their friends. Keep the twenty-fourth open, she'd told them. He was going to be fifty. She was making a surprise party.

A few of their friends groaned. They knew he did not like surprises. After six years together, they figured, she ought to know that. He was gonna be mad as hell.

Well—not exactly. The surprise party was his idea. The surprise was going to be on the guests.

On Thursday she goes over to Albertson's, where a new deli section has just opened. She orders a couple of party platters: the assorted meats and cheeses (large), the vegetable tray (small). The woman behind the counter beams.

"It's our very first party platter," the woman says.

She wonders if she did the right thing.

The next day, Friday, he and she and the kid pick up two friends who are in on the secret. They drive to the Judicial Complex. Inside, Steve Herrera, who was elected a district judge in November, is waiting in his chambers, in his loose black robe.

"There's a standard little oath," the judge says. "Do you want me to leave out the part about obeying?"

"Yes," he says. He squeezes her hand, her left hand, the hand that's wearing the ring he gave her the night before. The ring that nearly sixty years ago his father gave to his mother. "Leave out the part about obeying."

The judge begins: "This is a very great honor for me. . . ."

He wonders. They really don't need a speech, here in the small chamber, just them and the two witnesses and the kid.

". . . because this is my very first wedding."

They all smile appreciatively. It's a rare wedding, he thinks, where the virgin is the judge.

The ceremony is short and sweet. A few minutes later, husband and wife now, they go home and drink champagne, and wait for the guests to show up. For his surprise fiftieth-birthday party.

Two by two they arrive. She explains his presence simply: "He found out." There are hugs all around, and birthday gifts.

When everyone is there in the living room, the kid disappears into the back of the house. She returns humming the Wedding March. And carrying the cake: a three-tiered wedding cake.

The guests don't get it at first. *There must be some mistake. Somebody gave them the wrong goddamn cake!*

Then, slowly, comes the dawn. And his words: "La Donna and I were married this afternoon."

Hugs for both, now, real embraces . . . and some tears . . . and a party!

The judge arrives with his wife and kid. The judge's kid and her kid are friends. The judge offers to take both kids home for the night. The very best present. . . .

In the morning they want to get out of town. Do something special. He gets an idea. "Let's drive out to the petroglyphs."

They drive down the highway for twenty miles. She dips between the strands of barbed wire. He climbs over the fence. Hand in hand in the warm February sun, as warm as it was that other February day six years before, they walk the dirt path toward the rocks. Soon the glyphs appear. Handprints. Snakes. Wolves. Stick figures. Ancient sacred drawings of the Anasazi.

They stand in the sun and gaze with renewed awe. They climb to the place where the towering rocks form an open grotto, in front of another stone that towers like an altar. They cannot find a climbing stalk of blue corn. But perhaps it is there nonetheless, they think. Perhaps it is merely invisible.

"Now we're married in the eyes of the gods," he says.

They continue to climb, to prowl. They are looking for a calendar. On one visit, a few years back, they had stumbled upon an ancient calendar carved on the back of a boulder. It is their secret treasure among the petroglyphs; they have never been able to find it again.

She wants to find it today. They hunt and hunt along the twisting ridge, in vain.

"I just realized why I wanted to come here today," he says. "It makes me feel young. I may be fifty, but these glyphs must be five hundred."

"More like a thousand," she says.

Then he has a deeper realization. A glimpse of rebirth in himself. At twenty-five he was a desperate seeker. At fifty he tries, as much as possible, to cherish what is given. He doesn't always succeed, but he tries. And much, this day, has been given.

Hand in hand they walk back toward the car, the years of their love inscribed on a calendar they are not permitted to see.

The Second Coming

Gene Smith was suffering from cataracts, which were causing him double vision. He was the starting shortstop for the Santa Fe Springs, but every time he backed up for a high pop fly and looked up into the falling twilight, into the lights that had not yet taken full effect, he would see two balls coming down, and Jon Richards, in short center, would yell at him: "The one on the left! Catch the one on the left!" Smith played the entire season that way and never dropped a pop-up. Talk about baseball instincts.

His double vision also came into play in a less literal respect. He took one look at me, with my ailing shoulder and my torn ribs, perceived that I would be a part-time player at best, and he saw me in a different role. "How would you like to be the manager?" he asked.

I pondered the tradition. Connie Mack of the Athletics. McGraw of the Giants. Durocher of the Dodgers. A long and hallowed trust. *Mayer of the Santa Fe Springs.* Why the hell not? As a kid I had always felt that, when my playing days were over, I would like to manage. Put my baseball knowledge to good use. Remain a part of the game. Strategy. Strategy had always been cool. I told Smith I would do it. I would be the manager—the one on the left.

In late April of that year we filed with the "Softball Men's Division—Fun League" a roster of sixteen players—an assortment of middle-aged writers, artists, photographers, cabinet-makers, scientists, real estate men, and one token lawyer. Though only ten men could play in the field, plus, according to league rules, an Eleventh Hitter—the phrase somehow reminded me of Death in *The Seventh Seal*—we knew we needed at least five substitutes because of the inevitable weaning process of summer vacations, business trips, pulled muscles, and children-in-a-play-at-school. It would be the manager's job—mine—to decide not only on strategy and each game's batting order, but on who played the entire game, who played half a game, who might not get to play at all. I would have power, pure, heady, and undiluted. It would be a growth experience. Maybe even pleasant.

My first task was to develop a starting lineup. Like Don Baylor a few years later, I lay awake into the middle of the night, pondering. Unlike Baylor I did have players, but that only made the task more complicated. As the leadoff batter, playing shortstop, I put Smith. *What the hell*, I figured: *You don't bite the hand that hires you.* In the crucial positions of left field and center field I put two of our trimmer, cockier players, Thad and Thad. (If nothing else, we were the only team in the league with two Thads.) Moving down the lineup, I mentally penciled heavy-hitter Butch Smith—Amara's nemesis—at first base, Richards in short-center. Right field was reserved for Daniel Morper, a painter who was married to my ex-wife. No offense was taken, and none was intended; I like the guy. It's just that his favorite sport is tennis.

But with all the positions taken, what was I to do with Elliott? Elliott, who had put up the money for our caps, and had now added matching T-shirts; Elliott, whose mineral-water spring south of town was surrounded, for metaphysical purity, by pyramids and crystals. Elliott, who at Christmas parties played a wonderful Santa Claus. I decided, by dawn's early light, that Elliott would, for metaphysical purity, be the Eleventh Hitter. It was the natural spot for his sometimes crystal glove. I popped a couple of antacid tablets and tried to get some sleep—perchance to dream of Casey Stengel, or at least Burt Shotten. Looking back, I don't recall what dream I had. It may have had to do with the Inquisition.

On Opening Day we were resplendent in our caps and T-shirts of baby blue, a shade apparently chosen by Eliott's wife. A number of the wives came to sit in the wooden bleachers to make a show of support and to talk about shopping. Two came to watch the game: Carol and La Donna.

The opposing team had full uniforms. The players were all in their twenties, young, lean, rugged, with pregnant wives in the stands holding babes in arms, or no wives at all. In the top half of the first inning, while I kept score on the bench, these young guns scored six runs. I chewed several more antacids.

That lovely twilight, however, age prevailed, like fine wine, over beauty. We battled back with eleven runs in the bottom of the first. We treated the young guns like young 'uns. We slaughtered them, 25–14. The next day we filled the springtime air with eager rehashings. We were nine years old again, and I was headed for some managerial hall of fame in the sky.

Right then was when a certain lack of timing came into play. Right then was the moment I should have quit.

In that wondrous first game I had only one small concern from my managerial perch on the bench. It was with the positioning of the Thads. All through the game they had been playing left and center field way out in the next county. Most of the runs we gave up had come from pop-ups that fell in front of them, which the backpeddling, double-sighted Smith had no chance in heaven or hell to reach. Only our mighty bats had made the problem moot. Now another game was at hand. Quietly I took the two Thads off to one side, out of earshot of the others, near a picnic bench off the third-base line. Gently, I suggested that they play in closer this time. Patiently, I explained my reasoning, about all the weak hitters in the league, about all the pop-fly singles.

"I hate it when balls go over my head!" Thad the First said. And he spun on his cleated heel and stalked away.

"I hate it when balls go over my head!" Thad the Second echoed. And he too, spun away, stalked away, from the words of his manager.

They were a good deal younger than I was. What do persons named Thad know of shortstops from The Bronx named Robert? I was an old man with flecks of gray in my sideburns, with a bad shoulder and bad ribs. Egocentric above all, they feared that a ball hit over their heads would somehow make them look bad, and they were damned if they were going to look bad in front of the ladies.

I wanted to scream at them that softball was a team game. I wanted to point out that one ball hit over their heads might be a home run, but that ten singles hit in front of them was seven runs and the bases still loaded. Which is more or less what happened that second game. I wanted to scream at them, but this was called a "fun league." Instead I warmed my vocal cords with the volcano that was erupting in my chest.

When the twilight contest began, I could barely see the two Thads in the outfield—and my eyes have always been my strongest feature. Thad the First was playing left field in Arizona. Thad the Second was playing center field in Utah. Home plate, alas, was still in New Mexico. As ball after ball dropped to the innocent grass in front of them, I could feeling anew a burning in my gut, reminder of an ulcer long healed. I wouldn't even have minded if they'd caught the imaginary ball on the right instead of the real one on the left. If only they had caught something! In my gullet I upped the ante. I switched from store-bought antacids to Tagamet—this wonder drug that was invented, I now understood, with managers in mind.

Still, thanks to our potent offense, going into the last inning we had a two-run lead, 13–11. We were in good shape despite the two Thads, and despite the complaints of Albert. A scientist at Los Alamos National Laboratory, Albert was a substitute, which position he did not much cherish. Albert, scientificlike, had shown up at the game having forgotten to bring the only thing he needed to bring, which was his glove. Now he was bitching at me that he was not playing enough. Against my better judgment I put Albert in to catch. I shall assign no blame, but our opponents quickly scored two runs on close plays at the plate, to tie the game.

At that point the opposing players began to jump up and down in celebration. They claimed that they had won the game. We compared scorebooks to unearth the problem. They had given us only three runs back in the first inning, though my own scorebook showed very clearly how we had scored four. I knew that I was right. But since they were the home team that evening, the umpires ruled that their scorebook was the official one, and that we had lost.

I had learned a costly but crucial lesson: In this league it was necessary to agree on the score after every inning.

That week I lay awake night after night, managing in bed. How to win games while still keeping Albert happy. And Elliott, the "owner," a good sport who was nonetheless getting restless as Eleventh Hitter. And what to do about the Thads. Since it was a fun league, I could not actually scream at them or give them orders they would have to obey. But I could damn well bench them! I decided I would go with the Walker boys, young brothers, real estate agents, who had not been available the first two games. Pat Walker I would put in center. Jim Walker I would put in left. The Thads would ride the pines, like it or not.

The day before the game Jim's car was totaled—with Jim in it—by a newly licensed sixteen-year-old girl driving a van on the wrong side of the street while eating a salad that was perched insecurely on her lap. Jim hurt his back and would miss the next few games. Brother Pat couldn't make it, either, for business reasons, and my dream lineup crumbled.

Our opponents the next night were the police. The Thads returned to the outfield–and played in the Canadian league. The pop flies fell like Chinese water torture. We suffered our first genuine drubbing, 14–4.

My rib cage was aching. My shoulder was sore. My stomach was burning. My head was pounding. I called my doctor and made an appointment, to make sure my long-gone ulcer had not returned. Then I called Smith and I resigned.

Subtle as Uriah Heep, I suggested a likely successor. I suggested Daniel Morper, the husband of my ex-wife. And Daniel took the job. I consoled myself with a wry smile. You win some, you lose some.

After one game, Daniel, too, quit.

As I write this four years later, the Santa Fe Springs have long since trickled into the healing earth from whence they sprang. Even Smith doesn't catch the ball-on-the-left anymore. He's put his glove, like mine, on a shelf. He still has double vision, but no longer does he peer uncertainly into the fast-falling night.

How quickly the children grow confident, mature. More quickly, even, than we grow old. And that is with the speed of light. Or darkness.

Two years ago the child got her driver's license. A few months later she turned sixteen. She moaned that she had outgrown her small bedroom. She wanted to swap, to take over my larger office. My office with its separate entrance. It was a move we would have to ponder. A major milestone.

One morning she sat in her chemistry class at Santa Fe High. Outside, the parking lot was icy. Inside, the lesson was making her mind wander. As the other kids talked to each other, she wrote down snatches of what she heard, in an abstract tone poem.

Most days, after school she would chatter about a boy she had spoken with, or a teacher who'd been rude to her. But this day she pulled out her blue notebook to read to us the poem she had written.

"It's really weird," she said. And then she read:

What does a rat mean? A nothing that you can smoke tobacco out of. A very good way to find today. With twenty bucks you are able to run. The day-old dude forgot his money. Now he's drinking Bud and reading a shooting newspaper.

The front page has pushed the teacher away. The little guy caught him on his way to escape. He pulled out his shotgun and got an E for effort. Everyone was in line for five minutes before the Mace took effect. The sounds of our tastebuds had a change of heart. Thoughts are due tomorrow.

There's a sign on the door that says fifty dollars to anyone. How do you get to two? Mace is the shoplifter's dream. Doctors think it's easy to hit people. If I told you I had a toothpick would it still mean they're attached? What do you think is going to happen? Don't forget to do what you can.

When she finished reading, her mother and I sat in silence for a moment.

"Isn't that weird?" the child said.

"It's fantastic," her mother said.

"It's beautiful," I echoed, aglow with stepfatherly pride.

"But it doesn't mean anything," the child said. "It just came out that way."

We sat in the living room and discussed creativity, its direct line to the subconscious.

"Well, explain it to me, then," the child said. "The first line. 'What does a rat mean?' "

"That's the central question of life," I told her. "What does a rat mean? Why did God create rats? Why did God create man? It's the same question. I don't know the answer. Nobody does. That's what we spend our lives trying to find out."

"Okay, what about this line?" the child said. " 'There's a sign on the door that says fifty dollars to anyone.' "

"I don't know," I said. "Maybe there's a roomful of hookers behind the door. Or maybe you have to do something to get the money. Something good. Or something evil. We don't know, but that's the point of poetry, of all art. It makes you think. It makes you wonder."

I remembered specific scenes from her childhood. Some happened before I came along. I had only heard about them, but they were part of her life's mythology. How at less than two years of age she used to climb to the top of a woodpile, and then begin to cry because she could not get down. And then, lifted down by her mother, she would promptly climb to the top again. And begin to cry again.

I remembered how at the age of eight she went through a sleepwalking phase, getting out of bed in the night, unlocking the front door, heading out into the cold night before her terrified mother caught up with her. How when we put a heavy chair in front of the door she moved that in her sleep and still got out. Till we fastened a hook-and-eye near the ceiling to stop her unconscious wanderings.

I remembered that time I took her to play softball, the screaming line drive, how I yelled at her not to try to catch it. I remembered the blood pouring out of her mouth onto the hungry grass.

Always, this fierce determination.

Encouraged, perhaps, by our praise, she told us she had written something else that day. This one in drama class. She read again from her notebook:

The repetitious music is resonating in my mind. The music is caught in a whirlpool of my thoughts. Thoughts about life, about love, about death, about reality, and about nothingness. Everything is like some distant dream that is trying to become reality but not quite achieving it. Who are these people? What are these sounds? Where am I? One would say I'm sitting in the drama room with my friends and classmates that I'm with every day. But I don't know these people—how they feel, what they think, why they're here. Disembodied voices floating around in the nothingness with no one to catch them. People pretend to talk and carry on conversations, but they are just pretending. I often wonder if they even realize what they're doing, why they're doing it. I doubt it. I don't think they want to know. It scares them.

It was on a Friday afternoon that she read this to us. On Saturday we swapped rooms. Much heavy lifting through narrow passages: bed, dresser, vanity, desks, bookshelves. It took three days. The last things she moved were her dozens of stuffed animals: the seal, the dolphin, the dragon, all the others. Into her new room with its separate entrance.

What does a rat mean?

Thoughts are due tomorrow.

Jackie Robinson is racing around third, taking a wide turn that carries him halfway to the Ebbets Field boxes as he streaks full-throttle to the plate. Roy Campanella belts a long drive into the stands in left-center. Carl Furillo turns at the right field wall, catches a ball on the fly off the scoreboard, and rifles a throw to second. Carl Erskine's big overhand curve is mowing down Yankee hitters like a scythe in a wheat field. Preacher Roe is demonstrating how to load up a ball with spit. (Just a little dab'll do ya.) Joe Black is firing fastballs as flat as aspirin tablets. Duke Snider, his left-handed swing as smooth as an avocado pit, the only lefty in the lineup, is lofting one into Bedford Avenue. Billy Cox is picking grounders like a carefree girl in a field picking daisies. (I recall a classic headline from the Daily News *back then:* DODGERS DANGLE COX AS TRADE BAIT.*) Pee Wee Reese swipes second base. Gil Hodges stands on deck, regal as always. Clem Labine's sweeping curve saves a game.*

It is a cloudy Sunday afternoon. I am watching a tape that Philip has sent me, a television version of *The Boys of Summer*—I never knew one had been made—that first aired in 1982, a decade after the book came out.

When the old black-and-white baseball clips have done their emotional business in my chest, and behind my eyes, the former players are shown in their homes, most of them gray haired, in their late fifties or their sixties, talking about that team, their lives. Three quarters of the infield is dead already, the infield of this team of destiny: Hodges, Robinson, Cox. Only Pee Wee lives to tell the tale. The Duke is there, a baseball broadcaster, and Furillo, a security guard, proud he made it to the majors with only an eighth-grade education. Erskine, a distinguished, articulate, yet homespun bank vice-president in his hometown of Anderson, Indiana, playing with his son, who has Down syndrome. Labine, with far too much dark hair for his age, hugging his son, who lost a leg in Vietnam. Campy in his wheelchair, this grown man being lifted in and out of cars by attendants. This team that in its time was loved like no team before or since. This team of tragedy.

The most moving story of all is told by Joe Black. He played high school ball in Phoenix, he says, and batted around .370, and major league scouts came swarming around the team, signing up lots of players. But none of them approached him, and he was the best on the squad. Finally he asked one of the scouts why they weren't signing him. Negroes don't make it to the majors, he was told. Young Joe Black was incredulous. He ran all the way home, he ran to his room, he took down the scrapbook he was keeping of all the great major league ballplayers. There were Babe Ruth and Ty Cobb and Hank Greenberg and Joe Di-Maggio and Ted Williams. And every one of them was white. He had never noticed that before. In a tearful rage Joe Black tore up all the pictures, one by one. All except the picture of Hank Greenberg.

Choked yet again by this American verity that we can never overcome, I waited for one more minor fact. But there was no more: Joe Black was not asked and did not say why Hank Greenberg had been spared. Greenberg was Jewish; I know that, you know that, but surely Joe Black did not know that back then, and even if he had, why would that have made any difference? Of all the great players of history, why did this black boy in Phoenix spare only Hank Greenberg?

Thoughts are due tomorrow.

As the final credits began, a closing image showed Pee Wee Reese, white haired but trim and fit in his middle years, knowing full well his old ball yard is now a housing project, saying, "If you haven't seen a game in Ebbets Field, you just ain't lived."

The shortstop as Descartes.

It is a sentiment in which I may well seek refuge as the years roll by. I cheered: therefore I was.

Tony O'Brien is the only person in my set who has thrown out the first ball at a major league baseball game. The tale that hangs upon that honor is salutary; for a while we were afraid it was O'Brien himself who would hang.

A lean and lank six-foot-three-inch photojournalist, Tony was born in The Bronx, an only child, and became a Yankee fan. When he was about eight years old his father took a job with the Justice Department and the family moved to suburban Virginia, just outside of Washington. Young Tony became a fan of the Washington Senators, went to games at Griffith Stadium, played Little League Ball at second base and behind the plate. Since part of baseball is learning to hate well, he learned to hate the rival Baltimore Orioles down the road. When the Senators hightailed it to Minnesota and became Twins, O'Brien, betrayed, bid them a sad farewell. He had never wholly given up on the Yankees, so he rejoined their ranks and has been a Yankee fan ever since. The Orioles remained anathema. "They were in another state—light-years away," he recalls.

In Little League, Tony played with a pitcher named Pat Conroy, who would grow up to write *The Prince of Tides* and other luminous novels. "I was the only one who could catch Pat Conroy," Tony says, "because he was so wild. He threw the ball so fast, it was a joke—but he had no control. He was awesome. We played some really good teams. I remember one game Conroy was pitching and I was catching, and the first guy came up to the plate for the other team. I said to him, 'The ball's coming right at your head, man, you better be careful, this guy's gonna kill you.' The guy said, 'Yeah, yeah.' The first pitch came in and the guy turned white, whiter than he was. Because it almost took his head off. The next pitch was the same way. Then he struck the guy out. The team was so petrified—and he wasn't doing it on purpose."

At St. Anselm's Priory High School, a Benedictine school, O'Brien was not going to go out for baseball; he didn't think he was good enough. But when the team's first baseman got hurt, the coach asked him to fill in. He played first all through high school. Then he went to talent-rich Notre Dame and restricted his baseball to watching the Yankees on the tube. When he moved to Santa Fe after leaving Notre Dame, he sometimes played softball for the Green Onion, a sports bar of which he is one of the proudest alumni.

Tony did stints as a photographer for three New Mexico newspapers, then began to hit national markets. He went to perhaps half the prisons in America, taking pictures of tough cons in reform programs for *Corrections* magazine. He went to Mexico to photograph the poverty there, to northern Ireland to record the stress of people living under deadly strife, to the slums of New York and Washington and Los Angeles to capture on film the battered lives of prostitutes, drug addicts, street gangs. His engaging modesty, his sly sense of humor, won him acceptance wherever he went. People from slums to battle zones somehow seemed willing to help Tony O'Brien get his pictures—probably because, deep down, he never felt he was any better a person than they were. Then he would return to some distant hotel room—or to his house across from a mountain in Santa Fe—and he would hole up alone and get depressed about what he had seen.

Between trips he dated Seva Dubuar, and he got to know her son, the young Jaime Dean, and he took Jaime to his first Albuquerque Dukes game. For a couple of years he was like a second father to the boy, till all the travel and a certain fear of commitment in the man behind the camera led the adult relationship to dissolve, as those things will. But never would the fondness totally dissolve, and certainly not the fondness for the boy.

In 1986, something inside O'Brien called him to Pakistan, where hundreds of thousands of people were living in makeshift refugee camps, displaced from their homes by the continuing war in neighboring Afghanistan. Tony wanted to record their plight. He said good-bye to his friends and he flew off to Peshawar, a city in northeast Pakistan close to the Afghan border. He had been there less than two hours, was walking down a street crowded with oxen and rickshaw taxis, when he was approached in front of an Afghan rug shop by a stranger with dark eyes and a dark moustache, wearing baggy pants, a turban, sandals.

"Do you want to go in?" the man asked in broken English. "Do you want to cross over?"

O'Brien immediately felt himself flooded with fear—fear not of the man but of the question. He knew what the question meant. It meant: Do you want to be smuggled across the border—illegally—into Afghanistan, to take pictures of the war there?

Every fiber of his being was shouting NO. He was not a combat photographer; that's not what he had gone there for. What he said was, "What would I have to do?"

What followed was two days of negotiations that O'Brien describes with wry self-mockery. He was told that he would have to pass as an Afghani. He gazed down at his six-foot-three-inch white frame and wondered how he was going to do that. He was told he would have to get himself an Afghan outfit, complete with *patu*. He didn't know what a *patu* was; he didn't know if you wore it or ate it. Told to be sure to get pills for diarrhea, he groaned inwardly, but plunged on. A rickshaw driver helped him get outfitted at an Afghan bazaar. A *patu* turned out to be a cloth you wore on your head and wrapped around you. In his cheap hotel room he got himself tangled in knots while trying to put it on. Looking in the mirror, he thought, *I look like a geek.*

When he showed up at the Peshawar headquarters of the Afghan rebels—the *mujahideen*—they did just what he had expected: they laughed at him. But they showed him how to wear the *patu,* and they escorted him on a bumpy two-day bus ride to the border. Along the way the bus stopped frequently at filthy outdoor cafés. O'Brien and the others were served bowls of stew. At each stop he asked what kind of stew it was. At each stop the reply was the same: "Chicken." That was fine with O'Brien. But he could not help realizing that from the window of the bus, as he gazed out across the land, he had not seen a single chicken for three hundred miles.

The border crossing was successful, and O'Brien spent seventeen days holed up with a rebel Afghan unit. Then he returned to Pakistan, took his first shower in more than two weeks, ate his first meal with a knife and fork. His pictures were published in magazines in the U.S. and Europe, including *Life.* Most were portraits of the dark and handsome Afghan rebels. He had not seen much combat; that was fine; but as he languished at home in the States, he felt more and more that he had not really captured the truth of what was going on in that war-torn country; that he had to go back again. And he did.

For eighteen months, living in Peshawar, Tony slipped in and out of Afghanistan. On one trip the rebels took him all the way to Kabul, the capital. There, while he was staying at a rebel safe house, someone betrayed the cause. Tony was drinking green tea and eating candies with a group of rebels when the "safe house" was raided by the secret police. O'Brien had no visa, was in the country illegally. His cameras and film were seized, and he was taken in chains to a large prison, where he was put in a small cell with two Afghani prisoners. If the chicken stew on the outside was questionable, the prison meals were meager: tea, bread, and sugar for breakfast, rice with onions and radishes for lunch, for dinner soup they called "water grease." Twice a week there was meat, once in a while a piece of fruit. "Once they rapped on the door and threw in two cucumbers," he recalls. To pass the time he and his cell mates made worry beads out of cherry and peach pits or bread. One cell mate, Nader Ali, spoke a bit of English, and he and Tony soon became close.

O'Brien was taken out for questioning day after day as the Afghanis sought information. If they decided he was a spy they could execute him. Tony felt that just for being in the country illegally they would hold him for a year. Day after day passed with no news from outside. He had no idea if anyone in the West even knew of his arrest.

It would be convenient to report that he got through the days by thinking of Mickey Mantle, Frank Howard, some of his other favorite ballplayers: Jackie Robinson, or Al Kaline, perhaps. But he did not think of baseball for an instant. He thought instead of Gordon Liddy, the Watergate conspirator. He had read some-where that Liddy said the most important thing to do in prison was stay in shape. So O'Brien, day after day, to the consternation of his cell mates, did endless push-ups.

For days his capture was unknown in the West. Finally word got out to his fellow newsmen, and then to his friends at home. Senators, congressmen, journalists, and the Red Cross began working for his release, vouching for his character, giving assur-ances that he was no spy. One day, without warning, he was suddenly released. He had been in the small Afghani cell for six weeks.

When O'Brien had been in prison for four weeks, the Afghanis permitted two reporters to interview him. To break the ice one of the reporters asked if he'd heard how well the Baltimore Orioles were doing. Tony said he didn't know; he asked what was going on. "They're in the running, they're in first place," the reporter said. Tony had been following the baseball scores in the *Herald Tribune* in Peshawar at the start of the season, but that had been months ago. Tony recalls: "I'm sure I said something about 'Boy, I'd sure like to be watching a baseball game.'" By that point he was nostalgic for anything—for everything—American, includ-ing hot dogs, peanuts, and popcorn. Then the interview turned to more serious matters.

Later, at the hotel where the reporters stayed, other reporters demanded a briefing. The conversation about the Orioles was mentioned. An Associated Press writer from India wrote the story as if the first thing O'Brien wanted to do when he got out—his biggest wish—was go to a Baltimore Orioles baseball game. The story hummed across the overseas wires into the American newspapers. And when O'Brien got back to the States and got his bearings, one of the first things that happened was that a season box-holder invited him to an Orioles game. "I didn't give a shit about the Orioles," Tony recalls. "But I was really touched. He wasn't with the club or anything. It wasn't a promotion. I didn't have the heart to tell him I wasn't an Oriole fan. That's how it had come out in the papers—that I had loved the Orioles since I was seven years old." Then the guy called back; he had arranged with the ball club for Tony to throw out the first ball at a game.

Tony, not wanting to seem ungrateful, agreed. He invited along some of his childhood baseball companions. "You've got to come," he told them, "I don't know anything about this team."

On game night Tony was treated like a celebrity by the public-relations people, by the general manager. He got a standing ovation from the crowd. He didn't have the heart to confess he had little use for the home squad.

"They took me out onto the field," he recalls. "I'm standing on a major league field for the first time. They were playing the Minnesota Twins—who had fled from Washington years before. TV crews asked me who my favorite player was. I didn't know their names. I said, 'Oh, I love them all. It's great to be here. It's a dream come true.' It *was* a dream come true, in a sense. But I started getting real nervous. I had to throw the ball out. I mean, Holy Christ, I hadn't thrown a baseball in years. What if I threw it into the ground? How far away is this guy going to be? They asked me if I wanted anybody's autograph. I knew Frank Robinson was the manager so I asked for his. The PR guy says, 'Jeez, Frank never gives autographs. But let me try.' So he goes to the dugout where Frank is sitting, and he talks to him and Frank looks at the ball he's holding, and he looks at me, and then he signs the ball, And they bring it back to me. They ask who else I want. I say that's it, I don't want anybody else on that ball."

The third baseman, Craig Worthington, came over and told Tony not to worry, he would catch the ball just fine. Tony is standing behind third toward home plate. He is introduced to the crowd—a prisoner who has just been released from Afghanistan. "I'm listening to all this, and I look up, and there on the center-field screen I see myself, big, big, huge, and everybody is cheering. Then the national anthem begins and I'm standing there, worrying about throwing out the ball, and I look over and I see this big black fuckin' bird—with a wing around me. It was so bizarre—I just got out of prison two weeks before. Two weeks. And I'm standing on a baseball field with a baseball in my hand and a big black bird running around me. A huge thing!"

When the national anthem ended, Tony threw out the ball. Craig Worthington caught it. O'Brien's nightmare of failure was over.

He was led back into the stands amid the cheers of tens of thousands. The general manager of the Orioles shook his hand and said to Tony, "I hope you bring us luck." As he was standing there, the first batter for the Twins, Kirby Puckett, belted a triple off the distant wall. O'Brien said to the general manager of the Orioles, "Maybe you don't want me here."

For all the irony of his first-ball saga, however, that night, that game, was meaningful to him in a place beyond laughter. "There's something about going to the ballpark," he said later. "Watching baseball, for a night game, in the twilight like that. . . . I can't even express the feelings that I had sitting there for that entire game. Just watching baseball. Eating hot dogs. It was so bizarre. Two weeks earlier I'd been sitting in a ten-by-eight cell in Kabul. It was so wonderful. So wonderful. It was like you were home."

The coda to the story, happily, involves the big black fuckin' bird. When the next issue of *Life* magazine came out, the publisher's letter was about O'Brien's imprisonment and release. Published with it was a picture taken that night of O'Brien with the bird, the big black Oriole mascot. Across the country in Santa Fe, a beautiful and smart twenty-six-year-old woman named Petra Lang had taken a job waiting tables at the best newsstand and coffee bar in town, called Downtown Subscription. As she flipped through *Life* magazine, her eye was caught by the picture of the tall guy and the bird. She did not normally read the publisher's letter, but because of the picture, she did. She showed it to another worker, saying, "Look, this guy's from Santa Fe."

"He's a regular here, when he's in town," the other woman said.

When Tony returned to Santa Fe he resumed his former habit of going for coffee and a newspaper to Downtown Subscription. He noticed immediately the stunning new waitress; he was taken with her beauty, her quiet reserve. Petra was going out with someone else at the time, but the story in *Life* had piqued her curiosity. In time she and O'Brien began to talk; he discovered she was as smart as she was pretty. In much later time—nine months later, when the other guy was out of her life—Petra and Tony began to date.

Another war came. O'Brien, who is always afraid and seems never afraid, went off to the Persian Gulf for *Life* to photograph Desert Storm. He chafed at the restrictions, the censorship, set by the Pentagon. He and a reporter went off across the desert in a jeep by themselves, against the rules—and while they were alone out in the desert a group of Iraqi soldiers surrendered to them. O'Brien and the reporter drove the Iraqis back to a U.S. army base where they could be interned. The only thing our hero forgot to do was to take away the rifles and hand grenades of his prisoners. But it all worked out. The men were interned. His photos again were published around the world.

When he got back from that war, Tony and Petra began living together. This was something new for a confirmed forty-seven-year-old bachelor. In time, predictably, he got wanderlust again. He could not get his mind off Nader Ali, one of his cell mates in Kabul. They had become that close. Three years had passed, and Tony felt he needed to find out what had happened to his friend. He needed to return to Kabul.

This time he did it legally. After four days he located Nader, who had been released from the prison only three weeks before. Together they went to visit the cell they had shared. Nader took Tony to meet his wife, his kids. Also present was Nader's younger brother, Jaffa. Tony asked if Jaffa was married. Nader Ali said: "He should have been married at eighteen. But the war interfered.

Now he's thirty-three and he's still not married. That's our first order of business now. To get Jaffa married, he's so old." Jaffa smiled, and took the half-serious teasing graciously.

Call it the Epiphany of Kabul. Call it an act of God. This playful family setting, in this primitive land, became one more twist in a maze of contemplation through which O'Brien had been wandering for months. When he returned home from the personal journey, he summoned the courage that heretofore had carried him from one deadly combat zone to another, but had never yet hurled him to the summit, the summit of total commitment to another human soul. He held his breath, he plummeted from the peak. He popped the question at last to the beauteous Petra.

That lovely lady, a fool for love, said yes.

For months now they have been making plans. On the seventeenth of April, in Cristo Rey Church, Mr. Tony O'Brien and Miss Petra Lang will join their hands in holy matrimony. The wedding bells echoing off the Sangre de Cristo Mountains will gladden the hearts of all who know the man—both for his own happiness and for that of his chosen lady, but also for themselves—because perhaps now he will cease his annoying habit of trying to get himself killed. Or, at least, he'll try it a bit less often.

Two of Tony's baseball teammates from his boyhood in Virginia will be among the wedding party. The big black bird, I suspect, will send regrets.

La Donna and I are going to spring training. It's something I've wanted to do all my life and have never done; it's something most baseball fans have wanted to do all their lives and never do. The plane tickets, the reservations, are on my desk. The pitchers and catchers reported on February nineteenth; the rest of the players reported on the twenty-fourth—my birthday. Now it is early March, and the faint scent of baseball is in the air, like that of a garden about to burst into bloom. On a warm day last weekend La Donna for the first time this year went out and weeded a large chunk of her garden. The next day snow fell, postponing the true start of her own good season. So she is coming with me. Monday we head for Tucson—spring-training home of the Rockies.

The Colorado caps have not yet arrived in town, but a local radio station has announced that it will broadcast all 162 Rockies games. I find myself devouring every word I can find in the newspapers about the Rockies as they prepare in Tucson—but also about the Mets as they work out in Port St. Lucie. Where do my true loyalties lie? The issue remains unresolved, and in the playing fields of my psyche this is no small matter.

One simple solution presented itself a while back. I could root for the Mets in the eastern division and the Rockies in the western. The two are not likely to meet in the league play-offs anytime soon. But when I looked at the schedule, the eternal trickster informed me—as he has a habit of doing—that I was begging the question. On Opening Day, April 5, the Colorado Rockies will play the very first game in their history at Shea Stadium, against the Mets. The teams will play again at Shea two days later. When the Rockies go home to Denver the following week, they will play host to the Mets for four consecutive days. Half of the twelve games between the teams this season will be played during the first two weeks. For whom will I be rooting when they go head to head? That is the bottom line, the bedrock question, the ultimate test of loyalty, of faith. I owe nothing to Eric Young, to Jerald Clark, to these other new Rockies. Yet they are not competing for my affection against Gary Carter, Keith Hernandez, Tom Seaver. They are challenging for my affections a Mets squad now composed mostly of Pirates, Cardinals, Royals, and Blue Jays. Who's Jeff Kent to me or me to Jeff Kent that I should root for him?

I still don't know the answer. I suspect I will not know the answer until Doc Gooden, if his arm is well, steps onto the mound for the Mets, and Alex Cole or some other Rockies leadoff man steps into the batter's box on Opening Day at Shea. Not till Doc goes into his windup and lets the ball fly plateward will I truly know whether I am rooting for a ball or a strike, for a hit or an out; whether I have switched my loyalty to the Rockies or remain ever true to the Mets.

This lingering uncertainty has confirmed my belief that baseball fandom is indeed like religious faith. It is not something you choose, it is something that chooses you. It is something with which you must be blessed. It is not an act of will but an act of love.

A package arrives in the mail from Philip. It is a Mets cap, blue and orange. It does not seem quite new. I call him up to thank him, warily—and to ask if he is trying to influence the jury.

"No, not at all," he says. "Someone gave it to me once. I found it on top of a closet. I remember you saying you didn't have one, so I thought you'd want it."

The next day I wear the Mets cap around town. The sensation is awkward. A Santa Fe resident for twenty-one years, I feel as if I just got off the Interstate; as if I am one of those newcomers whom the locals love to hate.

"You don't understand," I want to tell people in the street. "This is from way back. This is the past. . . ."

I feel as if I am cheating on my wife.

Yesterday I met O'Brien for coffee at Downtown Subscription, something we try to do every couple of weeks. He has been busy with wedding plans, busy getting nervous. I said dryly that we had already bought the lettuce for the salad we would provide, so it was too late to turn back now. He told me that, in fact, he'd been getting calls from friends around the country, warning him that they have already bought their plane tickets for his wedding—so he'd better not change his mind.

As we chatted, a good-looking young man walked into the coffee bar, quite by coincidence. It was Jaime Dean. I had not seen him since I'd watched him and his friends working out last summer. Jaime and Tony—his second father—hugged fiercely, as if they had not seen each other in at least as long. Jaime joined our table, a fresh breeze of youth, and filled us in on some recent travails. The first day of spring practice at Santa Fe High, a grounder had taken a bad hop and fractured his collarbone. Two days later he'd been rushed back to the hospital with an appendix that had to come out. That had been three weeks ago; he felt fine now, but he would not be able to swing a bat for another three weeks. The school baseball season would be lost to him. But he'd be going to spring training in two weeks, with his baseball cards and his friend, Jeff Dailey.

"I'll guess you'll go to Phoenix, where most of the major league teams work out," I said.

"Actually, I'll be going to the minor league complexes," Jaime said. "Hang out with my friends there."

"I don't suppose you're switching to the Rockies," I said. "I suppose you're still a Detroit fan."

"I'm a Detroit fan for life," he said.

I told him I was going south to watch the Rockies, but also to find old men who had retired to Arizona just to see spring training every year. As a kid of eight or nine I'd already had my retirement home picked out—Vero Beach, Florida, spring training home of the Dodgers.

"You want to see old men, go to Chandler," Jaime said. "South of Phoenix, where the Milwaukee Brewers play. The stands there are filled with all these old men screaming for the Brewers."

I made a note of it. The kid knows everything.

Jaime said his girlfriend would be joining him for a weekend down there. I asked if it was the same girl he'd been seeing last summer. He said it was; that her name was Callie Batts; that she plays softball for Santa Fe High. "We met when we were on the same Little League team," he said.

This brave new age. I looked at the handsome young kid who should have been my son. Who should have been me. Who *was* me. I thought of all the innocent little girls of childhood, the ones that got away. I asked him one more question, and I knew the answer deep in my gut well before I asked, because there was only one possible answer forthcoming.

"When you and Callie played Little League," I asked, "where did Callie play?"

"Where?"

"What position?"

"Oh. Shortstop."

What else did I expect?

When I got home I asked Amara and her friend Nicole if they knew Callie Batts.

"Yeah. She's real sweet, real gentle," Nicole said.

"She's kind of quiet, reserved," Amara said. "Jaime Dean and Callie? That's a nice couple."

Yeah, I thought. *Nice. But can she go to her left?*

On the plane I started an old Spenser mystery by Robert B. Parker, in which Spenser goes undercover as a writer to investigate whether a Red Sox pitcher is throwing games. Spenser has been my flying companion for years—funny, diverting, mysterious enough to hold my attention over the droning of the engines. The book was called *Mortal Stakes;* if you want to know the outcome you'll have to read it yourself.

The Rockies were training at Hi Corbett Field, a ten-minute drive from the downtown Tucson arts district, where we were staying. It's the summertime home of the Tucson Toros of the Triple-A Pacific Coast League. The Arizona sun was already strong when we got to the field about ten the next morning. The Rockies were taking batting practice in their dashing uniforms— black shirts, black caps, white pants with a barely visible stripe. The batting cage was in place, and the protective screens at the mound and in front of first base. In the poetic morning light, small still-lifes, little groupings of caps and bats and gloves, dotted the grass like Emily Dickinson couplets. *Because I would not stop at third, He threw me out at home.* Don Baylor, the rookie manager, was surrounded by writers near first base. Don Zimmer, his belly hanging over his belt, sat in the shade of the dugout. Daryl Boston, number 6 on his back, leaned against the batting cage, awaiting his turn. Down the right field line I spotted the leonine features of Andres Galarraga. There were more than seventy players in camp hoping to make this first Rockies team, and those were the only faces I recognized.

In the shade behind the stands a vending booth had already opened for the day, selling four kinds of Rockies T-shirts, and spring training pennants. The coveted black caps were lined up on a high shelf, neatly marked by size. I bought two, both 7 ⅝, one for me, one that O'Brien had requested. La Donna donned Tony's against the brightening sun while I softened the flat peak of mine to the proper curve; tomorrow we would stash Tony's safely in the hotel room, and the second baseman from Oklahoma would wear my Brooklyn cap.

In the stands a scattering of spectators was watching the morning workout. High up by themselves in the shade behind home plate—shade that would disappear by game time—two friends sat together. Both were easterners who had retired to Tucson. Both had been lifelong Yankee fans. Clifton Burdon was a month shy of seventy-two years old. Herb Fehling was seventy-seven.

"I'm originally from Maine," Burdon said, with an accent that still spoke of that rugged coast. "Then I moved to Colorado. Been waiting for the Rockies for thirty years." In Maine he pitched high-school ball back in the 1930s. He used to listen to the Yankees on the radio. "I was listening when Babe Ruth hit that famous home run against Chicago in 1932. We had to imagine what was happening. But it's good for us to have to imagine things."

He remembered seeing Mickey Mantle play his first game at Yankee Stadium. "It was 1950, or '51—do you remember, Herb?"

"I'm not sure," Herb said. "I know that Joe D. was 1936."

Burdon moved from Maine to Colorado in 1953, and spent thirty-two years there, not far from Denver, as a school principal. He retired to Tucson in 1981, for the weather. "I always said if Denver got a major league team I would move into town to see the games." But now, he says, he will remain a Yankee fan. "I just hope I can outlast George Steinbrenner."

Burdon and his son, John, who also lives in Tucson, both coach American Legion ball in the summer. "We have a lot of scouts come to see our kids play. So I'm still involved in baseball. It's been very important to me. I like football, and I like basketball. But I still go back to baseball. There's nothing like it. The thing I enjoy the most is to come out here and see families, especially with kids. It's one thing you can take your kids to and it isn't all that expensive. We see a lot of that in the summertime, when the Toros are playing. I come to see the Toros play quite often. All the kids come, because school is out, and they don't have to get up the next morning."

As we talk, that most musical sound of spring, the crack of bat on ball—well, maybe the second most musical, after the singing of the birds—echoes from the batting cage and bounces off the ad-covered outfield walls, over which in left-center field a cutout of the Marlboro Man presides tall and stately against distant white clouds, a devil aping an angel. Beneath his gaze anonymous Rockie wannabes shag the drifting fly balls.

Burdon's friend Herb was born on New York's Lower East Side in 1916. His family moved to Yorkville when he was six, and later to the Bronx, to 166th Street, closer to Yankee Stadium than I was. "My dad worked in a bank, my mother was just a housewife," Herb says, the *just* revealing his unconcern with political correctness. "I didn't get involved in baseball till 1923, when my dad took me into the ballpark. When they opened the Yankee Stadium. I only knew one ballplayer at that time, and that was Ruth. But after a little while I got to know all the other Yankees." He started going to a lot of games, remembers paying $.50 to sit in the bleachers when he went by himself, $1.10 for grandstand seats when his dad took him. "Maybe I'm wrong, but I just don't enjoy the ballplayers today as I did then," he says. "They seemed to want to play a lot more baseball back then, just because they wanted to play baseball." He is still a Yankee rooter, though he, too, has no love for Steinbrenner.

Herb spent fifty years working for the Coca-Cola company before retiring to Tucson. "I played a lot of sandlot baseball," he recalls. "I had a tryout with the Dodgers. That was when I was about eighteen or nineteen, in the early thirties. They had right field with that stone wall out there. The guy was whacking them out to me against the wall. I used to back off and catch them off the wall. I caught three of them off the wall. He wanted to know how come I could play that wall like I did. I said as a kid I used to play off-the-wall with a rubber ball, and I got to know just about where they would bounce. He took my name and address, but I never did hear anything from them. I always felt that my mother didn't want me to leave home. But I never got any information on that." He chuckles ruefully.

"She's ninety-five today," he adds. "She's back in New Jersey. She's blind. And she's deaf. She's in a home up there."

Herb has a son and daughter-in-law who work for the Veterans Administration in Tucson. He still writes to his blind, aged mother. His brother and his sister-in-law live in New Jersey and read his letters to her. I ask if he writes his mother about coming to these baseball games. "No, she never liked baseball," he says. "Because my dad liked it, and we liked it, boys being boys. Man and boy—this is the ballpark."

In his voice is a mild accusation. In his words is the merest hint of a suspicion he appears to have harbored for sixty years now—the suspicion that perhaps the Dodgers did get in touch with him, way back then; and that his mother, not wanting her son to leave home, destroyed the letter, and with it his chance for a baseball career. But Herb Fehling does not say this in so many words; the likelihood is that it never happened. I picture his aged mother, frail, blind, deaf, in the home in New Jersey, and I do not press the point.

Last night I began reading *Leviathan,* a new novel by Paul Auster, one of the most provocative and intelligent of contemporary American writers. On page seventeen I came to the following paragraph; the protagonist, a writer, is explaining why he returned to the States after living for five years in Paris:

I woke up one morning last summer and told myself it was time to come home. Just like that. I suddenly felt I'd been there long enough. Too many years without baseball, I suppose. If you don't get your ration of double plays and home runs, it can begin to dry up your spirit.

In five previous novels by Auster I do not recall a single reference to baseball (though I may be mistaken); I was pleased to find its spiritual truth here. But I bring up Auster for a different reason. His books are filled with enigmas, internal mysteries, the certainty that nothing is what it seems. People turn up in places they could not possibly have been. And inadvertently, I have just done the same thing. I am setting down my recollections of spring training a week after our return, and a few paragraphs above, I placed Rockies coach Don Zimmer in the shade of the Colorado dugout.

The Second Coming

Once a slim shortstop/third-baseman, Zimmer is a graying man now with a large belly and the expression of a bulldog, and reminds me of La Donna's lumpish eighty-six-year-old grandfather in Oklahoma. But Zimmer was not in the dugout our first morning of spring training; the Rockies were playing the California Angels in a split-squad game that day; Zimmer was nowhere in sight; he was up near Phoenix, managing the other half of the split squad. With a blip of the computer I could instantly erase him, restore the verities, but I am loath to do that; he is/was a Brooklyn Dodger, he was even a teammate of Pee Wee Reese's, he has a metal plate in his head from being beaned, he is getting on in years, and in a parallel reality anything is possible. Let us leave him be, in two places at once. Tomorrow we will catch up with him in the dugout shade, when he really will be there; when I will touch his deceptive flesh.

Of the first Colorado Rockies exhibition game I ever saw (it was the fourth they ever played) there is little of interest to report, beyond the large number of old-timers filling the stands by game time—which was to be expected down here—and the large number of two-year-old children and one-year-old children and even unborn children in the stands in the company of their young mothers, which I did not expect. The Angels had sent a team of minor-leaguers for this split-squad game, and the Rockies, with a few exceptions, were a team of minor leaguers. Players shuttled in and out of the game every few innings, and at the end of seven innings the score was tied, 1–1. We were watching baseball, it was true, real live baseball, but by three in the afternoon we had been sitting in the relentless sun for five hours, our heads were aching despite the consumption of several hot dogs and Cokes, La Donna was bored—with good reason, I thought—and I was trying to figure out how to walk out on a tie game without violating my own baseball code, under which such a premature exit was a shameful offense. After serious thought I decided that my marriage came first, and I sent La Donna off to the shade behind the grandstand, and told her I would be along soon. The Rockies obliged by giving up two runs in the top of the eighth, so when, losing my own battle to the sun, I joined her at mid-inning, I did not feel too bad. Though I wanted the Rockies to win, the reality was that the final score of this practice game counted for nothing. We drove back to our hotel and drank wine and beer in the lobby, and when sometime later a bunch of fans down from Denver to watch their team returned from the game, I learned that the Rockies had rallied for four runs in the bottom of the eighth and won the game, 5–3. I was suitably impressed.

Clever woman that she is, La Donna said that the next morning, if it was all right with me, when I went off to the ball field I could drop her and her camera at the Gene C. Reid zoo that sprawled across seventeen acres a few hundred yards beyond the left field fence. We sealed the deal that night with Chinese food.

Far more important than the game that day, or our own maladaptation to the sun, was a feeling of camaraderie I sensed building among those at the ballpark who wore Colorado caps, those in the hotel lobby, those in the streets. The American West has never been one location, not geographically or in any other way. The green hills and Anglo population of Colorado have little in common with the high desert and Hispanic culture of New Mexico, or with the low desert and conservative politics of southern Arizona, or with the Mormon influence of Utah, or with the cowboys of Montana. I was beginning to believe that something more important was taking place here than the birth of just another baseball team. The Rockies would be the first major leaguers ever to go to bat between Texas and California. The breadth of their western radio network would be a linkage of humanity akin, in a small but symbolic way, to the early telegraph. The national pastime had been a long time in coming to this burgeoning part of the nation. Many baseball fans would remain loyal to their prior teams—I was still uncertain about myself—but many others would switch to the Rockies, and hundreds of thousands of westerners who had never particularly followed baseball, for lack of a rooting interest, would now have a team of their own, a common conversation piece more upbeat than "overdevelopment," more fun than "water rights." Perhaps I was merely enchanted with the glitzy hat; perhaps some small part of me still felt, after twenty years here, that I remained a dispossessed New Yorker, and wanted to belong, and could now truly be part of the West without skiing, without riding horses, without wearing cowboy boots, without even chopping wood; I could belong the easy way, by donning a Rockies cap. Whatever the reason, I became convinced that I was witnessing in Tucson something grand and significant: the birth-squall of the first true brotherhood of the American West.

One couple at our hotel, down from Denver, already owned season tickets to Mile High Stadium for the Rockies games. Despite that they had come to Tucson to watch a week of spring training. And they were planning to fly to New York the first weekend in April to see the Rockies' first real ball game, at Shea Stadium. The husband, who runs a restaurant in Denver, was originally from Rumania and had never been a baseball fan before, though his Ohio-born wife had rooted for Cleveland till now. I asked him why they were going so far as to fly to New York for the opener, when the Rockies would be in Denver four days later. "This is a once-in-a-lifetime occurrence," he said. "I figure you might as well do it right."

The Colorado Rockies, I began to believe, creating interest throughout a larger geographical region than any previous expansion team, might well have a manifest destiny of their own.

The Chinese food that night, at a restaurant voted best Oriental spot in Tucson by readers of a local weekly newspaper, featured American vegetables—carrots and peas and lima beans—mixed in with the garlic chicken, in the tradition of those restaurants originated by the families of Chinese railroad builders a century ago. We stuffed ourselves anyway. Garlic, though no recent invention, is the culinary equivalent of the split-fingered fastball; it can atone for a multitude of sins.

The next day Don Zimmer was in the Rockies' dugout in the flesh. Prowling the field with a yellow press pass dangling from my shirt, taking pictures for one of the newspapers back home, I clicked a shot of him with his hands spread wide on the back of the dugout bench, like a combination of Buddha and Christ; I moved away and circled back and shot him talking with Baylor while holding three baseballs in one hand; I kept moving away and coming back, as if the steel plate in his head was a magnet, at least for onetime Dodger fans. I remembered listening on the radio to the game more than forty years earlier when he had gotten beaned and lay unconscious. I remembered not knowing—as no one knew for some moments—if he would live. Now he was the last of the old Brooklynites still in major league ball.

I had not come to Tucson to talk to ballplayers or coaches—the daily press does enough of that—but when Zimmer was alone again I could not resist approaching him. "Mr. Zimmer," I said, "as an old Brooklyn Dodger fan, I would like to shake the hand of one of the Brooklyn Dodgers."

With nary a smile—he must have been through this thousands of times in his life—Zimmer dutifully extended his hand and we shook; his hand was plump and pudgy, yet strong. I tried to think of a brilliant conversational gambit to try next. After a long silence my ready wit came to the rescue. "Good luck with the Rockies," I said. Zimmer grunted quietly and hoisted his bulk up the dugout steps and walked onto the field carrying a bat, and he began to slam grounders to the infield with more ferocity than I could manage when I was young and certainly more than I can manage now, the tenderizing ministrations of Jayne-the-therapist notwithstanding. It almost seemed as if the old boy were making a point.

One day about twenty years ago, while traveling across southern New Mexico, Carol and I stopped to eat in a cafeteria. At a nearby table we saw an elderly couple, in their seventies at least, eating. They looked as if they had been together forever, they clearly were husband and wife, but they were not enjoying each other's company. As they chewed their food in silence, with dentures, each was extremely, silently, annoyed with the other. Carol and I had the same interpretation: they seemed to be upset with each other for having gotten so goddamned feeble, so goddamned old. We wondered, afterward, if we would be that way someday.

Carol and I won't—at least not with each other; circumstance has seen to that. But I recalled that irritated couple from years before when, leaving Don Zimmer to his fungoes, I climbed high up into the stands and began to chat with a very different couple, the Tollivers, who had come out early to watch the workouts. They were of a different breed, J. A. and Marie Tolliver. He was seventy-four and she was seventy-two, they had been married for fifty-four years, and they still seemed to be enjoying every minute of it. And many of the minutes had to do with baseball, with a passion for the game they seemed to share, a passion that went back to the playing days of Bob Feller and Ted Williams and Jackie Robinson. They lived in El Paso, they were retired—he from a brakeman's job with the Southern Pacific Railroad, she from teaching elementary school—and every spring since they retired nine years ago they had come to Phoenix or Tucson for a month or more and watched baseball nearly every day. "And we usually go early, to watch them practice," Marie Tolliver said. J.A. added, "I like to see infield practice." Sometimes they watched a day game and a night game the same day. They have four grandsons, they said—two seventeen, one twelve, one eight—and a week later, on school break, the four boys would be joining them here to watch the games, as they did every year. For all of them, they said, it is their favorite time of year. When we returned to Santa Fe I read yet another article—this one a front page story in *Variety*—about how baseball needs to modernize itself to keep its fans, to make new fans. A fury grew inside me as I thought of the Tollivers in their seventies and their grandkids in their teens and younger, sharing the same passion for the game as it has always been. The drive for modernization, for changing the rules of the game, for the farce of interleague play—a farce because no single baseball game proves anything, baseball is a game for the long haul—all this is media crap driven by the quest for the television dollar, by hollow club owners and hollow press lackies to whom no tradition is sacred. If the greedy bastards who now run the game prevail, I hope they will choke on their money. I can only trust that the poetry will survive the commodity.

From the point of view of the fan what has undermined baseball fervor more than anything else is free-agency. In the old days the Dodgers, the Yankees, the Red Sox, the Indians, fielded the same team year after year, the same familiar players, whom hometown fans grew to adore like family. Occasionally there was a major trade that stunned the hot-stove league and added a dash of spice, but more often the same teams toiled year after year, till a rookie up from the farm system got good enough to oust an aging veteran. Today the players fly from team to team on a shuttle whose oiled engine is cash. If you are the kind of person, as I am, who prefers to place his loyalty in people rather than institutions, this cannot help but water down the great escape of fanaticism.

Unfortunately, free-agency, a true fan's despair, is also a necessary good. The great ballplayers deserve their millions far more than the cowardly club owners. So we must live with it, in this postmodern age, just as we live with divorce and one-parent homes. As Author Wiggen reminded us, slavery went out with Lincoln.

Honest critics of the game—and especially profound ones— invariably end up admitting that, for all its problems, it is still the best game we have; that it is still, therefore, important. I plead guilty to being (in the phrase of one of our finest journalists, Robert Lipsyte) one of the Lost Boys of Literature—a writer who loves the game too much. But I believe that the poetry of baseball will long endure. Modern man has invented pesticides and the bomb. The birds still sing.

In the zoo the animals are being kind. An alligator winks one eye at La Donna's camera. A lioness obligingly crosses her yard and poses beside her newborn cub. An anteater flicks out its eellike tongue. A tortoise sheds a tear for her. A macaw spreads its colorful wings. Perhaps it's her gray-blue eyes, her gentle manner. Perhaps it is the Brooklyn cap she is wearing.

In the ballpark the Rockies are trailing Milwaukee, 4–2. When they rally in the bottom of the seventh, closing the gap to a run, the fans in the right field bleachers stomp their feet in unison, a metal thunder roars across the field toward left, and the animals in the zoo beyond must surely be wondering what rough new beast, its hour come round at last, is slouching from the dugout to be born.

I leave the game after the seventh, again, to get to the zoo before it closes, before La Donna is ejected. Closing time, I discover, has been moved back an hour, and we have time to tour the zoo together. The shade is thick and welcome, the bird-sound orchestra overhead is rich as Beethoven. Beneath the airborne symphony I hear again the ballpark thunder. I think: *The Rockies are coming from behind! Again!* Later I will learn that this time it was Brewer thunder; the 4–3 game I left, with the Rockies trailing, will end up 12 to 3.

An elephant peels a branch with his trunk. A rhinoceros, painted with dried mud, basks near a wall that offers little shade. Hundreds, maybe thousands, of dark fish cruise in a pool of turquoise water. I take La Donna's hand. Tomorrow's game with the Cubs is sold out. Tomorrow we will visit the galleries in the Tucson arts district. Tomorrow I will fall in love with a racehorse fashioned from baling wire, about sixteen inches long, about ten inches high, its musculature wrapped precisely, front hooves straining, its mane and tail flat out in the invisible breeze of its frozen speed, and after some hesitation I will buy this stirring sculpture and take it home, along with an inordinate liking for the running Rockies. This liking, I realize, is lodging itself deeper inside me than a month ago I would have believed possible.

It is the first day of spring, and the country girl, wearing shorts for the first time this season, her legs as white as her tennis shoes, as she is quick to point out, is digging in her garden. There is a section of the lawn behind the patio in which the grass has always grown only fitfully. She is out there toiling away, gloved hands ripping up the dead clumps. The garden areas that rimmed the lawn on three sides were, last spring and summer, a cornucopia of color; there was no room in which she could plant new shrubs, in which she could sow new seeds. Now, as she works, perspiring, a whole new section of rich brown earth, about eight feet by eighteen feet, is beginning to show itself hungrily to the afternoon sun. The woman, as we have seen, has a league of her own—as much so as J. Henry Waugh. Now it, too, is undergoing expansion.

In late afternoon we drive to several stores. Already a new peony bush, in a pot in the house awaiting the passing of the last evening frost, has produced a mammoth bright purple blossom, far ahead of schedule. Small bulbs of canna lilies are nestled in paper bags on the kitchen floor. Now in the stores she buys packets of seeds: white moonflowers, sweet peas, delphinium, alyssum, zinnias, Canterbury bells. At night, as we watch the evening news, she opens the packets one by one. In each are about a dozen seeds, some almost the size of cherry pits. She rolls them in her palms, lovingly, like dice, her expression vibrant with warm anticipation. Some people have green thumbs; the country girl has a nourishing soul.

It has been three decades at least since I listened to a baseball game on the radio; four decades—back to the early 1950s, to the days before we owned a TV set—since I did so on any regular basis. Now I have begun again to listen. To spring-training games. To the Colorado Rockies.

Friday night the Rockies were trailing, 6–0. They came from behind to win, 10–7. Saturday they won, 8–6. Sunday they won again, 11–3.

I begin to harbor a distant hope. Perhaps they will not finish last.

I warn myself against optimism. The average record of expansion teams in their first season is 59 wins and 102 losses. The Rockies have only one real pitcher, David Nied.

Still . . .

On Saturday a Mets exhibition game was being televised from Florida. I watched two innings, and grew bored. I snapped off the set. I turned on the radio.

With no conscious choice, with no free will, I seem to have abandoned the Mets, after thirty-one years—abandoned them for the Rockies, this gangly young colt, far ahead of schedule. A lifetime ahead of schedule.

Even as I am writing these words, the telephone rings. The photographs I took at spring training were published in the local paper yesterday, along with a bit of poetic text; the city girl is calling to tell me she liked the pictures, the words.

She volunteers, also, that she has rediscovered the exquisite pleasure of baseball on the radio. She has been listening to the

Rockies. It has taken her back to the days when she used to listen to the spring training games of the Mets on the radio, and to the days before that, when she used to walk the streets of her childhood with a portable radio at her ear, listening to the spring training games of the Dodgers. The Brooklyn Dodgers.

I ask the question that, a few months ago, would have been unimaginable. I ask if she is a Rockies fan.

She tells me that she is.

"Except when Gooden is pitching," she adds.

Of course. That is an ultimate given. Except when Doc Gooden is pitching.

In less than a week the new season will start. In the garden dull roots are stirring with spring rain. My friends, too, are stirring. Mixing memory and desire.

Tom Collins has left his job with the art gallery. He has been living with a young woman named Syd Fenwick, a photographer whose specialty is black-and-white photographs of baseball parks. She has just learned that her pictures have been accepted for display in July at the annual sports art show in Cooperstown, which coincides with the induction of baseball's new Hall-of-Famers. Collins, who has written much art criticism, has decided that he is really a frustrated sportswriter. He and Syd are planning to head south, to Memphis and beyond, to do a words-and-picture book on the Class AA Southern Association, where, in Tom's words, "baseball is still pure." I wish him well on the project. I don't have the heart to warn him that being a writer of books is worse than being a White Sox fan. Writers stare death in the face every hour.

Jorge Ramirez is getting together his Little League team. He plans to manage Ramirez Construction himself this season, hoping to boost the team out of the cellar.

Gene Smith appears to have given up his flirtation with the Rockies. He moved from New Jersey to New Mexico before the Dodgers left Brooklyn, so when they landed in Los Angeles in 1958 they were closer to him than before. He still likes to watch Dukes games, to follow the progress of the players to the big club.

Once a bolink, always a bolink. When we have lunch three days before the start of the season, Smith recalls an umpire named Shlitsky who used to call balls and strikes for a sandlot league back in Bayonne. Shlitsky had one leg that was crippled from polio, Smith says, and he used to call balls and strikes on crutches from behind the pitcher. If you didn't like one of his calls, you tried to blast the next pitch right back at him, tried to knock him off his crutches.

The childhood recollections of baseball fans could fill a very fat encyclopedia. . . .

Jerry Ortiz y Pino is mourning the loss of Steve Olin and Tim Crews of his beloved Cleveland Indians, killed last week in a boating accident in Florida. He saw the headlines of their deaths as he stepped off a plane from El Salvador, where he had been attending a political protest meeting. Despite the coming of the Rockies to his backyard, Jerry will stick with the distant Tribe, as he has since 1948. "The mood of the country is shifting to the Indians," he says, tongue lodged smoothly in cheek.

Jaime Dean, having missed high school ball this spring because of his appendix, is talking about spending the summer at a baseball camp.

Tony O'Brien, who will be marrying his Petra in two weeks, has arranged for them to honeymoon in Egypt, where bombs planted by Muslims—the side he hung out with in Afghanistan—have recently been blowing up tourist buses. Petra is looking forward to the trip. Once more O'Brien's friends will have to worry, till the lad and his lass come safely home.

Probably, I figure, he just wants to throw out another first ball.

Two summers ago La Donna and the child went to Oklahoma for a week to visit her parents. I was busy with some deadline or other and stayed home. I came down with a minor stomach ailment. I was depressed about my work. To jolt myself out of an onset of self-pity, I went to the nearby mall and rented a tape of *Field of Dreams*.

When the film came out in 1989 I had taken the family to see it. For the last fifteen minutes of the movie my throat was choked, I found myself fighting back tears. I am rarely so moved by films. The last time it had happened so strongly was back when I was a senior in college and saw *Citizen Kane* for the first time only hours before I was to report to the *New York Post* for my first night as a copyboy. I've seen *Kane* a dozen times since and have never failed to be stirred, beyond all reason, by the final flaming image.

When, two summers ago, alone in the darkened house, I watched *Field of Dreams* again, my reaction was even stronger than it had been in the crowded theater a few years earlier. Though I am cynical in many respects, tears streamed down my face during much of the film. There were moments when, unheard by anyone, huge sobs burst forth without warning, without explanation, from someplace deep inside me.

My purpose in writing this book, I understand now, was to discover why I cry at *Field of Dreams*.

One could suggest that Pee Wee Reese and the old Brooklyn Dodgers are my own vanished Rosebud. But that much I knew going in. Like the journalists in *Kane* I am no closer to the answer at the end than I was at the beginning. Something lies buried still in the mind's dark Xanadu.

The last week of spring training I catch parts of two Mets games on television. I see them come from behind to beat the Dodgers. I see them come from behind to beat the Yankees. How can I abandon a team that does that?

I used to feel that anyone who roots for two teams is only half a fan. Now I rationalize the opposite. If I root for two teams, I can be twice the fan! There will be 162 Rockies games on the radio. There will be 75 Mets games on the tube. . . .

The night before Opening Day I memorize carefully the face of La Donna, my wife. The features of Amara, my daughter, I imprint firmly in my brain. I want to be sure I will recognize them both, come October.

April 5. Opening Day, 1993. The sun is shining brightly in Shea Stadium. I see this on the TV set in my office. I push the "mute" button. The crowd at Shea is cheering wildly as the Mets take the field. I hear this on the radio, on the Rockies baseball network.

Eric Young, the first batter in the history of the Colorado Rockies, this new pantheon in the parallel reality that stretches into the invisible future, this new pantheon whose origins I will describe in croaking tones to my grandchildren, should I be so blessed—Eric Young steps into the batter's box. On the mound Doc Gooden blows into his hands. On the bookshelf in my office my old Brooklyn cap, my New York cap, my Colorado cap, sit side by side by side, like three old men on a sunny park bench, three old men with stories to tell.

Doc Gooden places his right foot on the rubber. Eric Young, the second baseman, a right-handed hitter, holds his bat high. Gooden goes into his smooth, lanky windup. He fires. The first pitch of the new baseball season catches the inside corner for a strike.

Epilogue:
Extra Innings

It is past midnight. He is sitting in his wing chair beside a lighted lamp, gazing, as he often does, at the painting on the far wall. It is, in his view, the best painting Smith ever did. He is proud to own it. The canvas is a silent symphony of golds and yellows and ochres, a small wisp of pink and white here, a mellow madness of incoming turquoise and dark blue blowing in from the right, balanced not by color but by line on the left. The painting is both representational and abstract. In the foreground molten waves leap. Beyond the golden sea there are what look like mountain peaks disappearing toward an infinite center. But the peaks glow in hallowed light high above the clouds. The vantage point, indeed, is above the clouds. Months after he—they—acquired the painting, Smith said it showed a storm approaching. That might be the artist's interpretation, but what do mere creators know? The blue is too blue for a storm, the peaks too golden, too Platonic, to be an earthly mountain range. As he gazes at the canvas now, it becomes what it always becomes for him—a high and distant dreamscape beyond seeing. The place—if there is such a place—to which human essences ultimately repair.

He does not know if there is a soul, if death is a final nailing in a box, an all-consuming chaos in the flames, leaving nothingness, a flat finality— or if there is, indeed, more. Far greater minds than his have debated this question and come to opposing views. This night he recalls what a wise woman, a psychologist, once told him when he asked if she were afraid to die. "I'm looking forward to it," the woman said. "I can't wait to find out what's next."

He does not know if there is a Next. But if there is, then what Smith has painted is the place where Next begins. Here in the golden light above the glowing peaks, the essence, the spirit, the soul—choose your own word—glides in freedom, having left the mortal remains behind. He wishes he could give himself wholly to this view, because in this view, here amid the glowing haze he will meet again with other essences—with his mother, with his father, with his grandpa Max, who took him to the bench in the park to feed the pigeons, who died when he was four. Here he will abide for however long such reunions are tolerated. Here he will be refreshed. Then, he imagines, the souls that must choose their Nexts move on, flow out into the stratosphere, from where the earth is that blue-green marble—the same one, perhaps, that he struck one day from far across the street, while an angel perched on his shoulder—and hover and glide and peer at the bustle of earthly days, in Tokyo and Singapore, in Iceland and Copenhagen, in Lima and Rio and The Bronx. Until they weigh and debate within themselves and choose—or cast all thought to the winds and choose at random.

Sitting in the wing chair in the after-midnight, the child asleep in one room, the woman asleep in another, he already knows what his choice will be. He will glide the world like the others—he has never traveled as much as he would have liked—but when the time comes to commit, he already knows. He will glide toward a large island, an island in the Caribbean. There in a shack of thatch he will find sprawled sleepily on sunlit morning sheets a dusky woman, long legged, beautiful. There is the hint of a smile on her lips; she has been well satisfied the night before by the man who sleeps soundly beside her. There is a vacancy, he knows; the womb behind the smooth curve of her belly is calling. There his essence will enter and take up residence, there in the vacancy of mingled seed. There in the beginning of the child-to-be. When he is born, his father will place tiny gloves, bats, balls, beside his crib, as is the local custom.

The island is called Hispaniola. The country is called by men the Dominican Republic. The city is known as San Pedro de Macorís. He has chosen it with specific intent. In the past two decades nearly a dozen boys from this one Dominican town have matured into major league short-stops. Fifty others from the same city have made it to the major leagues as pitchers or outfielders—more major leaguers by far from this city than from any other city in the world. This is as strange a phenomenon as there is in all of baseball. He does not know if the source is the earth or the water or the air, or the genes of the dusky woman and the lithe and wiry man. All he knows is that major league shortstops grow here like sugar cane. And so here he will choose for his Next. He may as well maximize the odds.

"There is only one possible reason for reincarnation," Smith said to him once, "and that's to come back as a major league shortstop."

He smiles at the recollection. His gaze withdraws from the painting, he returns to his own self. His eyes feel sleepy now. The child is silent behind the wall on which the painting hangs. He clicks off the light, he finds his way in the other direction, to the bedroom where the woman lies. He climbs into bed beside her, careful not to disturb her sleep. He closes his eyes in the darkness, he waits for the dreamy golden haze to fade.

Suddenly his eyes spring open. He has had a terrible thought. With a maddening sense of futility, of anger, of fear, he stares at the darkness of the ceiling.

What if . . . he has thought. What if?

He does not know if there is a Next, but of one thing he is certain. If there is a Next, it does not remember. It does not remember the Previous. It does not recall the Before. Two different women in the same small western city have told him that in past lives they were victims of Nazi concentration camps; they have claimed they remember. He attributes this not to memory but to psychology, however complex. If there is a Next, you do not remember.

And now, lying in the darkness, he thinks: What if?

What if, Before, he already was a major league shortstop?

This catastrophe keeps him awake till the first gray light of dawn.